Measuring up: Canadian Results of the OECD PISA Study

The Performance of Canada's Youth in Science, Reading and Mathematics

2006 First Results for Canadians aged 15

Authors

Patrick Bussière, *Human Resources and Social Development Canada*
Tamara Knighton, *Statistics Canada*
Dianne Pennock, *Council of Ministers of Education, Canada*

Published by authority of the Minister responsible for Statistics Canada

December 2007

Catalogue no. 81-590-XPE — No. 3
ISBN 978-0-660-19780-7
ISSN 1712-5464
Catalogue no. 81-590-XIE — No. 3
ISBN 978-0-662-47372-5
ISSN 1712-5472

Également offert en français sous le titre : *À la hauteur : Résultats canadiens de l'étude PISA de l'OCDE — La performance des jeunes du Canada en sciences, en lecture et en mathématiques — Premiers résultats de 2006 pour les Canadiens de 15 ans*

Frequency: Occasional

Ottawa

Human Resources and Social Development Canada, Council of Ministers of Education, Canada and Statistics Canada

Library and Archives Canada Cataloguing in Publication Data

Bussière, Patrick
  The performance of Canada's youth in science, reading and mathematics :
2006 first results for Canadians aged 15

(Measuring up : Canadian Results of the OECD PISA Study; no. 3)
Issued also in French under title: La performance des jeunes du
Canada en sciences, en lecture et en mathématiques : premiers résultats de 2006
pour les canadiens de 15 ans.

Available also on the Internet.
ISBN 978-0-660-19780-7 (paper)
ISBN 978-0-662-47372-5 (Internet)
CS81-590-XPE
CS81-590-XIE

1. Academic achievement – Canada – Statistics.
2. Educational evaluation – Canada.
3. High school students – Rating of – Canada.
4. High school students – Rating of – Canada – Statistics.
5. High school students – Rating of – OECD countries – Statistics.
I. Bussière, Patrick. II. Knighton, Tamara. III. Pennock, Dianne. IV. Statistics Canada.
V. Canada. Human Resources and Social Development Canada.
VI. Council of Ministers of Education (Canada). VII. Series.

LB3054.C3 B87 2007   373.126'20971
C2007-988001-0

Acknowledgements

We would like to thank the students, parents, teachers and principals who gave of their time to participate in the 2006 OECD PISA study. The support for this Federal-Provincial collaborative project provided by members of the PISA Steering Committee and by the coordinators in each participating Ministry or Department of Education during all steps of the study is gratefully acknowledged. The dedication of the survey development, implementation, processing and methodology teams was essential to the project's success and is appreciated.

This publication was prepared jointly by Statistics Canada, Human Resources and Social Development Canada and the Council of Ministers of Education, Canada and was supported financially by Human Resources and Social Development Canada.

The report has benefited from the input and comments of reviewers in provincial Ministries and Departments of Education; the Council of Ministers of Education, Canada; Human Resources and Social Development Canada and Statistics Canada. A very special thank you is extended to Danielle Baum for her indispensable help in preparing the manuscript for publication. The contribution of editorial, com-munications, translation and dissemination services staff of Statistics Canada, Human Resources and Social Development Canada and the Council of Ministers of Education, Canada was essential to the project's success and is appreciated.

Note of Appreciation

Canada owes the success of its statistical system to a long-standing partnership between Statistics Canada, the citizens of Canada, its businesses, governments and other institutions. Accurate and timely statistical information could not be produced without their continued cooperation and goodwill.

Acronyms

The following acronyms are used in this publication:

OECD	Organisation for Economic Co-operation and Development
PISA	Programme for International Student Assessment
HRSDC	Human Resources Social Development Canada
SES	Socio-economic status

Table of contents

Table of contents

Table of contents

List of tables

Table of contents

List of charts

Introduction

In the spring of 2006, Canadian students participated in the Programme for International Student Assessment (PISA) which seeks to measure how well young adults, at age 15, are prepared to meet the challenges of today's knowledge societies. PISA was first conducted in 2000 with an emphasis on reading achievement and again in 2003 with an emphasis on mathematics achievement. The third survey of PISA conducted in 2006 completes the first set of three-yearly assessment surveys of knowledge and skills with a focus on science achievement. This report summarizes the results for Canada and the provinces in an international context.

The Programme for International Student Assessment

The Programme for International Student Assessment (PISA) is a collaborative effort among member countries of the Organisation for Economic Co-operation and Development (OECD). PISA is designed to provide policy-oriented international indicators of the skills and knowledge of 15-year-old students[1] and sheds light on a range of factors that contribute to successful students, schools and education systems. It measures skills that are generally recognized as key outcomes of the educational process. The assessment focuses on young people's ability to use their knowledge and skills to meet real life challenges. These skills are believed to be prerequisites to efficient learning in adulthood and for full participation in society.

PISA has brought significant public and educational attention to international assessment and related studies by generating data to enhance the ability of policy makers to make decisions based on evidence. In Canada, it is carried out through a partnership consisting of Human Resources and Social Development Canada, the Council of Ministers of Education Canada and Statistics Canada.

The project began in 2000 and focuses on the capabilities of 15-year-olds as they near the end of compulsory education. It reports on reading literacy, mathematical literacy and scientific literacy every three years and provides a more detailed look at each domain in the years when it is the major focus. For example, science was the major domain of PISA in 2006 when the focus was on both overall (or combined) scientific literacy and three scientific sub-domains (identifying scientific issues, explaining phenomena scientifically and using scientific evidence). As minor domains in PISA 2006, only single measures of reading and mathematics were available. On the other hand, more detailed information was available on reading and reading sub-domains in 2000 and mathematics and mathematics sub-domains in 2003.

Box 1

The PISA Assessment Domains

PISA measures three domains: mathematical literacy, reading literacy, and scientific literacy. The domains were defined as follows by international experts who agreed that the emphasis should be placed on functional knowledge and skills that allow active participation in society.

Scientific literacy (hereafter referred to as science):

An individual's scientific knowledge and use of that knowledge to identify questions, to acquire new knowledge, to explain scientific phenomena, and to draw evidence based conclusions about science-related issues, understanding of the characteristic features of science as a form of human knowledge and enquiry, awareness of how science and technology shape our material, intellectual, and cultural environments, and willingness to engage in science-related issues, and with the ideas of science, as a reflective citizen.

Reading literacy (hereafter referred to as reading):

An individual's capacity to understand, use and reflect on written texts, in order to achieve one's goals, to develop one's knowledge and potential and to participate in society.

Mathematical literacy (hereafter referred to as mathematics):

An individual's capacity to identify and understand the role that mathematics plays in the world, to make well-founded judgements and to use and engage with mathematics in ways that meet the needs of that individual's life as a constructive, concerned and reflective citizen.

Why do PISA?

The skills and knowledge that individuals bring to their jobs, to further studies and to our society, plays an important role in determining our economic success and our overall quality of life. The importance of skills and knowledge is expected to continue to grow. The shift to knowledge and information intensive industries, to communication and production technologies, to falling trade barriers and to the globalization of markets have precipitated increases in the knowledge and skills that the present and future economy requires. These include a rising demand for a strong set of foundation skills upon which further learning is built.

Elementary and secondary education systems play a central role in laying a solid base upon which subsequent knowledge and skills can be developed. Students leaving secondary education without a strong foundation may experience difficulty accessing the postsecondary education system and the labour market and they may benefit less when learning opportunities are presented later in life. Without the tools needed to be effective learners throughout their lives, these individuals with limited skills risk economic and social marginalization.

Governments in industrialized countries have devoted large portions of their budgets to provide high quality universal elementary and secondary schooling. Given these investments, governments are interested in the relative effectiveness of their education systems. To address these issues, member governments of the Organisation for Economic Co-operation and Development (OECD) developed a common tool to improve their understanding of what makes young people—and education systems as a whole—successful. This tool is the Programme for International Student Assessment (PISA).

Information gathered through PISA enables a thorough comparative analysis of the performance of students near the end of their compulsory education. PISA also permits exploration of the ways that achievement varies across different social and economic groups and the factors that influence their level and distribution within and among countries.

Why did Canada participate?

Canada's participation in PISA 2006 stems from many of the same questions motivating other participating countries. Canada invests significant public resources in the provision of elementary and secondary education. Canadians are interested in the quality of education provided to their youth by elementary and secondary schools. How can expenditures be directed to the achievement of higher levels of knowledge and skills upon which lifelong learning is founded and to potentially reduce social inequality in life outcomes?

Canada's economy is also evolving rapidly. Between 2006 and 2015, the fastest labour market growth is among occupations requiring higher skills.[2] Even employees in traditional occupations are expected to upgrade their knowledge and skills to meet the rising demands of new organisational structures and production technologies. Elementary and secondary education systems play a key role in generating the supply of skills to meet this demand. The competencies acquired by the end of compulsory schooling provide individuals with the essential foundation necessary to further develop human capital.

Questions about educational effectiveness can be partly answered with data on the average performance of Canada's youth. However, two other questions with respect to equity can only be answered by examining the distribution of competencies: Who are the students at the lowest levels? Do certain groups or regions appear to be at greater risk? These are important questions because, among other things, acquisition of knowledge and skills during compulsory schooling influences access to postsecondary education, eventual success in the labour market and the effectiveness of continuous, lifelong learning.

What is PISA 2006?

Fifty-seven countries participated in PISA 2006, including all 30 OECD countries[3]. Between 5,000 and 10,000 students aged 15 from at least 150 schools were typically tested in each country. In Canada, approximately 22,000 15-year-olds from about 1,000 schools participated across the ten provinces[4]. The large Canadian sample was required to produce reliable estimates representative of each province and for both French and English language school systems in Nova Scotia, New Brunswick, Quebec, Ontario and Manitoba.

The 2006 PISA assessment was administered in schools, during regular school hours in April and May 2006. This assessment was a two hour paper-and-pencil lasting. Students also completed a 20-minute student background questionnaire providing information about themselves and their home and a 10-minute questionnaire on information technology and communications, while school principals completed a 20-minute questionnaire about their schools. As part of PISA 2006, national options could also be implemented. Canada chose to add a 5-minute student questionnaire to collect more information on the school experiences of 15-year-olds, their work activities and their relationships with others.

Box 2

Overview of PISA 2006

	International	Canada
Participating countries/provinces	• 57 countries	• 10 provinces
Population	• Youth aged 15	• Same
Number of participating students	• Between 5,000 and 10,000 per country with some exceptions for a total of close to 400,000 students	• Approximately 22,000 students
Domains	• Major: science • Minor: reading and mathematics	• Same
Amount of testing time devoted to domains	• 390 minutes of testing material organized into different combinations of test booklets 120 minutes in length • 210 minutes devoted to science • 60 minutes each devoted to reading, mathematics	• Same
Languages in which the test was administered	• 43 languages	• English and French
International assessment	• Two hours of direct assessment of science, reading and mathematics • Twenty minute contextual questionnaire administered to youth • A school questionnaire administered to school principals	• Same
International options	• Ten-minute optional questionnaire on information technology and communications administered to students • Ten-minute optional questionnaire on educational career administered to students	• Ten-minute optional questionnaire on information technology and communication administered to students
National options	• Grade based assessment • Other options were undertaken in a limited number of countries	• Five minutes of additional questions administered to students regarding their school experiences, work activities and relationships with others.

Objectives and organization of the report

This report provides the first pan-Canadian results of the PISA 2006 assessment of science, reading and mathematics by presenting at the national and provincial results in order to complement the information presented in "Learning for Tomorrow's World - First Results from PISA 2006"[5]. Results are compared to other participating countries and across Canadian provinces.

Chapter 1 provides information on the relative performance of Canadian 15-year-old students on the PISA 2006 assessment in science. It presents the average level of performance on the combined science scale as well as the three science sub-domains; the distribution of achievement scores and proficiency levels in science for Canada as a whole and for the provinces; and results for the English-language and French-language school systems. Chapter 2 discusses information on the mean performance of Canada and the provinces in reading and mathematics, compares results for the English-language and French-language school systems and examines change in performance over time. Chapter 3 examines the relationship between performance and selected student characteristics. Chapters 4 provides an overview of three key themes explored in PISA 2006 – student engagement in science, science and the environment and contexts for the learning of science. Finally, the major findings and opportunities for further study are discussed in the conclusion.

Notes

1. OECD (1999), Measuring Student Knowledge and Skills: A New Framework for Assessment, Paris.

2. Lapointe, Mario, Kevin Dunn, Nicolas Tremblay-Côté, Louis-Philippe Bergeron, and Luke Ignaczak (May 2007) *Looking-Ahead: A 10-Year Outlook for the Canadian Labour Market (2006-2015)*, HRSDC, SP-615-10-06E .

3. OECD countries include Australia, Austria, Belgium, Canada, Czech Republic, Denmark, Finland, France, Germany, Greece, Hungary, Iceland, Ireland, Italy, Japan, Korea, Luxembourg, Mexico, Netherlands, New Zealand, Norway, Poland, Portugal, Slovak Republic, Spain, Sweden, Switzerland, Turkey, United Kingdom, and United States. Partner countries are: Argentina, Azerbaijan, Brazil, Bulgaria, Chile, Chinese Taipei, Columbia, Croatia, Estonia, Hong Kong – China, Indonesia, Israel, Jordan, Kyrgyzstan, Latvia, Liechtenstein, Lithuania, Macao – China, Montenegro, Qatar, Romania, Russian Federation, Serbia, Slovenia, Thailand, Tunisia, and Uruguay.

4. No data were collected in the three territories and on First Nations schools.

5. OECD (2007), PISA 2006: Science competencies for tomorrow's world. Paris.

Chapter 1

The performance of Canadian students in science in an international context

This chapter compares the Canadian results of the PISA 2006 assessment in terms of average scores, variation in performance and proficiency levels. First, the performance of Canadian 15-year-old students is compared to the performance of 15-year-old students from other countries that participated in PISA 2006. Second, the results of student performance in the ten Canadian provinces are analyzed. Following this, the performance of students enrolled in English-language and French-language school systems are compared for the five provinces in which the two groups were sampled separately.

Defining science

The definition of science in PISA 2006 focuses on the competencies that clarify what 15-year old students know, value and are able to do within personal, social and global contexts.

In addition to reporting on combined science performance through a combined science scale, PISA 2006 reports on three scientific competencies that underpin the PISA 2006 definition of scientific literacy. The features of each of these three competencies are described in Box 3[6].

Box 3

PISA 2006 scientific competencies

Identifying scientific issues

- Recognizing issues that are possible to investigate scientifically

- Identifying keywords to search for scientific information

- Recognizing the key features of a scientific investigation

Explaining phenomena scientifically

- Applying knowledge of science in a given situation

- Describing or interpreting phenomena scientifically and predicting changes

- Identifying appropriate descriptions, explanations and predictions

Using scientific evidence

- Interpreting scientific evidence and making and communicating conclusions

- Identifying the assumptions, evidence and reasoning behind conclusions

- Reflecting on the societal implications of science and technological developments

---

The combined science score is expressed on a scale with an average of 500 points for the OECD countries[7] and about two-thirds of the students scoring between 400 and 600 (i.e. a standard deviation of 100).

While PISA is a not a test of learned curriculum, the points on the science scale can be interpreted in the context of the school environment. For example, 28 of the 30 OECD countries that participated in PISA 2006 had a sizable number of 15-year-olds in the sample who were enrolled in at least two different, but consecutive grades. For these 28 countries combined, the OECD analyses revealed that one additional school year corresponds to an increase of 34 score points on the PISA 2006 combined science scale[8].

One way to summarize student performance and to compare the relative standing of countries is by examining their average test scores. However, simply ranking countries based on their average scores can be misleading because there is a margin of error associated with each average score. This margin of error should be taken into account in order to identify whether differences in average scores exist when comparing countries (see text box 4 'A note on statistical comparisons').

Box 4

A note on statistical comparisons

The averages were computed from the scores of random samples of students from each country and not from the population of students in each country. Consequently it cannot be said with certainty that a sample average has the same value as the population average that would have been obtained had all 15-year-old students been assessed. Additionally, a degree of error is associated with the scores describing student performance as these scores are estimated based on student responses to test items. A statistic, called the standard error, is used to express the degree of uncertainty associated with sampling error and measurement error. The standard error can be used to construct a confidence interval, which provides a means of making inferences about the population averages and proportions in a manner that reflects the uncertainty associated with sample estimates. A 95% confidence interval is used in this report and represents a range of plus or minus about two standard errors around the sample average. Using this confidence interval it can be inferred that the population mean or proportion would lie within the confidence interval in 95 out of 100 replications of the measurement, using different samples randomly drawn from the same population.

When comparing scores among countries, provinces, or population subgroups the degree of error in each average should be considered in order to determine if averages are different from each other. Standard errors and confidence intervals may be used as the basis for performing these comparative statistical tests. Such tests can identify, with a known probability, whether there are actual differences in the populations being compared.

For example, when an observed difference is significant at the 0.05 level, it implies that the probability is less than 0.05 that the observed difference could have occurred because of sampling or measurement error. When comparing countries and provinces, extensive use is made of this type of test to reduce the likelihood that differences due to sampling or measurement errors will be interpreted as real.

Only statistically significant differences at the 0.05 level are noted in this report, unless otherwise stated. This means averages did not differ when the 95% confidence intervals for the averages being compared do not overlap. Where confidence intervals did overlap an additional t-test was conducted to test for differences.

Canadian students performed well in science

Overall, Canadian students performed well in science, as illustrated in Chart 1.1. Listed in Table 1.1 are the countries that performed significantly better than Canada or equally as well as Canada on the combined science scale and the three science competency sub-domains. The average scores of students in the remaining countries that took part in PISA 2006 were statistically below that of Canada. Among 57 countries, only Finland and Hong Kong-China performed better than Canada on the combined science scale.

Canadian students also performed well in the three science competency sub-domains (Charts 1.2 to 1.4; Table 1.1). Only Finland outperformed Canadian 15-year-olds in 'identifying scientific issues' and 'using scientific evidence' while four countries outperformed Canadian 15-year-olds in 'explaining phenomena scientifically'.

As the full assessment of science took place for the first time in 2006 and was only measured as a minor domain previously, it is not possible to directly compare science performance over time since PISA 2000. However, insights can be provided by looking at Canada's relative position across the assessments. In PISA 2003, four countries outperformed Canadian 15-year-olds in combined science compared to only two countries in PISA 2006. The relative change in ranking for Canada between 2003 and 2006 may be attributable to an improvement in performance in Canada, a decrease in performance in other countries or a combination of both factors.

Table 1.1

Countries performing better than, or the same as Canada

	Countries performing significantly better than Canada	Countries performing as well as Canada
Science – combined scale	Finland, Hong Kong-China	Chinese Taipei, Estonia, Japan, New Zealand
Science – identifying scientific issues	Finland	New Zealand, Australia, Netherlands, Hong Kong-China
Science – explaining phenomena scientifically	Finland, Hong Kong-China, Chinese Taipei, Estonia	Czech Republic, Japan
Science – using scientific evidence	Finland	Japan, Hong Kong-China, Korea, New Zealand, Liechtenstein

Chart 1.1

Average scores and confidence intervals for provinces and countries: Combined science

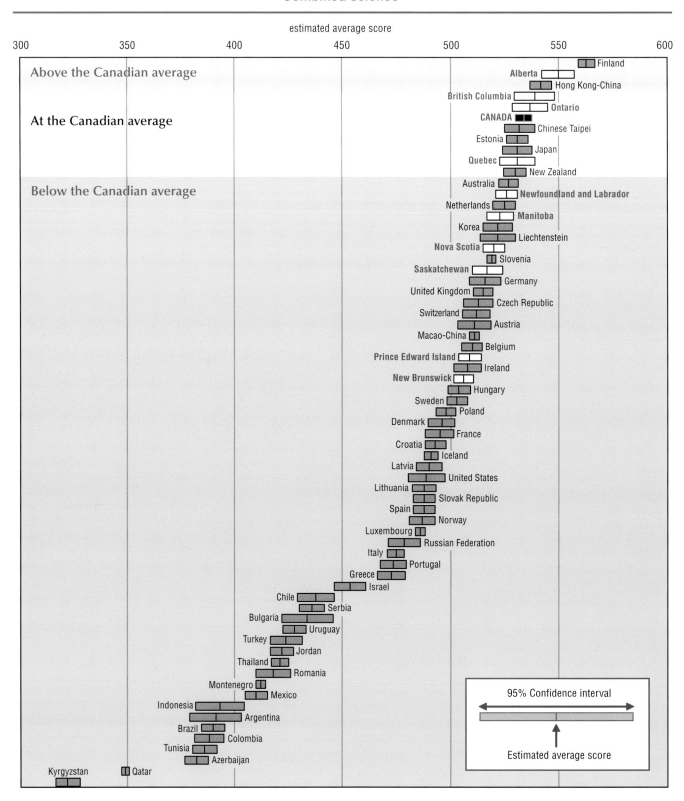

Note: The OECD average is 500 with a standard error of 0.5.

Chart 1.2

Average scores and confidence intervals for provinces and countries: Identifying scientific issues

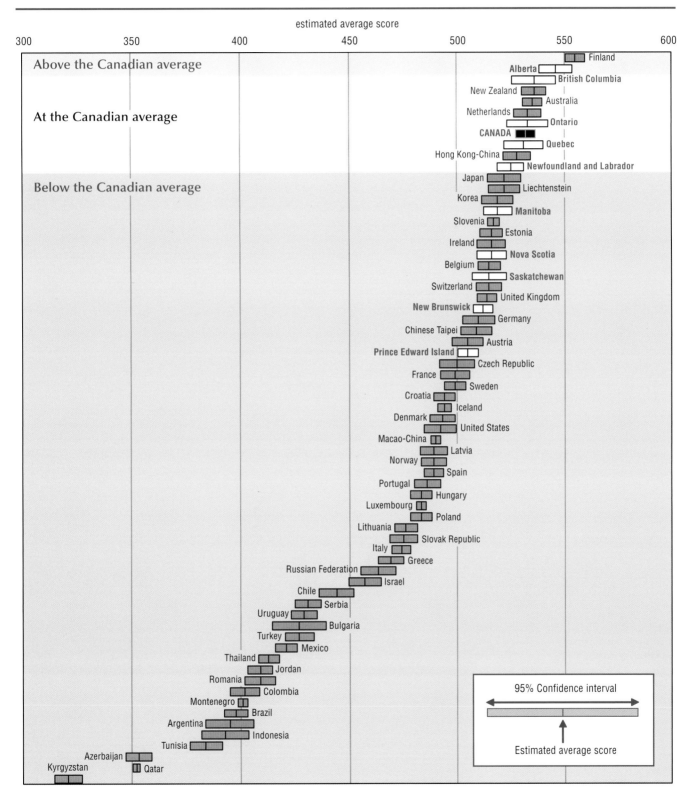

Note: The OECD average is 500 with a standard error of 0.5.

Chart 1.3

Average scores and confidence intervals for provinces and countries: Explaining phenomena scientifically

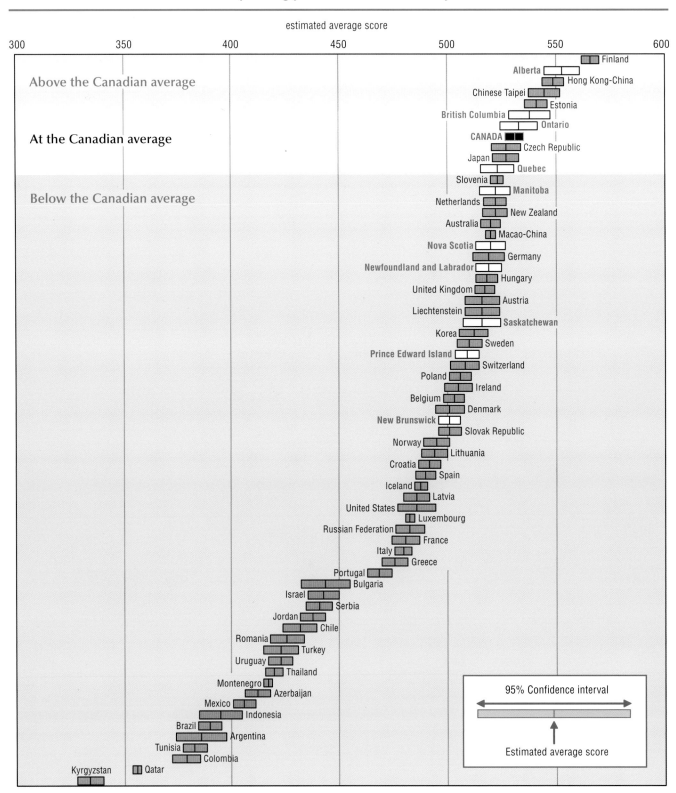

Note: The OECD average is 500 with a standard error of 0.5.

Chart 1.4

Average scores and confidence intervals for provinces and countries: Using scientific evidence

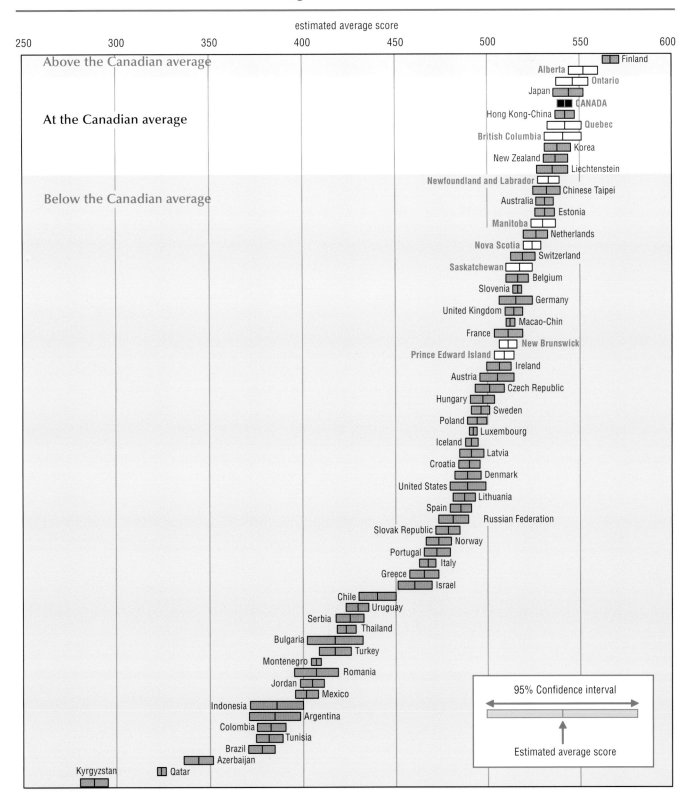

Note: The OECD average is 499 with a standard error of 0.6.

All provinces performed at or above the OECD average

Fifteen year-old students in all the Canadian provinces performed well in science which contributed to Canada's standing in international comparisons (Charts 1.1 to 1.4). All provinces performed at or above the OECD mean in the combined science scale and science competency sub-scales.

Generally, provinces fell into one of three groups when compared to the Canadian averages for combined science and the three science sub-domains (Table 1.2). The average performance of students in Alberta was significantly above the Canadian average. Quebec, Ontario and British Columbia performed about the same as the Canadian average while students in Newfoundland and Labrador, Prince Edward Island, Nova Scotia, New Brunswick, Manitoba and Saskatchewan performed significantly below the Canadian average. Students in Newfoundland and Labrador performed at the Canadian average in the sub-domain of 'identifying scientific issues' and below the Canadian average on the combined science scales and the other two science sub-domains.

Table 1.2			
Provincial results in science in relation to the Canadian average			
	Provinces performing significantly better than the Canadian average	Provinces performing as well as the Canadian average	Provinces performing significantly lower than the Canadian average
Science – combined scale	Alberta	Quebec, Ontario, British Columbia	Newfoundland and Labrador, Prince Edward Island, Nova Scotia, New Brunswick, Manitoba, Saskatchewan
Science – identifying scientific issues	Alberta	Newfoundland and Labrador, Quebec, Ontario, British Columbia	Prince Edward Island, Nova Scotia, New Brunswick, Manitoba, Saskatchewan
Science – explaining phenomena scientifically	Alberta	Quebec, Ontario, British Columbia	Newfoundland and Labrador, Prince Edward Island, Nova Scotia, New Brunswick, Manitoba, Saskatchewan
Mathematics – using scientific evidence	Alberta	Quebec, Ontario, British Columbia	Newfoundland and Labrador, Prince Edward Island, Nova Scotia, New Brunswick, Manitoba, Saskatchewan

Note: Provinces within each cell are ordered from east to west.

Canada has more equity in performance compared to all OECD countries combined

While mean performance is useful in assessing the overall performance of students, it can mask significant variation within a country/province. Further light on the performance within countries/provinces can be shed by examining the relative distribution of scores or the gap that exists between students with the highest and lowest levels of performance within each jurisdiction. This is an important indicator of the equity of educational outcomes in science. Chart 1.5 shows the difference in average scores between those in the lowest quarter (25th percentile) of student achievement and those in the highest quarter (75th percentile) of student achievement on the combined science scale. While in Canada, those in the highest quarter scored 127 points higher than those in the lowest quarter, this variation ranged from approximately 124 to 134 points across the provinces.

The amount of within-country variation in performance in science varied widely among OECD countries (Appendix tables B.1.5 to B.1.8). Both Canada and the majority of the provinces were among the few jurisdictions with above-average science performance and below-average level of disparity in student performance (as measured by score point differences between the 75th and 25th percentile) – both of these outcomes being desirable.

Chart 1.5

Difference in average scores in science between students who performed in the bottom quarter of performance and students who performed in the top quarter of performance

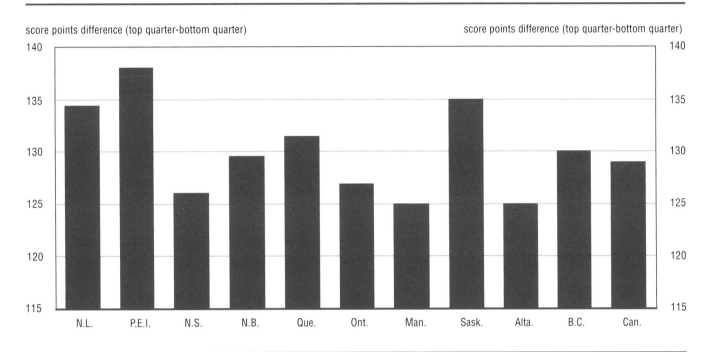

score points difference (top quarter-bottom quarter)

score points difference (top quarter-bottom quarter)

Canada has a high percentage of high achievers in science

The average scores reported in the previous section provide a useful but limited way of comparing performance of different groups of students. Another way to compare performance is to examine the proportions of students who can accomplish tasks at various proficiency levels. This kind of analysis allows a further breakdown of average scores and an examination of groups of students who show similar abilities. In PISA, science proficiency is a continuum – that is, science proficiency is not something a student has or does not have, but rather every 15-year-old shows a certain level of proficiency. The science proficiency levels used in

PISA 2006 are described in the text box 5 'Science Proficiency levels'.

Chart 1.6 (based on data from Appendix table B.1.9) shows the distribution of students by proficiency level by country and includes the Canadian provinces. Results for countries and provinces are presented in descending order according to the proportion of 15-year-olds who performed at Level 2 or higher. The OECD defined Level 2 proficiency as a baseline as it represents a critical level of science literacy on the PISA test. It is at Level 2 that students begin to demonstrate the kind of science knowledge and skills that enable them to actively and effectively use science competencies.

Chart 1.6

Percentage of students at each level of proficiency on the combined science scale

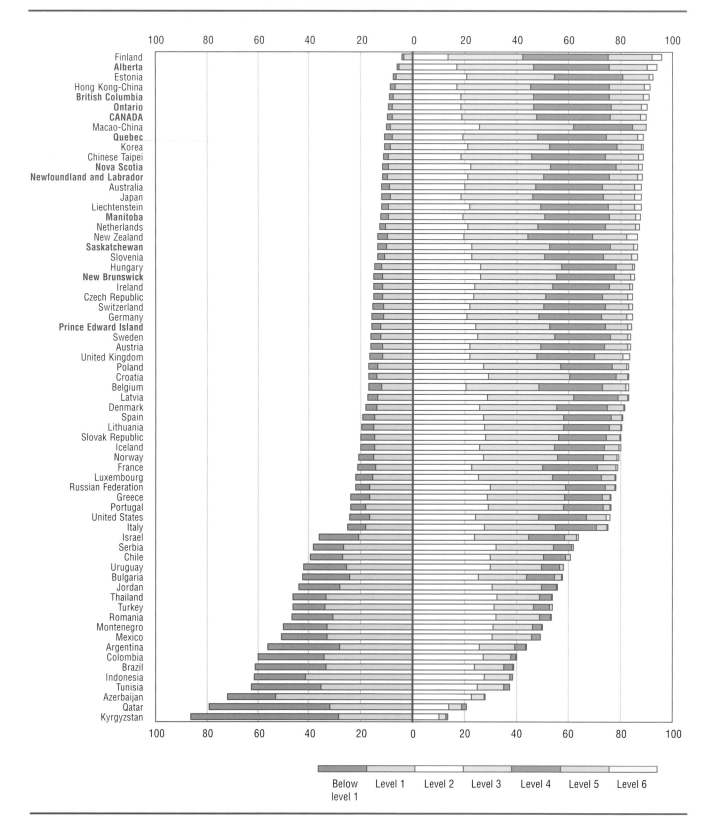

Box 5

Science proficiency levels

Science achievement was divided into six proficiency levels representing a group of tasks of increasing difficulty with Level 6 as the highest and Level 1 as the lowest. Students performing below Level 1 (science score below 334.5) are not able to demonstrate routinely the most basic type of knowledge and skills that PISA seeks to measure. Such students have serious difficulties in using science literacy as a tool to advance their knowledge and skills in other areas. Placement at this level does not mean that these students have no science knowledge and skills. Most of these students are able to correctly complete some of the PISA items. Their pattern of responses to the assessment is such that they would be expected to solve less than half of the tasks from a test composed of only Level 1 items.

In PISA 2006, Level 2 has been identified as the 'baseline proficiency' level or the level of achievement on the PISA scale at which students begin to demonstrate the scientific competencies that will enable full participation in life situations related to science and technology.

Students were assigned to a proficiency level based on their probability of answering correctly the majority of items in that range of difficulty. A student at a given level could be assumed to be able to correctly answer questions at all lower levels. To help in interpretation, these levels were linked to specific score ranges on the combined science scale. Below is a description of the abilities associated with each proficiency level. (Source: Organisation for Economic Cooperation and Development, Programme for International Student Assessment, PISA 2006).

Level 6 (score above 707.81)

At Level 6, students can consistently identify, explain and apply scientific knowledge and knowledge about science in a variety of complex life situations. They can link different information sources and explanations and use evidence from those sources to justify decisions. They clearly and consistently demonstrate advanced scientific thinking and reasoning, and they are willing to use their scientific understanding in support of solutions to unfamiliar scientific and technological situations. Students at this level can use scientific knowledge and develop arguments in support of recommendations and decisions that centre on personal, social or global situations.

Level 5 (score from 633.14 to 707.81)

At Level 5, students can identify the scientific components of many complex life situations, apply both scientific concepts and knowledge about science to these situations, and can compare, select and evaluate appropriate scientific evidence for responding to life situations. Students at this level can use well-developed inquiry abilities, link knowledge appropriately and bring critical insights to these situations. They can construct evidence-based explanations and arguments based on their critical analysis.

Level 4 (score from 558.48 to 633.14)

At Level 4, students can work effectively with situations and issues that may involve explicit phenomena requiring them to make inferences about the role of science or technology. They can select and integrate explanations from different disciplines of science or technology and link those explanations directly to aspects of life situations. Students at this level can reflect on their actions and they can communicate decisions using scientific knowledge and evidence.

Level 3 (score from 483.81 to 558.48)

At Level 3, students can identify clearly described scientific issues in a range of contexts. They can select facts and knowledge to explain phenomena and apply simple models or inquiry strategies. Students at this level can interpret and use scientific concepts from different disciplines and can apply them directly. They can develop short communications using facts and make decisions based on scientific knowledge.

Level 2 (score from 409.14 to 483.81)

At Level 2, students have adequate scientific knowledge to provide possible explanations in familiar contexts or draw conclusions based on simple investigations. They are capable of direct reasoning and making literal interpretations of the results of scientific inquiry or technological problem solving.

Level 1 (score from 334.48 to 409.14)

At Level 1, students have such a limited store of scientific knowledge that it can only be applied to a few, familiar situations. They can present scientific explanations that are obvious and follow concretely from given evidence.

Using these proficiency levels, students with high and low levels of proficiency can be identified. Listed in Table 1.3 are the percentages of students who performed at Level 1 or below and the percentages of students who performed at Level 5 or 6 for each country and the ten provinces.

Students performing at Level 1 or below would have great difficulty continuing studies in science and in daily life activities involving the application of science skills. In contrast, the students performing at Level 5 or above are likely to be well qualified to do so.

Compared to the OECD average, a significantly smaller proportion of Canadian students performed at Level 1 or below in science. The Canadian proportion at Level 1 or below was almost half the proportion of the OECD average (10% versus 19% respectively). Only Finland and Estonia had a significantly smaller proportion of students at Level 1 or below than Canada.

In contrast, a significantly higher proportion of Canadian students performed at Level 5 or above in science. The OECD average was approximately 9%, six percentage points lower than the average of 15% for Canada. Two countries (Finland and New Zealand) had significantly greater percentages of students with higher skills than Canada.

Turning to the provinces, the percentages of students who performed at Level 1 or below on the combined science scale were similar to the percentage for Canada in six of the Canadian provinces (Newfoundland and Labrador, Nova Scotia, Quebec, Ontario, Manitoba and British Columbia). The percentages of students in Alberta who performed at Level 1 or below was significantly lower than the Canadian average. While the percentage of students who performed at Level 1 or below was higher that the Canadian average in Saskatchewan, New Brunswick and Prince Edward Island, the percentage was below the OECD average.

The percentages of students in Alberta at Level 5 or higher (18%) were significantly greater than the Canadian percentage (15%). The percentages of students in Newfoundland and Labrador, Quebec, Ontario, Manitoba and British Columbia who performed at Levels 5 or higher were comparable to the percentage for Canada.

Lower percentages of students in Prince Edward Island, Nova Scotia, New Brunswick and Saskatchewan performed at Level 5 or higher compared to the Canadian percentage (Table 1.3). However, the provincial percentages were statistically the same or higher than as the OECD average.

Table 1.3

Percentage of students with high and low proficiency levels in science, by country and province

Percentage significantly higher than the Canadian percentage	Percentage not significantly different from the Canadian percentage	Percentage significantly lower than the Canadian percentage

Percentage of students with low level proficiency (level 1 or below)		Percentage of students with high level proficiency (level 5 or above)	
Country and province	percentage	Country and province	percentage
Finland	4	Finland	21
Alberta	6	Alberta	18
Estonia	8	New Zealand	18
Hong Kong-China	9	British Columbia	16
British Columbia	9	Hong Kong-China	16
Ontario	9	Japan	15
Canada	10	Australia	15
Macao-China	10	Chinese Taipei	15
Korea	11	Canada	15
Quebec	11	Ontario	14
Chinese Taipei	12	Quebec	14
Nova Scotia	12	United Kingdom	14
Newfoundland and Labrador	12	Newfoundland and Labrador	14
Japan	12	Netherlands	13
Manitoba	12	Slovenia	13
Australia	13	Manitoba	13
Netherlands	13	Liechtenstein	12
Liechtenstein	13	Germany	12
Saskatchewan	14	Czech Republic	12
New Zealand	14	Estonia	12
Slovenia	14	Saskatchewan	11
Hungary	15	Switzerland	11
New Brunswick	15	Korea	10
Germany	15	Belgium	10
Ireland	15	Nova Scotia	10
Czech Republic	15	Austria	10
Switzerland	16	Prince Edward Island	10
Prince Edward Island	16	Ireland	10
Austria	16	United States	9
Sweden	16	France	8
United Kingdom	17	New Brunswick	8
Croatia	17	Sweden	8
Poland	17	Denmark	7
Belgium	17	Hungary	7
Latvia	17	Poland	7
Denmark	18	Iceland	6
Spain	20	Norway	6
Slovak Republic	20	Luxembourg	6
Lithuania	20	Slovak Republic	6
Iceland	20	Macao-China	5
Norway	21	Croatia	5
France	21	Israel	5
Luxembourg	22	Lithuania	5
Russian Federation	22	Spain	5
Greece	24	Italy	5

Table 1.3 (concluded)

Percentage of students with high and low proficiency levels in science, by country and province

Percentage significantly higher than the Canadian percentage		Percentage not significantly different from the Canadian percentage		Percentage significantly lower than the Canadian percentage	
Percentage of students with low level proficiency (level 1 or below)			Percentage of students with high level proficiency (level 5 or above)		
Country and province	percentage		Country and province		percentage
United States	24		Russian Federation		4
Portugal	24		Latvia		4
Italy	25		Greece		3
Israel	36		Portugal		3
Serbia	38		Bulgaria		3
Chile	39		Chile		2
Uruguay	42		Uruguay		2
Bulgaria	43		Turkey		1
Jordan	44		Serbia		1
Thailand	46		Brazil		1
Turkey	46		Jordan		1
Romania	47		Argentina		1
Montenegro	50		Romania		1
Mexico	51		Thailand		0
Argentina	56		Mexico		0
Colombia	60		Montenegro		0
Brazil	61		Qatar		0
Indonesia	61		Colombia		0
Tunisia	63		Tunisia		0
Azerbaijan	72		Azerbaijan		0
Qatar	79		Indonesia		0
Kyrgyzstan	86		Kyrgyzstan		0

Students in minority language school systems had lower performance in combined science compared to those in majority language school systems

This section examines the science performance of students in the French-language and English-language school systems for the five Canadian provinces in which these populations were separately sampled. The performance of the minority language group (students in French-language school systems in Nova Scotia, New Brunswick, Ontario and Manitoba, and students in the English-language school system in Quebec) are compared to the majority group.

Results from PISA 2006 found that for science in the combined scale, students enrolled in the French-language school systems in Nova Scotia, New Brunswick, Ontario and Manitoba performed significantly lower than students in the English-language school systems. The differences ranged from 29 to 46 score points. In Quebec there was a small but statistically significant difference with results favouring the French-language system.

With respect to science performance in the three science sub-domains, significant differences favouring the English-language school system were observed in the four provinces where the French-language school systems are found in minority settings. In Quebec, there was a small but statistically significant difference with results favouring the French-language system in the sub-domains of 'explaining phenomena scientifically' while no significant difference was observed in the other two sub-domains.

Table 1.4

Average science scores by province and language of the school system

	English-language school system		French-language school system		Difference between French-language and English language school system	
	average	standard error	average	standard error	difference[1]	standard error
Science – combined scale						
Nova Scotia	521*	(2.5)*	475*	(5.6)*	46*	(6.1)*
New Brunswick	516*	(3.0)*	482*	(3.1)*	34*	(4.4)*
Quebec	519*	(3.2)*	532*	(4.7)*	-13*	(5.7)*
Ontario	538*	(4.3)*	498*	(3.5)*	40*	(5.4)*
Manitoba	524*	(3.3)*	495*	(5.7)*	29*	(6.7)*
Science – identifying scientific issues						
Nova Scotia	517*	(3.6)*	465*	(6.1)*	52*	(7.0)*
New Brunswick	524*	(3.0)*	483*	(3.3)*	41*	(4.7)*
Quebec	523	(3.7)	532	(5.3)	-9	(6.6)
Ontario	534*	(5.1)*	495*	(3.8)*	40*	(6.3)*
Manitoba	520*	(3.4)*	485*	(5.7)*	35*	(6.7)*
Science – explaining phenomena scientifically						
Nova Scotia	520*	(3.4)*	474*	(6.3)*	46*	(7.4)*
New Brunswick	510*	(3.4)*	479*	(3.3)*	31*	(4.8)*
Quebec	509*	(3.6)*	524*	(4.5)*	-16*	(6.0)*
Ontario	534*	(4.6)*	492*	(3.5)*	42*	(5.8)*
Manitoba	523*	(3.6)*	496*	(5.6)*	27*	(6.7)*
Science – using scientific evidence						
Nova Scotia	525*	(2.5)*	481*	(6.1)*	45*	(6.8)*
New Brunswick	521*	(3.0)*	487*	(3.6)*	35*	(4.7)*
Quebec	531	(3.4)	543	(5.3)	-12	(6.3)
Ontario	547*	(4.5)*	508*	(3.9)*	39*	(5.8)*
Manitoba	531*	(3.5)*	502*	(6.0)*	29*	(7.1)*

* Statistically significant differences.

1. This difference may be slightly different from that obtained by subtracting the averages due to rounding.

Summary

In this chapter performance in combined science and in the three science sub-scales of identifying scientific issues, explaining phenomena scientifically and using scientific evidence are presented for Canada and the provinces.

In an increasingly technology-based society, knowledge and skills in science are critical to economic progress. Canada's performance in PISA 2006 suggests that, on the whole, Canadian 15-year-olds are equipped with the science knowledge and skills to participate in a society in which science and technology play a significant role.

However, while all provinces scored above the OECD average, there were differences in performance among provinces. While the comparative approach taken in this chapter does not lend itself to developing explanations for these differences, further analysis could explore how resources, schools and classroom conditions, as well as individual and family circumstances, affect variation in achievement.

Notes

6. Further detail on scientific literacy and the scientific competencies are available in the PISA 2006 framework: 'Assessing Scientific, Reading and Mathematical Literacy, A Framework for PISA 2006'. OECD (2007).

7. The OECD average for the combined score was established with the data weighted so that each OECD country contributed equally. As the anchoring of the scale was done for the combination of the three competency sub-domain scales, the average mean and standard deviation for the sub-domain scales differ from 500 and 100 score points.

8. OECD (2007), Learning for Tomorrow's World – First results from PISA 2006. Paris.

Chapter 2

The performance of Canadian students in reading and mathematics in an international context

This chapter presents the overall results of the PISA 2006 assessments in the minor domains of reading and mathematics. First, the average performance of Canadian 15-year-old students is compared to the performance of 15-year-old students from countries that participated in PISA 2006. Second, students' performance in the ten Canadian provinces are presented and discussed. Third, the performance of students enrolled in English-language and French-language school systems are compared for the five provinces in which the two groups were separately sampled. Lastly, the results of PISA 2006 are compared with those of PISA 2003 and PISA 2000 for reading and mathematics.

Defining reading and mathematics

Both reading and mathematics were minor domains in PISA 2006. On the other hand, reading was the major domain of PISA 2000 while mathematics was the major domain in PISA 2003. Definitions for both domains are provided in the Introduction.

The scores for reading and mathematics are expressed on a scale with an average or mean of 500 points and a standard deviation of 100. This average was established in the year in which the domain became the main focus of the assessment - 2000 for reading and 2003 for mathematics. Approximately two-thirds of the students scored between 400 and 600 (i.e. within one standard deviation of the average) for the OECD countries. Due to change in performance over time, the OECD average scores for mathematics and reading in PISA 2006 differ slightly from 500.

Canadian students performed well in reading and mathematics

One way to summarize student performance and to compare the relative standing of countries is by examining their average test scores. However, simply ranking countries based on their average scores can be misleading because there is a margin of error associated with each score. As discussed in Chapter 1, when interpreting average performances, only those differences between countries that are statistically significant should be taken into account. Table 2.1 shows the countries that performed significantly better than or the same as Canada in reading and mathematics. The averages of the students in all of the remaining countries were significantly below those of Canada. Overall, Canadian students performed well. Among the countries that participated in PISA 2006, only Korea, Finland and Hong Kong-China performed better than Canada in reading and mathematics. Additionally Chinese Taipei performed better than Canada in mathematics.

Chart 2.1

Average scores and confidence intervals for provinces and countries: Reading

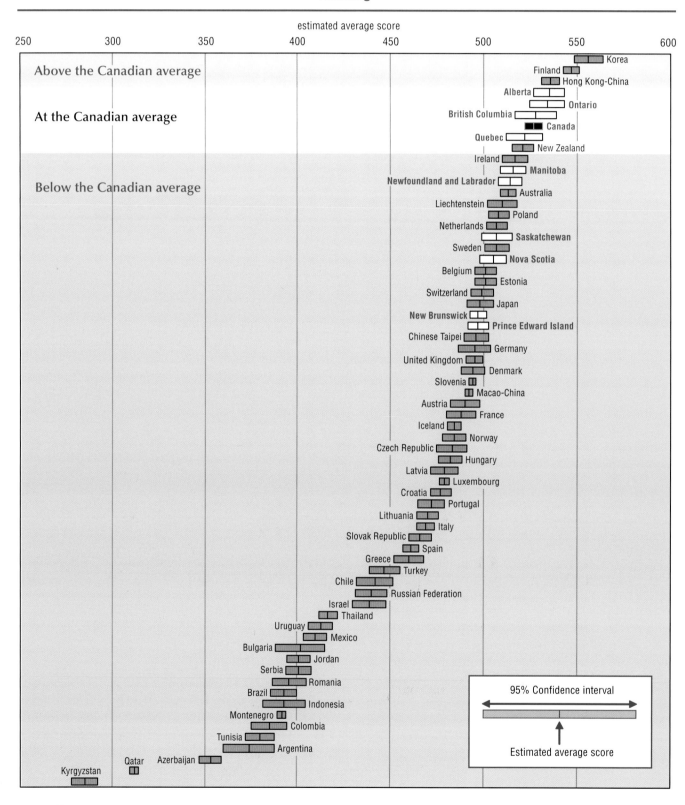

Note: The OECD average in 2006 is 492 with a standard error of 0.6.

Chart 2.2

Average scores and confidence intervals for provinces and countries: Mathematics

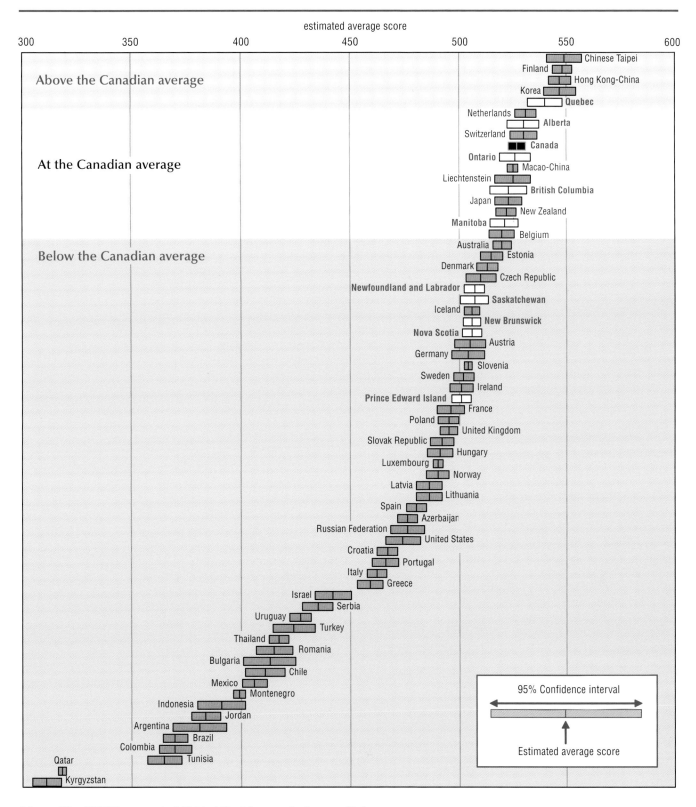

Note: The OECD average in 2006 is 498 with a standard error of 0.5.

Table 2.1		
Countries performing better than, or the same as Canada		
	Countries performing significantly better than Canada	Countries performing the same as Canada
Reading	Korea, Finland, Hong Kong-China	New Zealand
Mathematics	Chinese Taipei, Finland, Korea, Hong Kong-China	Netherlands, Switzerland, Macao-China, Liechtenstein, Japan, New Zealand, Belgium

All provinces performed at or above the OECD average in reading and mathematics

Across the two minor domains of PISA 2006 the performance of students in all provinces was, with a few exceptions, above the OECD average. Students in Prince Edward Island and New Brunswick performed at the OECD average in reading while students in Prince Edward Island performed at the OECD average in mathematics.

As shown in Table 2.2, students in Quebec performed above the Canadian average in mathematics and at the Canadian average in reading. Students in Ontario, Alberta and British Columbia performed at the Canadian average in both minor domains. Students in Newfoundland and Labrador, Prince Edward Island, Nova Scotia, New Brunswick and Saskatchewan performed below the Canadian average in both minor domains. Students in Manitoba performed below the Canadian average in Reading and at the Canadian average in mathematics.

Table 2.2			
Provincial results in reading and mathematics in relation to the Canadian average			
	Provinces performing significantly better than the Canadian average	Provinces performing the same as the Canadian average	Provinces performing significantly lower than the Canadian average
Reading		Quebec, Ontario, Alberta, British Columbia	Newfoundland and Labrador, Prince Edward Island, Nova Scotia, New Brunswick, Manitoba, Saskatchewan
Mathematics	Quebec	Ontario, Manitoba, Alberta, British Columbia	Newfoundland and Labrador, Prince Edward Island, Nova Scotia, New Brunswick, Saskatchewan

Note: Provinces within each cell are ordered from east to west.

Canada has more equity in performance compared to all OECD countries combined

While mean performance is useful in assessing the overall performance of students, it can mask significant variation within a jurisdiction. Further light on the performance within jurisdictions can be shed by examining the relative distribution of scores or the gap that exists between students with the highest and lowest levels of performance within each jurisdiction. This is an important indicator of the equity of educational outcomes in reading and mathematics. Chart 2.3 shows the difference in average scores between those in the lowest quarter (25th percentile) of student achievement and those in the highest quarter (75th percentile) of student achievement in reading and mathematics. For Canada overall, those in the highest quarter scored 124 points higher on reading and 117 points higher in mathematics compared to those in the lowest quarter. This compares to 147 and 127 points respectively for reading and mathematics across all OECD countries

The amount of within-country variation in performance in reading and mathematics varied widely among countries (Appendix tables B.2.3 and B.2.4). Canada was one of the few countries with above-average performance and below-average disparity in student performance (as measured by score point differences between the 75th and 25th percentile) – both of these outcomes being desirable.

Chart 2.3

Difference in average scores in reading and mathematics between students who performed in the bottom quarter of performance and students who performed in the top quarter of performance

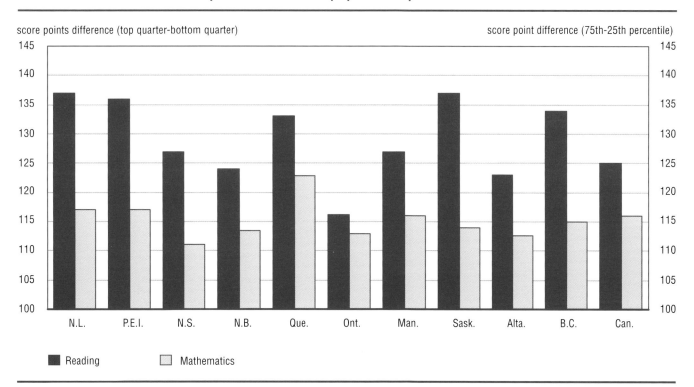

score points difference (top quarter-bottom quarter)

score point difference (75th-25th percentile)

Reading   Mathematics

Across the provinces, differences between the lowest and highest quarter ranged from 112 to 123 in mathematics and 116 to 140 in reading. All provinces had below-average levels of variation in mathematics performance compared to the OECD average. Generally speaking, provinces that performed better in reading and mathematics tended to have less variation between the highest and lowest quartile of student performance.

Achievement of Canadian students in reading and mathematics differ by language of the school system

This section examines the performance of students in the English-language and French-language school systems for the five Canadian provinces that sampled these population groups separately. The performance of the minority language group (students in French-language school systems in Nova Scotia, New Brunswick, Ontario and Manitoba and students in the English-language school system in Quebec) are compared to he majority language group.

A comparison of PISA 2006 results within each province is given in Table 2.3. As was the case in PISA 2000 and PISA 2003, students enrolled in the French-language school systems in Nova Scotia, New Brunswick, Ontario and Manitoba performed significantly lower in reading than did students in the English-language system in the same province. In Quebec, student performance did not differ between the English-language and French-language school systems.

For mathematics, there were significant differences favouring the English-language system in New Brunswick and Ontario however these differences were much less pronounced than those observed for reading. There were significant differences favouring the French-language school system in Quebec. No significant differences in mathematics were observed in Nova Scotia and Manitoba.

Table 2.3

Average reading and mathematics scores by province and language of the school system

	English-language school system		French-language school system		Difference between French-language and English-language school system	
	average	standard error	average	standard error	difference[1]	standard error
Reading						
Nova Scotia	506*	(3.6)*	442*	(5.7)*	64*	(6.5)*
New Brunswick	510*	(2.6)*	465*	(3.7)*	45*	(4.2)*
Quebec	520	(3.2)	522	(5.7)	-3	(6.8)
Ontario	536*	(4.8)*	485*	(3.3)*	51*	(5.9)*
Manitoba	518*	(3.6)*	465*	(5.8)*	53*	(6.8)*
Mathematics						
Nova Scotia	506	(2.3)	496	(5.3)	11	(5.8)
New Brunswick	509*	(2.8)*	499*	(3.2)*	10*	(4.4)*
Quebec	530*	(2.8)*	541*	(4.8)*	-12*	(5.6)*
Ontario	527*	(3.8)*	507*	(3.0)*	19*	(4.9)*
Manitoba	521	(3.4)	516	(5.0)	4	(6.2)

* Statistically significant differences.
1. This difference may be slightly different from that obtained by subtracting the averages due to rounding.

Student performance in reading and mathematics remained stable since 2000 for Canada overall and for most provinces

PISA 2006 provides the third assessment of reading since 2000 when the first full assessment of reading took place, and the second assessment of mathematics since 2003 when the first full assessment of mathematics took place. While this section looks at change over time, performance differences should be interpreted with caution for several reasons. First, while the measurement approach used in PISA is consistent across cycles, small refinements were made so small changes should be interpreted prudently. Secondly, since data is available for three points in time for reading and two points in time for mathematics since being assessed fully in 2003, it is not possible to determine the extent to which observed differences are indicative of longer-term changes.

The OECD average of 492 points in reading in 2006 represents a decrease in the average score of 500 for the OECD countries that participated in 2000[9]. In Canada, as well as across OECD countries, reading performance did not change between 2003 and 2006. Reading performance also remained stable in Canada between 2000 and 2006. In comparing change between 2000 and 2006, reading performance remained stable in 16 countries including Canada, decreased in 15 countries and increased in 8 countries. The improvement in reading performance observed in Hong Kong-China and Korea explains why these two countries, for the first time, outperformed Canada in 2006.

Mathematics performance remained unchanged across all countries between PISA 2003 and PISA 2006 and the OECD average change of 2 score points was not statistically significant.

Tables 2.4 and 2.5 show the confidence intervals for performance in reading and mathematics for Canada and the provinces. The confidence intervals take into account the sampling, linkage and measurement errors that are introduced when assessments are linked with a limited number of common assessment tasks over time. Changes are only statistically significant when the confidence intervals around scores do not overlap.

Performance in reading and mathematics remained stable across jurisdictions with the following exceptions: reading performance decreased between 2000 and 2006 in Prince Edward Island, Nova Scotia and Saskatchewan while mathematics performance decreased between 2003 and 2006 in Alberta and British Columbia.

Table 2.4

Comparison of performance confidence intervals in reading, PISA 2000, 2003 and 2006, Canada and the provinces

| | PISA score with 95% confidence interval | | | | | |
| | 2000 | | 2003 | | 2006 | |
	average score	standard error	average score	standard error with linkage error	average score	standard error with linkage error
Newfoundland and Labrador	517	(2.8)	521	(4.9)	514	(5.4)
Prince Edward Island	517*	(2.4)	495*	(4.4)	497*	(5.1)
Nova Scotia	521*	(2.3)	513	(4.4)	505*	(5.7)
New Brunswick	501	(1.8)	503	(4.3)	497	(5.0)
Quebec	536	(3.0)	525	(5.7)	522	(6.7)
Ontario	533	(3.3)	530	(5.1)	535	(6.4)
Manitoba	529	(3.5)	520	(5.0)	516	(5.7)
Saskatchewan	529*	(2.7)	512*	(5.6)*	507*	(6.3)*
Alberta	550	(3.3)	543	(5.7)	534	(6.1)
British Columbia	538	(2.9)	535	(4.5)	528	(7.1)
Canada	534	(1.6)	528	(4.1)	527	(5.1)

* Statistically significant differences compared to PISA 2000.
Note: The linkage error is incorporated into the standard error for 2003 and 2006.

Table 2.5

Comparison of performance confidence intervals in mathematics, PISA, 2003 and 2006, Canada and the provinces

| | PISA score with 95% confidence interval | | | |
| | 2003 | | 2006 | |
	average score	standard error with linkage error	average score	standard error with linkage error
Newfoundland and Labrador	517	(2.5)	507	(3.1)
Prince Edward Island	500	(2.0)	501	(2.7)
Nova Scotia	515	(2.2)	506	(2.8)
New Brunswick	512	(1.8)	506	(2.5)
Quebec	537	(4.7)	540	(4.4)
Ontario	530	(3.6)	526	(4.0)
Manitoba	528	(3.1)	521	(3.6)
Saskatchewan	516	(3.9)	507	(3.7)
Alberta	549*	(4.3)*	530*	(4.0)*
British Columbia	538*	(2.4)*	523*	(4.7)*
Canada	**532**	**(1.8)**	**527**	**(2.4)**

* Statistically significant differences.

Note: The linkage error is incorporated into the standard error for 2006.

Summary

Because reading and mathematics were considered to be minor domains in PISA 2006, a smaller proportion of students were assessed in those domains compared to the science assessment, which was the major focus of the 2006 assessment. Additionally, a smaller number of items were included in each of these assessments than were included in the science assessment. Consequently, this chapter focuses on providing an update on overall performance in these two domains.

While performance in reading remained stable in Canada since PISA 2000, improved performance in reading in Hong Kong-China and Korea resulted in these two countries outperforming Canada for the first time since PISA was implemented. This suggests that although Canada's performance in reading is strong, in order to maintain its' competitive edge in the future Canadian 15-year-olds will need to improve at the rate of the top performing countries, rather than simply maintain their competencies in reading.

Note

9. Three OECD countries (The Netherlands, the Slovak Republic and Turkey) were not included in the PISA 2000 assessment.

Chapter 3

Differences in performance by selected student characteristics

Introduction

As shown in Chapter 1, the science performance of students differed considerably across countries and across provinces. In this Chapter, selected student characteristics that are related to performance are explored beginning with an examination of performance by gender and immigrant status followed by an examination analysis of the impact of parental education and of socio-economic status.

Boys outperform girls in 'explaining phenomena scientifically' while girls outperform boys in 'identifying scientific issues'

Policy makers have an interest in reducing gender disparities in educational performance. Such performance coupled with their motivation and attitudes towards learning influence both educational and occupational pathways of boys and girls.

PISA 2006 shows that gender differences on the combined science scale, which varied across countries, were small in absolute terms when compared with the large gender gap in reading. In Canada, no gender difference was observed on the combined science scale with the exception of Newfoundland and Labrador where girls performed better than boys by 12 score points. Across all countries participating in PISA 2006, ten countries showed an advantage of boys over girls while thirteen countries showed an advantage of girls over boys. For the remaining countries there were no significant gender differences on the combined science scale.

In Canada, although overall there were no gender differences on the combined science scale or on the sub-scale of using scientific evidence, there were substantial gender differences on the other two science sub-scales as summarized in Table 3.1. In Canada, most countries and eight of the ten provinces, boys out performed girls in the sub-domain of 'explaining phenomena scientifically'. Canadian boys outperformed girls by 17 score points and this difference ranged from 0 to 21 points across provinces (Appendix table B.3.1) while across all OECD countries boys outperformed girls by 15 score points. In contrast, in Canada, most countries and all of the provinces, girls outperformed boys in the sub-domain 'identifying scientific issues'. The magnitude of this difference was 14 points for Canada overall, 17 points across all OECD countries and ranged from 12 to 36 score points across provinces.

The performance patterns on these two sub-scales suggest that boys and girls have very different levels of performance in different areas of science. It appears that boys demonstrate better performance at mastering scientific knowledge whereas girls demonstrate better performance at seeing the larger picture that enables them to identify scientific questions that arise from a given situation.

Table 3.1

Summary of gender differences for Canada and the provinces

	Girls performed significantly higher than boys	Boys performed significantly higher than girls	No significant differences between boys and girls
Science – combined scale	Newfoundland and Labrador		Canada, Prince Edward Island, Nova Scotia, New Brunswick, Quebec, Ontario, Manitoba, Saskatchewan, Alberta, British Columbia
Science – using scientific evidence	Newfoundland and Labrador, Saskatchewan		Canada, Prince Edward Island, Nova Scotia, New Brunswick, Quebec, Ontario, Manitoba, Alberta, British Columbia
Science – explaining phenomena scientifically		Canada, Prince Edward Island, Nova Scotia, New Brunswick, Quebec, Ontario, Manitoba, Alberta, British Columbia	Newfoundland and Labrador, Saskatchewan
Science- identifying scientific issues	Canada, All provinces		
Reading	Canada, All provinces		
Mathematics		Canada, Nova Scotia, Quebec, Ontario, Manitoba, Alberta, British Columbia	Newfoundland and Labrador, Prince Edward Island, New Brunswick, Saskatchewan

Note: Provinces within each cell are ordered from east to west.

Gender differences across the minor domains of mathematics and reading were consistent with results from previous PISA assessments with boys outperforming girls in mathematics and girls outperforming boys in reading. As was also the case in previous PISA assessments, the gap between girls and boys in reading was much larger than the gap between boys and girls in mathematics. In Canada, while boys outperformed girls by 14 points in mathematics, girls outperformed boys by 33 points in reading. At the provincial level, boys outperformed girls in mathematics in six of the ten provinces while girls outperformed boys in reading in all provinces.

When examining patterns of gender differences for the domains across provinces, some interesting patterns emerge. In contrast to that observed for Canada overall and the remaining provinces, in Newfoundland and Labrador, Prince Edward Island and Saskatchewan, no gender differences were observed in mathematics or on the sub-scale of 'explaining phenomena scientifically'. In three of the largest provinces, Quebec, Ontario and British Columbia, the magnitude of the gender differences across domains were more pronounced in domains where boys outperformed girls and less pronounced in domains where girls outperformed boys (Appendix tables B.3.1 and B.3.2).

Immigrant students perform lower in science than non-immigrant students

Immigration has long been integral to Canada's social, cultural and economic development and it is expected that immigrants will constitute a larger share of the growth of Canada's labour force in the future. Results of the 2003 International Adult Literacy and Skills Survey[10] revealed that a larger proportion of adult immigrants performed at a lower level in literacy, numeracy and problem solving than Canadian-born. PISA data can also be explored to see if performance differences exist between immigrant and non-immigrant students.

PISA identifies two groups of immigrants: **second-generation immigrants** are those born in Canada from immigrant parents; and **first generation immigrants** are those born outside of Canada. Students born in Canada from parents also born in Canada are defined as non-immigrant students.

Twenty one percent of the Canadian youth that participated in PISA 2006 were immigrants. Ten percent were first generation and 11% second generation. Immigrant youth represent 10% or more of the 15-year-old youth in five provinces: Quebec, Ontario, Manitoba, Alberta and British Columbia (Appendix table B.3.3). Detailed results about immigrant youth are presented only for these five provinces.

Table 3.2

Distribution of 15-year olds by immigrant status and difference in performance on the combined science scale. PISA 2006

	Percentage of Students by Immigrant Status			Performance on the combined science score		
	Non-immigrants	Second-generation immigrants	First-generation immigrants	Non-immigrants	Second-generation immigrants	First-generation immigrants
	percentage			average score		
Quebec	87	7	6	540	501	483
Ontario	69	16	15	546	538	520
Manitoba	88	7	5	529	509	496
Alberta	83	10	6	553	543	548
British Columbia	72	15	14	544	519	536
Canada	79	11	10	541	528	519
OECD Average	91	5	5	506	468	450

Second-generation immigrants completed all their education in Canada, having been born in this country. However this is not necessarily the case for first-generation immigrants depending on their age of arrival to Canada. Even if PISA is not measuring knowledge and skills specifically acquired in school, one would expect that the differences in scores between second-generation immigrants and non-immigrant students would be small, particularly in an area like science, where youth are more likely to develop their knowledge and skills in school rather than in their family or community. However, as shown in Table 3.2, non-immigrant students outperformed second generation immigrants who were born and educated in Canada. In three provinces (Manitoba, Quebec and British Columbia) the performance differences between non-immigrant youth and their second generation peers were significant.

Within Canada, the difference ranged from 20 points in Manitoba to 39 points for Quebec.

A similar pattern is observed when looking at differences in performance between first generation immigrants and non-immigrant students. In Canada, non-immigrant youth outperformed their first-generation peers by 23 points in science. Performance differences were significant in Ontario (27 points) and Manitoba (32 points) and were most pronounced in Quebec at 57 points.

When comparing performance between first and second generation immigration youth, there were similar levels of performance in four provinces. However, for Canada overall and Ontario second generation immigrant students outperformed first generation immigrant students by 10 points and 19 points respectively.

It should be noted that immigrant youth in Canada have much higher performance than immigrants across all OECD countries (Appendix table B.3.3) and also perform above the OECD average of 500. In addition, the magnitude of performance differences of immigrant students compared to non-immigrant students is less pronounced in Canada compared to across all OECD countries as whole. The only exception is observed in Quebec where the difference in scores is at the OECD average. In contrast, in Alberta there were no differences in performance between immigrant and non-immigrant students.

Higher levels of parental education are associated with higher performance in science

Parents play an important role in how students learn. Aside from being actively involved in their children's education, parents also provide a home environment that can impact on learning. Parents serve as a model for learning, determine the educational resources available in the home and hold particular attitudes and values towards education.

Parental education is a factor that has been shown to be related to important transitions in youth life. For example, Knighton and Bussière (2006) found that youth whose parents highest level of education was high school or less were less likely to complete high school or to go to post-secondary education by age 19.

Thirty percent of the Canadian youth that participated in PISA 2006 had parents whose highest level of education was high school or less while 70% of students had a parent with at least some post secondary education. Parental education varied across provinces (Appendix table B.3.4): students whose parents had some postsecondary education ranged from 56% (Newfoundland and Labrador) to 77% (Ontario).

Youth with at least one parent who had post-secondary education outperformed their peers whose parents had high school education or less (Chart 3.1). In Canada, this difference amounted to 32 score points which is roughly equivalent to one year of education. While differences existed across all of the provinces the magnitude of this difference varied, ranging from 21 and 22 points in British Columbia and Manitoba respectively to 41 points in Quebec and Newfoundland and Labrador.

Chart 3.1

Difference in score points of the combined science scale between students whose parents had some post secondary education and students whose parents had high school or less

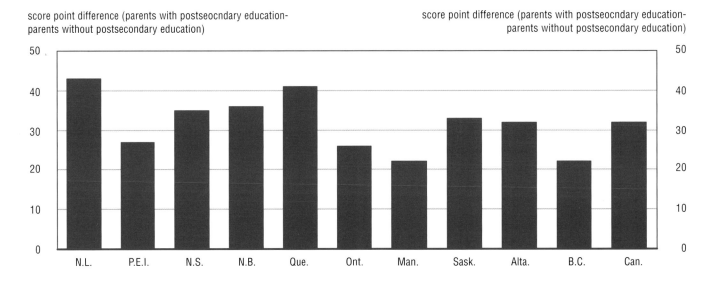

Socioeconomic status is related to performance but to a lesser extent in Canada when compared to other countries

How equitable the benefits of schooling are to students from different socio-economic backgrounds can be understood from the relationship between socio-economic background and student performance. Socio-economic status (SES) is a term used to summarize a variety of factors, including parental education and occupation, which influence student performance. In PISA 2006, SES was measured by an index that includes information describing family structure, parental education and occupation, parental labour market participation and whether a student's family has specific educational and cultural possessions at home. This index

is standardized to have an average of 0 and standard deviation of 1 across all OECD countries.

The averages of SES for Canada and the provinces are reported in Table 3.3. As was the case in previous PISA assessments, the average student in Canada had a relative socio-economic advantage compared to 15-year-olds in all OECD countries with a score on the mean index being higher than the OECD average of 0. Students in the four Atlantic provinces had scores below the Canadian average while the remaining provinces had scores that did not differ significantly from the Canadian average. Though the differences were not significant, Ontario, Alberta and British Columbia had higher scores than Canada. While students in all provinces tend to be more advantaged than 15-year-olds in other OECD countries, the differences across provinces suggest that all students in Canada may not have access to the same resources or opportunities.

Table 3.3

Socio-economic status in Canadian provinces

	Mean index score		Performance on the science scale, by national and provincial quarters of Socioeconomic status			
	mean index	standard error	bottom quarter	second quarter	third quarter	top quarter
	percentage		average score			
Newfoundland and Labrador	0.11	(0.02)	481	511	538	574
Prince Edward Island	0.21	(0.02)	481	499	522	536
Nova Scotia	0.24	(0.03)	484	504	531	555
New Brunswick	0.20	(0.04)	472	495	517	545
Quebec	0.21	(0.03)	495	522	537	574
Ontario	0.48	(0.05)	506	530	557	567
Manitoba	0.34	(0.04)	494	516	534	556
Saskatchewan	0.28	(0.04)	479	508	530	550
Alberta	0.43	(0.05)	519	541	560	584
British Columbia	0.40	(0.04)	507	538	545	563
Canada	0.37	(0.02)	501	527	548	569
OECD average	0.00	(0.00)	430	481	512	549

The relationship between SES and performance can be measured by the average performance levels by quarter of the index. Table 3.3 shows the relationship between student performance and SES; students are grouped into 4 quarters based on their score on the SES index, those in the bottom quarter have lower levels of SES while those in the highest quarter have higher levels of SES.

As shown in Table 3.3 there is a positive relationship between SES and science performance. In Canada, those in the top quarter of SES score 68 points higher, equivalent to one proficiency level higher, than those in the lowest SES quarter. The effect of SES on performance is much lower than that observed across all OECD countries where the difference between those in the top and bottom quarter was 119 points.

At the provincial level, the SES performance gap between the bottom and top quarters ranged from 55 and 56 points in Prince Edward Island and British Columbia respectively to 93 points in Newfoundland and Labrador. The fact that all provinces had SES performance gaps below the OECD average and average performance above the OECD average in science can be an indication that jurisdictions are able to mitigate the effects of SES and achieve relative equity in the distribution of learning performance. However, as seen by provincial differences in performance related to SES, it appears that there is still room for improvement. Across jurisdictions, British Columbia represents an example of a jurisdiction that has minimized the relationship between student SES and performance while still maintaining high levels of student performance.

Summary

This chapter examined the relationship between various student background characteristics and achievement.

While no gender differences exist on the combined science scale, the performance patterns on two sub-scales suggest that boys and girls have very different levels of performance in different areas of science. It appears that boys may be better at mastering scientific knowledge whereas girls may be better at seeing the larger picture that enables them to identify scientific questions that arise from a given situation. Additionally, girls continue to outperform boys in reading while boys outperform girls in math.

Immigrant status, parental education and socio-economic background are all related to performance but to a lesser extent in Canada compared to OECD countries as a whole. However, differences observed across the jurisdictions, suggest that further improvements are possible. For example, Alberta represents a jurisdiction with higher performance and no differences in performance between immigrants and non-immigrant Canadians and British Columbia represents an example of a jurisdiction that has minimized the relationship between student SES and performance while still maintaining high levels of student performance.

While this chapter has only looked at the relationship between student background characteristics examined individually on performance, further multivariate research can determine the relative performance of student background characteristics impacting performance.

Note

10.   Building on our Competencies: Canadian Results of the International Adult Literacy and Skills Survey, HRSDC and Statistics Canada 2005.

Chapter 4

Themes explored through PISA 2006

Introduction

In addition to assessing student performance, PISA also collected data on student, family and institutional factors that can help to explain differences in performance. These factors are organized around themes or research areas that will be further expanded upon in future thematic reports released by the OECD and can be further explored nationally through subsequent analysis with PISA 2006 data.

In this chapter, three key themes related to science are explored. First an examination of students' engagement in science and its relationship to science achievement is presented. Next, science and the environment are explored. This is followed by a look at the contexts for the learning of science.

The focus of this chapter is to provide a first glance at the breadth of information collected through PISA 2006. While this chapter does not explore these themes in depth, it does provide an overview of the relationships of these themes with student achievement and provides detailed data tables summarizing these results at the provincial level in the Appendix tables that can be further used by policy makers for informing decisions.

Box 6

Reporting PISA indices

Several themes presented in this chapter are based on questions collected through the student and school questionnaire and on indices that were derived based on these questions. A description of each index is provided in the text and each index was constructed so that the average score across the OECD countries is 0 and so that two-thirds of the scores are between -1.0 and 1.0 (i.e. a standard deviation of 1). Positive scores on each index are associated with higher levels of the attribute being measured whereas negative scores on each index are associated with lower levels of the attribute being measured.

In this section, relationships between indices and performance are presented in terms of differences in average performance between the top quarter and bottom quarter on the indices. In addition, the Appendix tables present the difference in student performance per unit (one standard deviation) of the index.

Science engagement

The level of student engagement in science is important for acquiring skills and knowledge in science. Students who are engaged in the learning process will tend to learn more and be more receptive to the pursuit of knowledge. Further, student engagement in science has an impact upon course selection, educational pathways and career choices.

PISA 2006 collected information on a variety of dimensions of student engagement relating to thier belief that they can succeed in science, their value of science, their interest in science and their perceptions and attitudes regarding environmental issues. Based on student responses to a series of questions, PISA 2006 constructed the following engagement indices:

Students' belief that they can success in science:

- Science self-efficacy measures confidence to perform science-related tasks
- Science self-concept measures their perception of their ability to learn science

Students' value of science:

- General value of science measures their general appreciation of science as important and valuable to society at large.
- Personal value of science measures their appreciation of science as being relevant and useful for their own purposes.

Students' interest in science:

- General interest in science refers to interest in learning about broad science topics.
- Enjoyment of science measures enjoyment in learning and reading about science, solving science problems and acquiring new knowledge in science.
- Instrumental motivation to learn science measures their belief that science will be useful for future employment or education.
- Future-oriented science motivation measures their belief that they will study and work in the field of science as an adult.
- Science activities outside school measure the extent to which they participate in activities outside of the school.

Student engagement results are summarized in Table 4.1 which shows the mean index score and relationship to science performance and in Table 4.2 which summarizes provincial differences in relationship to the Canadian average. Detailed results are presented in Appendix tables B.4.1 to B.4.9.

Students believe that they can succeed in science

The belief in their ability to succeed in science is an important outcome of education and highly relevant to successful learning by the student. Canadian youth more strongly believe that they can succeed in science compared to the beliefs of their international peers. As indicated by the average index scores compared to the OECD average of 0 (Table 4.1), Canadian 15-year-olds reported higher levels of confidence in performing science-related tasks (science self-efficacy) and a higher perception of their ability to learn science (science self concept). Compared to Canadian 15-year-olds as a whole, students in Newfoundland and Labrador and Alberta reported higher levels of confidence in performing science-related tasks while students in New Brunswick, Quebec and Saskatchewan reported levels lower than the Canadian average (Appendix table B.4.1). Students in Manitoba and Saskatchewan reported lower levels of perception of their ability to learn science (science self concept) compared to the Canadian average (Table 4.1, Appendix table B.4.2).

Table 4.1 shows the relationship between the engagement indices and science performance. Students are grouped into four quarters based on their score on each index, those in the bottom quarter reported lower levels while those in the top quarter reported higher levels of the respective index. Among all the student engagement indices, the two indices relating to a student's belief that they can succeed in science had the strongest relationship with science achievement. Those with higher levels of belief that they can succeed in science (i.e. those in the top quarter in the index of science self-efficacy and science self-concept) had much higher average scores, equivalent to more than one proficiency level higher, relative to those with lower levels of belief that the can succeed in science (i.e. those in the bottom quarter on these indices). This relationship also held true across the provinces (Appendix tables B.4.1 and B.4.2).

Students' value of science

The value that students place on science concerns their general appreciation of science as being important and valuable to society at large and that they personally value of science as being relevant and useful for their own purposes. Compared to 15-year-olds across all OECD countries, Canadian youth believed more strongly that science is important and valuable to society at large as well as for their own purpose (Table 4.1). Compared to the Canadian average, youth in Quebec were less likely to believe that science is relevant and useful for them personally while students in Newfoundland and Labrador, Prince Edward Island and Alberta were more likely to believe that science is relevant and useful for them personally. Youth in Nova Scotia, New Brunswick and Saskatchewan were less likely to believe in the value of science for the society (Table 4.2).

There was a relationship between students' value of science and their science performance. Youth in the top quarter on the indices of general value of science and personal value of science scored 62 and 69 points higher respectively than their counterparts who scored in the bottom quarter of each index. This relationship also held true across the provinces (Appendix tables B.4.3 to B.4.4).

Students' interest in science

Students' general interest in science was included in PISA because of its established relationship with achievement, course selection, career choice and lifelong learning[11] Five scales measured various aspects of their interest in science. Compared to students across all OECD countries, as shown in Table 4.1, Canadian students reported higher levels of general interest in science, higher levels of enjoyment of science, higher levels of belief that science will be useful for future employment or education (instrumental motivation) and higher levels of belief that they will study and work in the field of science as an adult (future oriented science motivation). In contrast, Canadian youth were less likely to participate in science activities outside of the school than their peers in other OECD countries.

Relative to the Canadian average, scores on the indices of general interest in science varied across provinces (Table 4.2). Youth in New Brunswick had higher scores than the Canadian average on four scales and youth in Newfoundland and Labrador had higher scores than the Canadian average on three scales. In contrast, youth in Saskatchewan and Manitoba had scores below the Canadian average on three scales.

Two of the indices – Instrumental motivation and Future-oriented science motivation – had particularly high provincial variation. While youth in Newfoundland and Labrador and Prince Edward Island believed more strongly that science will be useful for future employment or education or that they will study and work in the field of science, youth in Quebec held these beliefs less strongly compared to the Canadian average. However, youth from Quebec and from New Brunswick were more likely than their other Canadian peers to participate in science activities outside of the school.

The relationship between students' interest of science and their science performance is summarized in Table 4.1. Youth in the top quarter on the indices of interest in science scored between 54 to 88 points higher than their counterparts in the bottom quarter of the indices. This relationship between interest in science and science performance also held true across the provinces and tended to be more pronounced in Newfoundland and Labrador and Prince Edward Island (Appendix tables B.4.5 to B.4.9).

Table 4.1

Mean index score of science engagement and relationship of science performance in Canada

| | Science performance by indices quarter | | | | | Difference in science performance between students in the top quarter versus students in the bottom quarter |
	mean index score	bottom quarter	second quarter	third quarter	top quarter	
	index					
Students' belief that they can succeed in science						
Science self efficacy	0.21	480	523	551	589	109
Science self-concept	0.27	494	519	553	592	98
Students' value of science						
General value of science	0.14	502	526	552	565	62
Personal value of science	0.20	504	529	538	575	69
Students' interest in science						
General interest in science	0.11	502	532	551	560	58
Enjoyment of science	0.17	493	523	548	581	88
Instrumental motivation to learn science	0.32	514	527	540	578	64
Future oriented science motivation	0.20	508	518	547	573	65
Science activities outside school	-0.15	507	528	548	561	54

Table 4.2

Provincial scores on indices of student engagement in science relative to the Canadian average

	Provinces performing significantly higher than the Canadian mean	Provinces performing as well as the Canadian mean	Provinces performing significantly lower than the Canada mean
Students' belief that they can succeed in science			
Science self-efficacy	Newfoundland and Labrador, Alberta	Prince Edward Island, Nova Scotia, Ontario, Manitoba, British Columbia	New Brunswick, Quebec, Saskatchewan
Science self-concept		Newfoundland and Labrador, Prince Edward Island, Nova Scotia, New Brunswick, Quebec, Ontario, Alberta, British Columbia	Manitoba, Saskatchewan
Students' value of science			
General value of science		Newfoundland and Labrador, Prince Edward Island, Quebec, Ontario, Manitoba, Alberta, British Columbia	Nova Scotia, New Brunswick, Saskatchewan
Personal value of science	Newfoundland and Labrador, Prince Edward Island, Alberta	Nova Scotia, New Brunswick, Ontario, Manitoba, Saskatchewan, British Columbia	Quebec
Students' interest in science			
General interest in science	New Brunswick	Newfoundland and Labrador, Prince Edward Island, Nova Scotia, Quebec, Ontario, Alberta, British Columbia	Manitoba, Saskatchewan
Enjoyment of science	Newfoundland and Labrador, British Columbia	Prince Edward Island, Nova Scotia, New Brunswick, Quebec, Ontario, Alberta	Manitoba, Saskatchewan
Instrumental motivation to learn science	Newfoundland and Labrador, Prince Edward Island, Nova Scotia, New Brunswick, Alberta	Ontario, Manitoba, Saskatchewan, British Columbia	Quebec
Future-oriented science motivation	Newfoundland and Labrador, Prince Edward Island, Nova Scotia, New Brunswick, Alberta	Ontario, Manitoba, Saskatchewan, British Columbia	Quebec
Science activities outside school	New Brunswick, Quebec	Newfoundland and Labrador, Nova Scotia, Ontario, Alberta, British Columbia	Prince Edward Island, Manitoba, Saskatchewan

Note: Provinces within each cell are ordered from east to west.

Science and the environment

Science and the environment is a key theme explored in PISA 2006. PISA 2006 collected information on the learning context for environmental issues and on students' perceptions and attitudes regarding environmental issues.

PISA 2006 provides insight into how environmental topics are taught to 15-year-olds in school. As shown in Appendix table B.4.10 and summarized in Table 4.3, environmental education was reported as a part of the science curriculum. In Canada and in all OECD countries combined, teaching of environmental topics most frequently occurred in a natural science course. Strategies for teaching about the environment vary across jurisdictions as summarized in Table 4.3.

Table 4.3

School reports on the teaching of environmental topics

	OECD percent	Canada percent	Provinces above the Canadian percent	Provinces at the Canadian percent	Provinces below the Canadian percent
In a specific environmental studies course	21	27	Newfoundland and Labrador, Prince Edward Island, New Brunswick	Quebec, Ontario, British Columbia	Nova Scotia, Manitoba, Saskatchewan, Alberta
In the natural sciences courses	94	92	Newfoundland and Labrador, Prince Edward Island, Manitoba, Saskatchewan, Alberta	Nova Scotia, New Brunswick, Ontario, British Columbia	Quebec
As part of a geography course	75	67	Newfoundland and Labrador, Prince Edward Island, Nova Scotia, Ontario, Manitoba	Quebec, British Columbia	New Brunswick, Saskatchewan, Alberta
As part of another course	63	56		Newfoundland and Labrador, Prince Edward Island, Nova Scotia, Quebec, Ontario, Manitoba, Saskatchewan, Alberta, British Columbia	New Brunswick

Note: Provinces within each cell are ordered from east to west.

Students may also acquire knowledge through environmental education opportunities that take place outside the classroom as summarized shown in Table 4.4. The majority of students participated in school activities to promote the learning of environmental topics while the mix of activities varied from the OECD. Canadian students were less likely to participate in outdoor education activities and trips to museums and were more likely to participate in trips to science/technology centres, extracurricular environmental projects, and lectures and seminars. Within Canada, the mix of activities also varied across jurisdictions as summarized Table 4.4 and Appendix table B.4.11.

Table 4.4

Percentage of students participating in school activities to promote the learning of environmental topics

	OECD percent	Canada percent	Provinces above the Canadian percent	Provinces at the Canadian percent	Provinces below the Canadian percent
Outdoor education	77	61	Newfoundland and Labrador, Saskatchewan	Prince Edward Island, Nova Scotia, Ontario, Manitoba, Alberta, British Columbia	New Brunswick, Quebec
Trips to museums	75	68		Prince Edward Island, Nova Scotia, Ontario, Manitoba, Saskatchewan, Alberta, British Columbia	Newfoundland and Labrador, New Brunswick, Quebec
Trips to science and/or technology centres	67	76		Newfoundland and Labrador, Ontario, Manitoba, Saskatchewan, Alberta, British Columbia	Prince Edward Island, Nova Scotia, New Brunswick, Quebec
Extracurricular environmental projects	45	65		Newfoundland and Labrador, Prince Edward Island, Nova Scotia, Quebec, Ontario, Manitoba, Alberta, British Columbia	New Brunswick, Saskatchewan
Lectures and/or seminars	53	73	Prince Edward Island, Ontario	Newfoundland and Labrador, Nova Scotia, New Brunswick, Manitoba, Saskatchewan, Alberta, British Columbia	Quebec

Note: Provinces within each cell are ordered from east to west.

PISA 2006 also collected information on students' perceptions and attitudes regarding environmental issues from which the following four indices were created:

- Awareness of environmental issues measures students' awareness of environmental issues such as genetically modified organisms, acid rain, nuclear waste, deforestation and greenhouse gases.
- Perception of the importance of environmental issues measures students' perception of the importance of environmental issues such as air pollution, energy shortages, extinction of plant and animals, deforestation, acid rain and nuclear waste.
- Optimism regarding environmental issues measures students' belief that problems associated

with environmental issues will improve over the next 20 years.

- Responsibility for sustainable development measures students' responsibility for sustainable development.

As seen in Table 4.5, compared to the OECD average of zero, Canadian students reported higher levels of awareness of environmental issues and lower levels of optimism regarding environmental issues. Canadian students reported similar levels of perception of the importance of environmental issues and responsibility for sustainable development as students across all OECD countries.

Table 4.5

Provincial results on indices of students' perceptions and attitudes regarding environmental issues relative to the Canadian average

	Mean index score	Provinces above the Canadian mean	Provinces at the Canadian mean	Provinces below Canadian mean
Awareness of environmental issues	0.27	Ontario, Alberta	Newfoundland and Labrador, Manitoba	Prince Edward Island, Nova Scotia, New Brunswick, Quebec, Saskatchewan, British Columbia
Perception of the importance of environmental issues	-0.10	Quebec	Prince Edward Island, Nova Scotia, New Brunswick, Ontario	Newfoundland and Labrador, Manitoba, Saskatchewan, Alberta, British Columbia
Optimism regarding environmental issues	-0.22	Newfoundland and Labrador, Manitoba, Saskatchewan, British Columbia	Prince Edward Island, Nova Scotia, New Brunswick, Ontario, Alberta	Quebec
Responsibility for sustainable development	0.02	Quebec	Ontario	Newfoundland and Labrador, Prince Edward Island, Nova Scotia, New Brunswick, Manitoba, Saskatchewan, Alberta, British Columbia

Note: Provinces within each cell are ordered from east to west.

Table 4.6 shows the relationship between the various indices on environmental issues and science performance. Students are grouped into four quarters based on their score on the respective index where those in the bottom quarter reported lower levels while those in the top quarter reported higher levels of the respective index. There was a strong association between science achievement and students' level of awareness of environmental issues and responsibility for sustainable

development. Those in the top quarter of these indices had much higher average scores compared to those in the bottom quarter of these indices. In contrast, there was a negative relationship between science performance and environmental optimism: those with higher science performance tended to have lower levels of environmental optimism. No relationship existed between perception of environmental issues and science performance.

Table 4.6

Relationship between indices on environmental issues and science performance

	Science performance, by quarter on the indices of environmental issues				Difference in science performance between students in the top quarter versus students in the bottom quarter
	bottom quarter	second quarter	third quarter	top quarter	
Index of awareness of environmental issues	482	529	554	580	98
Index of perception of environmental issues	527	541	545	533	6
Index of environmental optimism	540	545	542	520	-20
Index of responsibility for sustainable development	508	519	549	570	62

Contexts for the learning of science

For the first time, PISA 2006 collected details about science-teaching and learning in order to shed light on the learning environment in which students have the opportunity to engage in science activities and to develop scientific literacy. Principals were asked questions about the availability of science teachers and laboratory equipment, activities to promote science learning, teaching of environmental topics at schools, activities to promote the learning of environmental topics and teacher emphasis on science-related careers. Students reported on how science was taught to them, the amount of time they spend learning science through in-school lessons, out of school lessons and homework and study. Students also reported on their perceptions of the usefulness of schooling for preparing them for science-related careers and for keeping them informed on science-related careers.

It should be noted that the characteristics of the current learning environment of 15-year-olds which is reported in this section may differ from that in their earlier school years and thus may not necessarily reflect their cumulative learning environment. Nonetheless, the breadth of information collected from both principals and students provides unique insights into the ways in which jurisdictions implement their educational objectives.

Science learning time

As shown in Chart 4.1, the majority of Canadian 15-year-olds (79%) were enrolled in a compulsory general science course while at least one-quarter of students were enrolled in a specific (chemistry, physics, biology) compulsory science course. A much smaller percentage of Canadian students were enrolled in optional science courses. Patterns of participation varied across jurisdictions as shown in Appendix table B.4.16.

Chart 4.1

Percentage of Canadian students taking various science courses

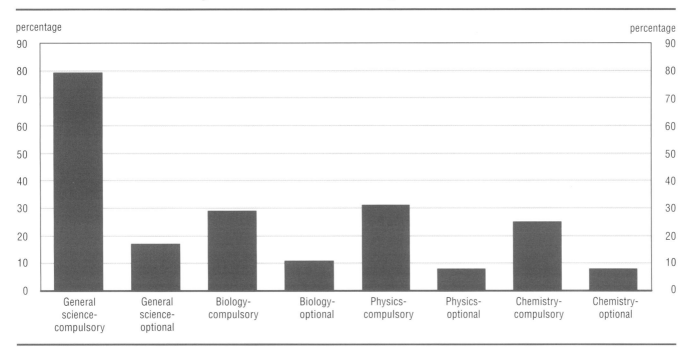

Table 4.7 shows the amount of time dedicated to learning science. It should be noted that science learning time is also associated with grade levels. With the exception of students in Quebec, the majority of Canadian students spend at least 4 hours or more a week learning science in school. The amount of time spent learning science in school was significantly related to science achievement. For Canada as a whole, students who spent 4 or more hours a week in science lessons performed 65 points higher, equivalent to almost one proficiency level than those who spent less than 2 hours. This difference varied by province ranging from 48 points in New Brunswick to 90 points in Quebec.

Table 4.7

Percentage of students and performance on the science scale, by time spent on learning

	Less than 2 hours a week	Four hours a week or more	Performance difference (4 hours or more-less than 2 hours)
	percentage	percentage	difference
Newfoundland and Labrador	15	63	80
Prince Edward Island	26	61	62
Nova Scotia	19	66	55
New Brunswick	30	60	48
Quebec	28	39	90
Ontario	24	63	53
Manitoba	26	58	63
Saskatchewan	28	54	63
Alberta	19	69	60
British Columbia	17	59	67
Canada	24	57	65

How science is taught in schools

Students were asked about a variety of practices used when learning science at school; these questions were used to create the following four indices in science teaching:

Interaction measures students' reports on interactive teaching practices such as giving students the opportunity to explain their ideas, involving students' opinions, having class debates or discussion and having student discussions.

Hands-on-activities measures students' reports on the frequency of hands-on activities in science lessons such as doing practical experiments in the laboratory, drawing conclusions from conducted experiments, observing teacher experiments and doing experiments following teacher instructions.

Student Investigations measures students' reports on the frequency of student investigations in science lessons such as designing science questions, designing experiments, choosing their own investigation and doing investigations to test out their own ideas.

Focus on models or applications measures students' reports on the frequency of teaching science lessons with a focus on models and applications such as

students being asked to apply a science concept to everyday topics, teachers using science to help students understand the world outside school, teachers explaining the relevance of science concepts to one's life and teachers using examples of technology application to show how school science is relevant to society.

As shown in Table 4.8, Canadian students were more likely to engage in each of the science teaching practices – interaction, hands-on activities, student investigations and focus on models or applications compared to the OECD as a whole. Compared to Canada, scores on the science teaching interaction practices index were higher in Newfoundland and Labrador, Prince Edward Island and Alberta and lower in Quebec. Scores for the index of hands-on activities were lower than the Canadian average in Newfoundland and Labrador, Prince Edward Island, Nova Scotia, New Brunswick and Manitoba. Scores on the index of student investigation were higher than the Canadian average in Prince Edward Island and New Brunswick and lower than the Canadian average in Quebec.

Table 4.8

Summary of scores on teaching and learning practices in school

Index	Canadian mean	Provinces above the Canadian mean	Provinces at the Canadian mean	Provinces below the Canadian mean
Interaction	0.17	Newfoundland and Labrador, Prince Edward Island, Alberta	Nova Scotia, New Brunswick, Ontario, Manitoba, Saskatchewan, British Columbia	Quebec
Hands-on activities	0.46		Quebec, Ontario, Saskatchewan, Alberta, British Columbia	Newfoundland and Labrador, Prince Edward Island, Nova Scotia, New Brunswick, Manitoba
Student investigations	0.13	Prince Edward Island, New Brunswick	Newfoundland and Labrador, Nova Scotia, Ontario, Manitoba, Saskatchewan, Alberta, British Columbia	Quebec
Focus on models or application	0.39		Newfoundland and Labrador, Prince Edward Island, Nova Scotia, New Brunswick, Quebec, Ontario, Manitoba, Saskatchewan, Alberta, British Columbia	

Note: Provinces within each cell are ordered from east to west. The OECD average is 0.

With the exception of student investigation practices there was no relationship between the various teaching and learning practices and science achievement. The relationship between student investigation practices and science achievement was negative. As shown in Appendix table B.4.20, the average score for students who were in the bottom quarter of this index was 568 compared to 503 for students who scored high on this index.

In addition to science teaching practices, a variety of school activities were used to promote the learning of science. As show in Table 4.9, excursions and field trips were most commonly used, followed by science competitions and extracurricular science projects. The mix of school activities varied across jurisdictions (Appendix table B.4.22, summarized in Table 4.9). Compared to the Canadian average, in general students in the eastern provinces were more likely to participate in science fairs and extracurricular science projects and less likely to participate in science clubs. Students in Saskatchewan were less likely to participate in four of the five school activities to promote the learning of science; students in Manitoba were less likely to participate in science fairs and science competitions.

Table 4.9

Percentage of students participating in school activities to promote the learning of science

Index	Canadian percent	Provinces above the Canadian percent	Provinces at the Canadian percent	Provinces below the Canadian percent
Science clubs	48		Nova Scotia, Quebec, Ontario, Manitoba, Alberta, British Columbia	Newfoundland and Labrador, Prince Edward Island, New Brunswick, Saskatchewan,
Science fairs	55	Newfoundland and Labrador, Prince Edward Island, Nova Scotia, New Brunswick, Quebec	Ontario, Saskatchewan, Alberta, British Columbia	Manitoba
Science competitions	65	Newfoundland and Labrador, Prince Edward Island	Nova Scotia, New Brunswick, Quebec, Ontario, Alberta, British Columbia	Manitoba, Saskatchewan
Extracurricular science projects	64	Newfoundland and Labrador	Prince Edward Island, Nova Scotia, New Brunswick, Quebec, Ontario, Manitoba, Alberta, British Columbia	Saskatchewan
Excursions and field trips	95	Nova Scotia, Ontario	Newfoundland and Labrador, Prince Edward Island, Manitoba, Alberta, British Columbia	New Brunswick, Quebec, Saskatchewan

Note: Provinces within each cell are ordered from east to west.

Preparation for science-related careers

How well prepared are students for taking up science-related careers? To investigate this question, two indices were created based on student responses. The school preparation index measures students' perceptions of the usefulness of schooling for preparing them for science-related careers. The student information index measures students' perceptions of being informed about science-related careers.

Compared to all 15-year-olds from all OECD countries, Canadian 15-year-olds reported higher levels of preparedness in terms of both the usefulness of schooling as preparation for science-related careers and of being informed about science-related careers (Table 4.10). Compared to the Canadian average, students in Alberta reported higher levels of preparedness on both indices, students in Quebec reported lower levels of preparedness on both indices, students in Prince Edward Island and Ontario reported higher level of preparedness in being informed about science-related careers and Saskatchewan reported lower levels of preparedness in being informed about science-related careers. Students in Manitoba reported higher levels of preparedness in school preparation.

Table 4.10

Summary of scores on the indices of school preparation and student information

Index	Mean index score	Provinces above the Canadian mean	Provinces at the Canadian mean	Provinces below the Canadian mean
School preparation	0.33	Manitoba, Alberta	Newfoundland and Labrador, Prince Edward Island, Nova Scotia, New Brunswick, Ontario, Saskatchewan, British Columbia	Quebec
Student information	0.28	Prince Edward Island, Ontario, Alberta	Newfoundland and Labrador, Nova Scotia, New Brunswick, Manitoba, British Columbia	Quebec, Saskatchewan

Note: Provinces within each cell are ordered from east to west.

Being prepared for a science-related career was associated with science achievement. Canadian students who were in the bottom quartile in terms of being informed about science-related careers scored 58 points lower than those who were in the top quartile (Appendix table B.4.23). Canadian students who were in the bottom quarter in terms of usefulness of schooling as preparation for science-related careers scored 20 points lower than those in the top quarter (Appendix table B.4.24).

Summary

This chapter has provided an overview of science related themes included in PISA 2006. While this chapter does not explore these themes in depth, it does reveal that differences exist in student engagement in science, the environment and science and the contexts for learning science both between Canada compared with students across all OECD countries and across provinces. There are strong relationships between these themes, in particular student engagement in science and science performance. These themes will be further expanded upon in future thematic reports released by the OECD and can be further explored through subsequent Canadian analysis with PISA 2006 data.

Note

11. OECD 2006. Assessing scientific, reading and mathematical literacy. A Framework for PISA 2006.

Conclusion

Ensuring that Canadian students acquire the skills and knowledge to participate fully in a knowledge-based economy and society is a goal shared by all levels of government and by the Canadian population. Will Canadian youth be well equipped to compete in tomorrow's economy? Have they developed a foundation of knowledge and skills for lifelong learning?

The OECD Programme for International Student Assessment (PISA) was first conducted in 2000. It compares how 15-year-old students from Canada perform in three domains - mathematics, reading and science - in comparison with their peers from other countries. Each PISA assessment provides more detailed information on one of the three domains. Reading was the major domain in 2000, mathematics in 2003 and science in 2006.

When the PISA 2000 and 2003 results were released, the performances of Canadian students were among the highest. Results from this report on PISA 2006 also show that 15-year-old students in Canada performed well in all three domains assessed relative to their international peers. In other words, Canada has retained its high standards over the six year period relative to other participating countries.

Canadian 15-year-olds performed well in science

Science was the main focus of the PISA 2006 assessment and was measured on a combined science scale as well as three sub-scales corresponding to three science competencies. Students from only Finland and Hong Kong-China outperformed Canadian 15-year-olds in combined science. Relative to their performance in the science sub-scales of 'identifying scientific issues' and 'using scientific evidence', Canadian students performed less well on the science sub-scale of 'explaining phenomena scientifically'. They were outperformed by four countries in 'explaining phenomena scientifically' compared to only one country in the other two sub-scales.

The scientific abilities of students are also described using six proficiency levels where higher proficiency levels indicate a higher level of science knowledge and skills. A higher proportion of Canadian students performed at the two highest proficiency levels (Levels 5 and 6) in combined science compared to the OECD average. Furthermore, a lower proportion of 15-year-old Canadians performed at Level 1 or below. Additionally, Canadian 15-year-old students scored almost one-half of a proficiency level above the OECD average. Although Canada is one of the leading countries in science performance, there is a large difference in performance between Canada and the leading country, Finland, equivalent to almost one-half of a proficiency level.

At the provincial level, all provinces performed above the OECD average in science. Furthermore, students from Alberta, British Columbia, Ontario and Quebec were only out-performed by students in Finland. Examining provincial results in science by proficiency levels reveals some important differences. Students from Alberta performed almost two thirds of a proficiency level higher than students from Saskatchewan, Prince Edward Island and New Brunswick on the combined science scale.

Between 2003 and 2006, Canadian performance remained unchanged in reading and mathematics however more countries outperformed Canada

Canadian 15-year-old students maintained their level of achievement in reading as compared to PISA 2003; however, they were outperformed by Finland, Hong Kong-China and Korea as opposed to only one country in previous assessments. This suggests that although Canada's performance in reading is strong, in order to maintain its competitive edge in the future Canadian 15-year-olds will need to improve at pace with other leading countries, rather than simply maintain their competencies in reading.

In 2006 in mathematics Canadian students continued to perform well though they were outperformed by students in Chinese Taipei, Finland, Korea and Hong Kong-China. All provinces performed at or above the OECD average in the two minor domains of reading and mathematics. However differences in performance among the provinces in all three PISA domains raise interesting questions of equity.

Girls and boys do equally well in science though they excel in different science competencies

In science, across all participating countries gender differences varied. In Canada and most provinces no gender difference was observed on the combined science scale or in the sub-domain of using scientific evidence. However, it should be noted that there were significant gender differences for two of the science sub-domains with boys outperforming girls in 'explaining phenomena scientifically' and girls outperforming boys in identifying scientific issues'. The performance patterns in these two sub-domains suggest that boys and girls have very different levels of performance in different areas of science. It appears that boys may demonstrate better performance at mastering scientific knowledge whereas girls may demonstrate better performance at seeing the larger picture that enables them to identify scientific questions that arise from a given situation.

As was the case in PISA 2000 and 2003, there was a relatively large difference in average scores favouring girls in reading while there was a somewhat lesser difference favouring boys in mathematics. The patterns of gender differences in both reading and mathematics remain areas of interest and concern since these differences can have an impact on future learning and career planning.

Students in minority language school systems had lower performance in science compared to those in majority language school systems

In the five provinces in which students in the French-language and English-language systems were sampled, there were differences in the performance between students in the two language school systems. In Nova Scotia, New Brunswick, Ontario and Manitoba, students in the French-language school system performed less well in science and in reading than their peers in the English-language school system while in Quebec students in the English-language school system performed less well in science than their peers in the French-language school system. There were no differences in performance between language school systems in reading and mathematics in Quebec and in mathematics in Nova Scotia and Manitoba.

Family background characteristics are related to student performance

Immigrant status, parental education and socio-economic background were all related to performance but to a lesser extent in Canada compared to OECD countries as a whole.

In Canada, non-immigrant students (those born in Canada whose parents were also born in Canada) had higher science performance than first generation immigrant students (those born outside Canada) and second-generation immigrant students (those born in Canada with at least one parent born outside of Canada). Non-immigrant students outperformed first-generation and second-generation immigrant students in three of the five provinces that had 10% or more 15-year olds who were immigrants.

In all provinces, 15-year-old students whose parents had postsecondary education performed about two-thirds of a proficiency level higher than those whose parents had high school education or less. Students from families with higher socio-economic status (SES) also tended to perform better in science. However, socio-economic status had a smaller impact on science achievement in Canada than in all OECD countries as a whole and Canada is therefore held as a model for achieving both excellence and equity. The relationship between education and socioeconomic background and performance was less pronounced in Canada and the provinces than for all OECD countries as a whole. While the relationship between SES and performance was found to be less pronounced in provinces than for the OECD on average, average performance was above the OECD average in science. This fact indicates that provincial ministries and departments of education have been able to lessen the effects of SES and provide relative equity in learning opportunities across schools for their students.

The performance of Canadian 15-year-old students is praiseworthy. Nonetheless there is also reason for some concern. Overall, when compared with their peers in other participating countries, Canadian students continue to do well on the PISA assessment; however, the top performing country in each of the domains has a much higher performance than Canada. Furthermore, significant provincial differences across domains continue to exist. It is important to note, nevertheless, that the performance of Canadian youth in the PISA 2006 assessment and in an international context is most promising to their future and the future of Canada.

Appendix A

PISA 2006 sampling procedures and response rates

The accuracy of PISA survey results depends on the quality of the information on which the sample is based as well as the sampling procedures. The PISA 2006 sample for Canada was based on a two-stage stratified sample. The first stage consisted of sampling individual schools in which 15-year-old students were enrolled. Schools were sampled systematically with probabilities proportional to size, the measure of size being a function of the estimated number of eligible (15-year-old) students enrolled. While a minimum of 150 schools were required to be selected in each country, in Canada, a much larger sample of schools was selected in order to produce reliable estimates for each province and for each of the language systems in the five provinces where these populations were separately sampled (Nova Scotia, New Brunswick, Quebec, Ontario and Manitoba).

The second stage of the selection process sampled students within sampled schools. Once schools were selected, a list of 15-year-old students in each sampled school was prepared. From this list, up to 35 students were then selected with equal probability. All 15-year old students were selected if fewer than 35 were enrolled. Additionally, in Prince Edward Island, Nova Scotia and New Brunswick and in the French-language school system in Manitoba more than 35 students were selected in order to meet sample size requirements.

In order to minimize the potential for response bias, data quality standards in PISA require minimum participation rates for schools and students. At the national level, a minimum response rate of 85% was required for schools initially selected. School response rates were also considered acceptable where the initial school response rate was between 65% and 85% and replacement schools were used to achieve a school response rate of 85% or higher. Schools with student participation rates between 25% and 50% were not counted as participating schools, but data for these schools were included in the database. Schools with student participation rates of less than 25% were not counted as participating and their data were excluded from the database.

PISA 2006 also requires a minimum student participation rate of 80% within all participating schools combined (original sample and replacements) at the national level.

Table A.1 shows the response rates for schools and students, before and after replacement for Canada and the 10 provinces. At the national level 941 schools were selected to participate in PISA 2006 and 850 of these initially selected schools participated. Rather than calculating school participation rates by dividing the number of participating schools by the total number of schools, school response rates were weighted based on 15-year-old enrolment numbers in each school.

With the exception of Quebec and Ontario, school response rates across the provinces were 94% or higher and student response rates were 84% or higher.

Table A.1

PISA 2006 school and student response rates

Provinces	Total number of selected schools (participating and not participating)	School response rate before replacement		School response rate after replacement		Total number of students sampled (participating and not participating)		Total number of students participating		Weighted student participation rate after replacement (percent)
		number	weighted percentage[1]	number	weighted percentage[1]	un-weighted	weighted	un-weighted	weighted	
Newfoundland and Labrador	75	74	99.8	75	100	1,960	6,167	1,741	5,481	88.9
Prince Edward Island	26	26	100	26	100	1,863	1,863	1,573	1,573	84.4
Nova Scotia	87	86	100	86	100	2,441	10,097	2,114	8,682	86.0
New Brunswick	68	67	100	67	100	2,671	8,331	2,443	7,641	91.7
Québec	187	159	82.9	159	83.2	4,942	72,201	3,695	53,243	73.7
Ontario	151	112	72.2	120	78.5	3,573	130,409	2,928	105,095	80.6
Manitoba	92	84	93.9	84	94.2	2,285	12,358	1,990	10,695	86.5
Saskatchewan	87	83	95.3	83	95.7	2,046	11,788	1,851	10,715	90.9
Alberta	90	86	96.0	87	97.6	2,349	37,460	1,984	31,676	84.6
British Columbia	78	73	94.6	73	94.9	2,198	46,911	1,884	40,238	85.8
Canada	941	850	83.2	860	86.2	26,328	337,585	22,203	275,038	81.5

1. School response rates were weighted based on 15-year-old enrolment.

Appendix B

Tables

The enclosed tables are based on the Organisation for Economic Cooperation and Development Programme for International Student Assessment, 2006.

The *standard error* associated with the estimates presented is included in parenthesis. The *confidence interval*, when presented, represents the range within which the score for the population is likely to fall, with 95% probability.

Only statistically significant differences at the 0.05 level are noted in this report, unless otherwise stated. This means averages did not differ when that the 95% confidence intervals for the averages being compared do not overlap. Where confidence intervals did overlap an additional t-test was conducted to test for differences.

In some tables the performance of countries and provinces relative to Canada has been indicated as being higher, the same, or lower using the following legend.

Performed significantly higher than Canada

Performed the same as Canada

Performed significantly lower than Canada

Table B.1.1

Estimated average scores and confidence intervals for provinces and countries: Combined science

Country and province	estimated average score	standard error	confidence interval – 95% lower limit	confidence interval – 95% upper limit
Finland	563	(2.0)	559	567
Alberta	550	(3.8)	543	558
Hong Kong-China	542	(2.5)	537	547
British Columbia	539	(4.7)	529	548
Ontario	537	(4.2)	529	545
Canada	534	(2.0)	530	538
Chinese Taipei	532	(3.6)	525	539
Estonia	531	(2.5)	526	536
Japan	531	(3.4)	525	538
Quebec	531	(4.2)	522	539
New Zealand	530	(2.7)	525	536
Australia	527	(2.3)	522	531
Newfoundland and Labrador	526	(2.5)	521	530
Netherlands	525	(2.7)	519	530
Manitoba	523	(3.2)	517	530
Korea	522	(3.4)	516	529
Liechtenstein	522	(4.1)	514	530
Nova Scotia	520	(2.5)	515	525
Slovenia	519	(1.1)	517	521
Saskatchewan	517	(3.6)	509	524
Germany	516	(3.8)	508	523
United Kingdom	515	(2.3)	510	519
Czech Republic	513	(3.5)	506	520
Switzerland	512	(3.2)	505	518
Austria	511	(3.9)	503	519
Macao-China	511	(1.1)	509	513
Belgium	510	(2.5)	505	515
Prince Edward Island	509	(2.7)	503	514
Ireland	508	(3.2)	502	515
New Brunswick	506	(2.3)	502	511
Hungary	504	(2.7)	499	509
Sweden	503	(2.4)	499	508
OECD average	500	(0.5)	499	501
Poland	498	(2.3)	493	502
Denmark	496	(3.1)	490	502
France	495	(3.4)	489	502
Croatia	493	(2.4)	488	498
Iceland	491	(1.6)	488	494
Latvia	490	(3.0)	484	495
United States	489	(4.2)	481	497
Lithuania	488	(2.8)	483	493
Slovak Republic	488	(2.6)	483	494
Spain	488	(2.6)	483	493
Norway	487	(3.1)	480	493
Luxembourg	486	(1.1)	484	488
Russian Federation	479	(3.7)	472	487
Italy	475	(2.0)	471	479
Portugal	474	(3.0)	468	480
Greece	473	(3.2)	467	480
Israel	454	(3.7)	447	461

Table B.1.1 (concluded)

Estimated average scores and confidence intervals for provinces and countries: Combined science

Country and province	estimated average score	standard error	confidence interval – 95% lower limit	confidence interval – 95% upper limit
Chile	438	(4.3)	430	447
Serbia	436	(3.0)	430	442
Bulgaria	434	(6.1)	422	446
Uruguay	428	(2.7)	423	434
Turkey	424	(3.8)	416	431
Jordan	422	(2.8)	416	428
Thailand	421	(2.1)	417	425
Romania	418	(4.2)	410	427
Montenegro	412	(1.1)	410	414
Mexico	410	(2.7)	404	415
Indonesia	393	(5.7)	382	405
Argentina	391	(6.1)	379	403
Brazil	390	(2.8)	385	396
Colombia	388	(3.4)	381	395
Tunisia	386	(3.0)	380	391
Azerbaijan	382	(2.8)	377	388
Qatar	349	(0.9)	348	351
Kyrgyzstan	322	(2.9)	316	328

Note: The OECD average is 500 with a standard error of 0.5.

Table B.1.2

Estimated average scores and confidence intervals for provinces and countries: Science – identifying scientific issues

Country and province	estimated average score	standard error	confidence interval – 95% lower limit	confidence interval – 95% upper limit
Finland	555	(2.3)	550	559
Alberta	546	(3.9)	538	553
British Columbia	536	(5.2)	526	546
New Zealand	536	(2.9)	531	542
Australia	535	(2.3)	531	540
Netherlands	533	(3.3)	526	539
Ontario	533	(4.9)	523	543
Canada	532	(2.3)	527	536
Quebec	531	(4.6)	521	540
Hong Kong-China	528	(3.2)	522	534
Newfoundland and Labrador	525	(3.2)	519	531
Japan	522	(4.0)	514	530
Liechtenstein	522	(3.7)	515	530
Korea	519	(3.7)	512	526
Manitoba	519	(3.3)	512	525
Slovenia	517	(1.4)	514	520
Estonia	516	(2.6)	511	521
Ireland	516	(3.3)	509	522
Nova Scotia	516	(3.5)	509	523
Belgium	515	(2.7)	510	520
Saskatchewan	515	(4.1)	507	523
Switzerland	515	(3.0)	509	521
United Kingdom	514	(2.3)	509	518
New Brunswick	512	(2.3)	508	517
Germany	510	(3.8)	502	517
Chinese Taipei	509	(3.7)	501	516
Austria	505	(3.7)	498	512
Prince Edward Island	505	(2.5)	500	510
OECD average	500	(0.5)	499	501
Czech Republic	500	(4.2)	492	509
France	499	(3.5)	492	506
Sweden	499	(2.6)	494	504
Croatia	494	(2.6)	488	499
Iceland	494	(1.7)	491	497
Denmark	493	(3.0)	487	499
United States	492	(3.8)	485	500
Macao-China	490	(1.2)	488	492
Latvia	489	(3.3)	482	495
Norway	489	(3.1)	483	495
Spain	489	(2.4)	484	494
Portugal	486	(3.1)	480	493
Hungary	483	(2.6)	478	488
Luxembourg	483	(1.1)	481	485
Poland	483	(2.5)	478	488
Lithuania	476	(2.7)	471	481
Slovak Republic	475	(3.2)	469	481
Italy	474	(2.2)	470	478
Greece	469	(3.0)	463	475
Russian Federation	463	(4.2)	455	471
Israel	457	(3.9)	449	465

Table B.1.2 (concluded)

Estimated average scores and confidence intervals for provinces and countries: Science – identifying scientific issues

Country and province	estimated average score	standard error	confidence interval – 95% lower limit	confidence interval – 95% upper limit
Chile	444	(4.1)	436	452
Serbia	431	(3.0)	425	436
Uruguay	429	(3.0)	423	435
Bulgaria	427	(6.3)	415	440
Turkey	427	(3.4)	421	434
Mexico	421	(2.6)	416	426
Thailand	413	(2.5)	408	418
Jordan	409	(2.8)	403	414
Romania	409	(3.6)	402	417
Colombia	402	(3.4)	396	409
Montenegro	401	(1.2)	399	403
Brazil	398	(2.8)	393	404
Argentina	395	(5.7)	384	406
Indonesia	393	(5.6)	382	404
Tunisia	384	(3.8)	376	391
Azerbaijan	353	(3.1)	347	359
Qatar	352	(0.8)	351	354
Kyrgyzstan	321	(3.2)	315	328

Note: The OECD average is 500 with a standard error of 0.5.

Table B.1.3

Estimated average scores and confidence intervals for provinces and countries: Science – explaining phenomena scientifically

Country and province	estimated average score	standard error	confidence interval – 95% lower limit	confidence interval – 95% upper limit
Finland	566	(2.0)	562	570
Alberta	553	(4.1)	545	561
Hong Kong-China	549	(2.5)	544	554
Chinese Taipei	545	(3.7)	538	552
Estonia	541	(2.6)	535	546
British Columbia	538	(4.9)	528	547
Ontario	533	(4.4)	524	542
Canada	531	(2.1)	527	535
Czech Republic	527	(3.5)	521	534
Japan	527	(3.1)	521	533
Quebec	523	(4.0)	515	531
Slovenia	523	(1.5)	520	526
Manitoba	522	(3.5)	515	529
Netherlands	522	(2.7)	517	527
New Zealand	522	(2.8)	517	528
Australia	520	(2.3)	516	525
Macao-China	520	(1.2)	518	522
Nova Scotia	520	(3.4)	513	526
Germany	519	(3.7)	512	526
Newfoundland and Labrador	519	(3.0)	513	524
Hungary	518	(2.6)	513	523
United Kingdom	517	(2.3)	512	521
Austria	516	(4.0)	509	524
Liechtenstein	516	(4.1)	508	524
Saskatchewan	516	(4.4)	507	525
Korea	512	(3.3)	505	518
Sweden	510	(2.9)	504	515
Prince Edward Island	509	(2.7)	504	515
Switzerland	508	(3.3)	501	514
Poland	506	(2.5)	501	511
Ireland	505	(3.2)	499	512
Belgium	503	(2.5)	498	508
Denmark	501	(3.3)	495	508
New Brunswick	501	(2.6)	496	506
Slovak Republic	501	(2.7)	496	506
OECD average	500	(0.5)	499	501
Norway	495	(3.0)	489	501
Lithuania	494	(3.0)	489	500
Croatia	492	(2.5)	487	497
Spain	490	(2.4)	486	495
Iceland	488	(1.5)	485	491
Latvia	486	(2.9)	481	492
United States	486	(4.3)	478	495
Luxembourg	483	(1.1)	481	485
Russian Federation	483	(3.4)	477	490
France	481	(3.2)	475	487
Italy	480	(2.0)	476	484
Greece	476	(3.0)	471	482
Portugal	469	(2.9)	464	475
Bulgaria	444	(5.8)	433	456

Table B.1.3   (concluded)

Estimated average scores and confidence intervals for provinces and countries: Science – explaining phenomena scientifically

Country and province	estimated average score	standard error	confidence interval – 95% lower limit	confidence interval – 95% upper limit
Israel	443	(3.6)	436	450
Serbia	441	(3.1)	435	447
Jordan	438	(3.1)	431	444
Chile	432	(4.1)	424	440
Romania	426	(4.0)	418	434
Turkey	423	(4.1)	415	431
Uruguay	423	(2.9)	417	429
Thailand	420	(2.1)	416	424
Montenegro	417	(1.1)	415	419
Azerbaijan	412	(3.0)	406	418
Mexico	406	(2.7)	401	412
Indonesia	395	(5.1)	385	405
Brazil	390	(2.7)	385	396
Argentina	386	(6.0)	375	398
Tunisia	383	(2.9)	378	389
Colombia	379	(3.4)	372	386
Qatar	356	(1.0)	354	358
Kyrgyzstan	334	(3.1)	328	340

Note: The OECD average is 500 with a standard error of 0.5.

Table B.1.4

Estimated average scores and confidence intervals for provinces and countries: Science – issuing scientific evidence

Country and province	estimated average score	standard error	confidence interval – 95% lower limit	confidence interval – 95% upper limit
Finland	567	(2.3)	563	572
Alberta	552	(4.1)	544	560
Ontario	546	(4.4)	537	554
Japan	544	(4.2)	536	552
Canada	542	(2.2)	537	546
Hong Kong-China	542	(2.7)	537	548
Quebec	542	(4.7)	532	551
British Columbia	541	(5.1)	531	551
Korea	538	(3.7)	531	546
New Zealand	537	(3.3)	530	543
Liechtenstein	535	(4.3)	526	543
Newfoundland and Labrador	533	(2.9)	527	538
Chinese Taipei	532	(3.7)	525	539
Australia	531	(2.4)	527	536
Estonia	531	(2.7)	526	536
Manitoba	530	(3.4)	523	537
Netherlands	526	(3.3)	519	532
Nova Scotia	524	(2.4)	519	529
Switzerland	519	(3.4)	512	526
Saskatchewan	517	(3.7)	510	524
Belgium	516	(3.0)	510	522
Slovenia	516	(1.3)	513	519
Germany	515	(4.6)	506	524
United Kingdom	514	(2.5)	509	518
Macao-China	512	(1.2)	509	514
France	511	(3.9)	503	519
New Brunswick	511	(2.4)	507	516
Prince Edward Island	509	(2.7)	504	514
Ireland	506	(3.4)	499	513
Austria	505	(4.7)	496	514
Czech Republic	501	(4.1)	493	509
OECD average	499	(0.6)	498	500
Hungary	497	(3.4)	490	504
Sweden	496	(2.6)	491	501
Poland	494	(2.7)	489	499
Luxembourg	492	(1.1)	490	494
Iceland	491	(1.7)	488	494
Latvia	491	(3.4)	484	497
Croatia	490	(3.0)	485	496
Denmark	489	(3.6)	482	496
United States	489	(5.0)	479	498
Lithuania	487	(3.1)	480	493
Spain	485	(3.0)	479	491
Russian Federation	481	(4.2)	473	489
Slovak Republic	478	(3.3)	471	484
Norway	473	(3.6)	466	480
Portugal	472	(3.6)	465	479
Italy	467	(2.3)	462	472
Greece	465	(4.0)	458	473
Israel	460	(4.7)	451	470

Table B.1.4   (concluded)

Estimated average scores and confidence intervals for provinces and countries: Science – issuing scientific evidence

Country and province	estimated average score	standard error	confidence interval – 95% lower limit	confidence interval – 95% upper limit
Chile	440	(5.1)	430	450
Uruguay	429	(3.1)	423	435
Serbia	425	(3.7)	418	432
Thailand	423	(2.6)	418	428
Bulgaria	417	(7.5)	402	431
Turkey	417	(4.3)	409	426
Montenegro	407	(1.3)	404	409
Romania	407	(6.0)	396	419
Jordan	405	(3.3)	398	411
Mexico	402	(3.1)	396	408
Indonesia	386	(7.3)	371	400
Argentina	385	(7.0)	372	399
Colombia	383	(3.9)	375	391
Tunisia	382	(3.7)	375	389
Brazil	378	(3.6)	371	385
Azerbaijan	344	(4.0)	336	352
Qatar	324	(1.2)	322	326
Kyrgyzstan	288	(3.8)	280	296

Note: The OECD average is 499 with a standard error of 0.6.

Table B.1.5

Variation in performance: Combined science

Country and province	Percentile												Difference in score points between the 75th and 25th percentile
	5th		10th		25th		75th		90th		95th		
	score	standard error	score	standard error	score	standard error	score	standard error	score	standard error	score	standard error	
Azerbaijan	300	(3.1)	316	(2.4)	344	(2.6)	414	(3.5)	456	(6.4)	485	(7.3)	70
Indonesia	286	(4.1)	307	(3.5)	345	(4.2)	438	(8.0)	488	(11.8)	518	(11.7)	94
Thailand	300	(4.0)	325	(3.4)	368	(2.8)	471	(3.3)	524	(3.8)	554	(4.2)	103
Qatar	229	(2.1)	253	(1.4)	292	(1.8)	396	(1.4)	462	(2.6)	505	(4.1)	104
Kyrgyzstan	191	(4.9)	220	(3.8)	267	(3.2)	372	(3.3)	428	(5.0)	468	(6.7)	105
Macao-China	378	(3.6)	409	(2.5)	458	(1.9)	566	(1.8)	611	(1.8)	635	(2.6)	108
Turkey	301	(2.8)	325	(3.2)	366	(2.6)	475	(5.8)	540	(9.7)	575	(9.8)	109
Montenegro	286	(2.7)	312	(2.1)	355	(2.2)	466	(2.2)	517	(3.0)	549	(3.7)	111
Mexico	281	(4.4)	306	(4.2)	354	(3.6)	465	(2.9)	516	(3.0)	544	(3.5)	111
Tunisia	254	(4.2)	283	(3.4)	328	(2.9)	440	(4.2)	495	(6.0)	527	(6.9)	112
Romania	291	(4.5)	314	(5.0)	361	(5.2)	473	(5.7)	526	(5.7)	557	(8.2)	112
Colombia	247	(6.3)	280	(4.5)	332	(4.8)	445	(4.7)	496	(4.6)	528	(4.7)	113
Estonia	392	(4.7)	422	(3.8)	474	(3.2)	589	(3.1)	640	(3.3)	668	(3.7)	115
Latvia	348	(5.2)	380	(4.2)	432	(3.7)	547	(3.5)	597	(3.5)	627	(3.1)	115
Finland	419	(4.4)	453	(3.3)	506	(2.9)	622	(2.5)	673	(2.9)	700	(3.1)	116
Serbia	297	(4.9)	327	(4.0)	377	(3.8)	495	(3.9)	545	(3.8)	576	(4.0)	118
Brazil	254	(4.5)	281	(3.2)	328	(2.3)	447	(4.5)	510	(5.6)	549	(5.3)	119
Croatia	354	(4.5)	383	(3.8)	433	(3.1)	553	(2.7)	604	(3.2)	634	(3.5)	120
Jordan	276	(5.2)	309	(4.0)	362	(2.8)	484	(3.5)	537	(4.5)	568	(5.4)	122
Russian Federation	333	(5.6)	364	(5.4)	418	(4.4)	541	(4.2)	596	(3.9)	627	(4.2)	123
Hungary	358	(4.4)	388	(4.2)	442	(3.5)	566	(3.3)	617	(3.1)	646	(4.2)	124
Korea	367	(8.4)	403	(5.7)	462	(4.1)	586	(3.8)	635	(4.7)	662	(5.9)	124
Greece	317	(7.3)	353	(5.4)	413	(4.4)	537	(3.3)	589	(4.1)	619	(3.8)	124
Alberta	**400**	**(7.4)**	**433**	**(6.3)**	**489**	**(4.6)**	**614**	**(4.1)**	**665**	**(5.7)**	**695**	**(4.3)**	**125**
Manitoba	**356**	**(7.4)**	**394**	**(5.4)**	**463**	**(5.2)**	**588**	**(4.4)**	**643**	**(5.5)**	**673**	**(6.2)**	**125**
Spain	338	(4.1)	370	(3.7)	427	(3.0)	552	(3.1)	604	(3.0)	633	(3.1)	125
Nova Scotia	**370**	**(5.9)**	**400**	**(6.1)**	**457**	**(4.9)**	**583**	**(3.9)**	**634**	**(4.8)**	**668**	**(7.1)**	**126**
Lithuania	340	(3.8)	370	(3.2)	425	(3.3)	551	(3.5)	604	(4.2)	633	(5.5)	127
Hong Kong-China	380	(6.2)	418	(6.1)	482	(3.6)	609	(2.8)	655	(3.5)	682	(3.1)	127
Ontario	**378**	**(8.4)**	**412**	**(6.6)**	**475**	**(5.7)**	**602**	**(4.8)**	**650**	**(4.6)**	**679**	**(5.0)**	**127**
Chile	295	(4.8)	323	(4.1)	374	(4.0)	501	(5.9)	560	(6.5)	595	(6.1)	127
Portugal	329	(5.4)	357	(4.8)	411	(4.2)	539	(3.0)	588	(2.9)	617	(3.2)	127
Poland	352	(3.8)	381	(2.9)	434	(2.7)	562	(3.1)	615	(3.3)	645	(3.3)	128
Canada	**372**	**(4.7)**	**410**	**(3.7)**	**472**	**(2.5)**	**601**	**(2.2)**	**651**	**(2.4)**	**681**	**(2.8)**	**129**
Slovak Republic	334	(5.6)	368	(3.7)	426	(3.2)	555	(4.0)	609	(4.1)	638	(3.9)	129
Uruguay	274	(6.8)	306	(4.9)	363	(4.1)	493	(3.3)	550	(3.6)	583	(4.2)	129
Denmark	341	(5.9)	373	(4.8)	432	(4.3)	562	(2.9)	615	(3.7)	646	(4.3)	130
New Brunswick	**353**	**(5.3)**	**388**	**(4.9)**	**441**	**(3.4)**	**571**	**(3.7)**	**623**	**(4.3)**	**654**	**(6.2)**	**130**
British Columbia	**375**	**(10.4)**	**415**	**(7.0)**	**476**	**(6.4)**	**606**	**(4.8)**	**655**	**(5.3)**	**681**	**(5.4)**	**130**
Sweden	347	(3.8)	381	(4.0)	439	(3.3)	569	(2.8)	622	(2.6)	654	(3.4)	131
Quebec	**359**	**(10.4)**	**402**	**(7.3)**	**468**	**(5.0)**	**599**	**(4.2)**	**652**	**(4.7)**	**683**	**(4.8)**	**131**
Ireland	351	(5.8)	385	(4.4)	444	(4.6)	575	(3.4)	630	(3.7)	660	(4.9)	132
Norway	328	(7.8)	365	(5.6)	422	(3.9)	553	(3.0)	610	(3.5)	641	(3.4)	132
OECD average	**340**	**(1.1)**	**375**	**(0.9)**	**435**	**(0.7)**	**568**	**(0.6)**	**621**	**(0.7)**	**652**	**(0.8)**	**133**
Italy	318	(3.1)	351	(2.8)	409	(3.0)	543	(2.4)	598	(2.6)	630	(2.8)	134
Newfoundland and Labrador	**367**	**(7.1)**	**400**	**(4.1)**	**460**	**(4.0)**	**594**	**(4.8)**	**648**	**(5.4)**	**673**	**(5.5)**	**134**
Liechtenstein	358	(11.2)	393	(12.8)	457	(7.3)	591	(7.1)	643	(9.4)	675	(13.4)	134
Saskatchewan	**356**	**(9.9)**	**392**	**(7.8)**	**451**	**(5.5)**	**586**	**(4.0)**	**637**	**(5.0)**	**665**	**(4.9)**	**135**
Chinese Taipei	369	(4.5)	402	(5.0)	466	(5.3)	602	(3.4)	651	(2.7)	676	(3.4)	136
Iceland	328	(4.9)	364	(3.1)	424	(2.6)	560	(2.3)	614	(2.9)	644	(3.4)	136
Luxembourg	322	(3.9)	358	(2.8)	419	(2.0)	556	(2.4)	609	(2.8)	640	(2.6)	137
Argentina	218	(9.9)	259	(9.0)	324	(7.2)	461	(6.6)	520	(6.5)	555	(6.6)	137

Table B.1.5 (concluded)

Variation in performance: Combined science

Country and province	Percentile												Difference in score points between the 75th and 25th percentile
	5th		10th		25th		75th		90th		95th		
	score	standard error	score	standard error	score	standard error	score	standard error	score	standard error	score	standard error	
Japan	356	(6.1)	396	(6.2)	465	(5.1)	603	(3.1)	654	(3.1)	685	(3.6)	137
Prince Edward Island	**346**	**(5.7)**	**383**	**(5.6)**	**440**	**(4.3)**	**578**	**(4.0)**	**632**	**(4.4)**	**664**	**(6.6)**	**138**
Australia	358	(3.5)	395	(3.4)	459	(2.6)	598	(2.5)	653	(2.9)	685	(3.4)	138
Switzerland	340	(5.0)	378	(4.9)	445	(3.9)	584	(3.5)	636	(3.8)	665	(4.6)	139
Austria	341	(9.3)	378	(6.2)	443	(5.4)	582	(4.1)	633	(3.6)	663	(4.1)	139
Slovenia	358	(3.8)	391	(2.8)	449	(2.7)	589	(2.1)	647	(3.3)	680	(3.0)	140
Czech Republic	350	(6.0)	385	(5.2)	443	(4.6)	583	(3.9)	641	(4.3)	672	(4.7)	140
Netherlands	362	(5.9)	395	(5.4)	456	(4.7)	596	(2.6)	646	(3.4)	675	(3.6)	140
Germany	345	(8.1)	381	(7.0)	447	(5.3)	587	(3.6)	642	(3.2)	672	(3.6)	141
Belgium	336	(7.3)	374	(5.4)	442	(3.8)	584	(2.4)	634	(2.3)	660	(2.7)	142
France	320	(6.3)	359	(5.5)	424	(5.3)	570	(4.0)	623	(4.0)	653	(3.8)	146
United Kingdom	337	(5.4)	376	(4.3)	441	(3.2)	590	(3.1)	652	(2.9)	685	(3.5)	150
Bulgaria	266	(8.1)	300	(7.1)	358	(6.4)	509	(7.8)	577	(8.2)	612	(8.3)	152
New Zealand	347	(5.2)	389	(4.5)	455	(3.6)	608	(2.9)	667	(3.3)	699	(3.1)	153
United States	318	(4.5)	349	(5.9)	412	(5.4)	567	(4.6)	628	(4.3)	662	(4.8)	155
Israel	275	(5.7)	310	(5.2)	374	(4.8)	535	(4.6)	601	(4.5)	636	(5.5)	160

Note: Countries and provinces in ascending order by the difference in score points between the 75th and 25th percentiles.

Table B.1.6

Variation in performance: Science – identifying scientific issues

Country and province	Percentile												Difference in score points between the 75th and 25th percentile
	5th		10th		25th		75th		90th		95th		
	score	standard error	score	standard error	score	standard error	score	standard error	score	standard error	score	standard error	
Azerbaijan	247	(4.5)	271	(4.1)	310	(3.5)	395	(3.3)	435	(4.3)	461	(5.0)	84
Qatar	234	(2.5)	258	(1.8)	300	(1.6)	398	(2.2)	453	(2.6)	495	(2.7)	98
Indonesia	269	(5.2)	297	(3.9)	342	(4.2)	444	(7.1)	495	(10.5)	522	(9.2)	103
Romania	284	(6.2)	311	(5.1)	357	(4.2)	461	(4.9)	510	(6.4)	539	(6.4)	104
Estonia	387	(5.3)	415	(4.0)	464	(3.7)	570	(2.9)	613	(2.9)	639	(3.5)	105
Turkey	304	(5.1)	330	(3.8)	374	(3.2)	480	(4.7)	531	(6.7)	561	(8.5)	106
Macao-China	358	(3.5)	388	(2.5)	437	(2.4)	545	(2.0)	591	(2.5)	615	(3.1)	108
Hungary	347	(5.7)	378	(4.4)	430	(3.6)	539	(3.3)	583	(3.6)	610	(4.4)	109
Serbia	289	(6.9)	323	(4.9)	377	(3.6)	487	(3.0)	533	(3.4)	560	(3.4)	110
Finland	411	(4.0)	446	(3.5)	501	(3.1)	612	(2.9)	659	(2.8)	686	(3.2)	111
Thailand	276	(4.6)	307	(3.7)	358	(3.4)	469	(3.4)	520	(4.2)	551	(4.6)	111
Latvia	346	(6.1)	377	(5.2)	434	(4.2)	547	(3.4)	594	(3.5)	621	(4.1)	112
Mexico	280	(6.1)	312	(4.7)	365	(3.4)	479	(2.8)	529	(3.0)	559	(3.9)	113
Montenegro	263	(3.1)	294	(2.1)	344	(2.0)	460	(1.9)	508	(2.5)	537	(3.4)	115
Lithuania	336	(4.5)	366	(3.2)	419	(3.4)	535	(3.4)	583	(3.5)	609	(4.5)	116
Poland	344	(3.9)	374	(3.2)	425	(3.0)	542	(3.2)	591	(2.7)	619	(3.7)	117
Croatia	354	(5.2)	384	(4.1)	435	(3.2)	552	(2.8)	604	(3.5)	634	(4.9)	117
Tunisia	240	(6.0)	271	(3.7)	324	(4.2)	442	(4.7)	499	(7.1)	532	(8.2)	118
Jordan	262	(5.3)	297	(3.6)	351	(3.0)	470	(3.5)	522	(3.5)	550	(4.0)	118
Spain	341	(4.1)	374	(3.2)	431	(2.7)	550	(2.4)	599	(2.7)	627	(3.1)	119
Kyrgyzstan	167	(6.2)	203	(4.4)	263	(4.4)	382	(3.3)	436	(4.2)	473	(5.8)	119
Korea	361	(7.6)	400	(6.0)	461	(4.4)	583	(4.1)	630	(4.1)	657	(5.0)	121

Table B.1.6 (concluded)

Variation in performance: Science – identifying scientific issues

Country and province	5th		10th		25th		75th		90th		95th		Difference in score points between the 75th and 25th percentile
	score	standard error	score	standard error	score	standard error	score	standard error	score	standard error	score	standard error	
Chile	300	(6.1)	330	(3.9)	383	(4.1)	505	(5.0)	561	(5.4)	594	(6.8)	122
Slovenia	372	(3.1)	402	(4.0)	457	(2.3)	579	(1.9)	627	(2.6)	655	(3.3)	122
Russian Federation	315	(5.8)	348	(5.7)	402	(4.6)	524	(4.7)	576	(4.9)	607	(4.5)	122
Greece	309	(6.1)	347	(5.3)	411	(4.4)	533	(2.9)	581	(3.4)	608	(3.2)	122
Denmark	341	(5.5)	375	(4.5)	432	(4.0)	556	(3.2)	607	(3.2)	637	(4.4)	124
Colombia	234	(8.6)	274	(6.9)	343	(4.7)	468	(4.1)	519	(4.7)	551	(5.1)	124
Slovak Republic	315	(8.5)	356	(4.9)	416	(3.6)	541	(3.6)	592	(3.6)	622	(3.7)	125
Brazil	249	(4.6)	281	(2.8)	334	(3.1)	459	(3.8)	520	(5.5)	555	(5.5)	125
Alberta	**389**	**(9.9)**	**426**	**(6.2)**	**484**	**(4.9)**	**610**	**(4.0)**	**665**	**(5.0)**	**694**	**(5.3)**	**126**
Ontario	**365**	**(9.9)**	**406**	**(8.3)**	**472**	**(6.6)**	**599**	**(5.0)**	**649**	**(5.7)**	**680**	**(6.3)**	**127**
Luxembourg	329	(2.9)	362	(2.3)	421	(2.0)	548	(2.3)	600	(2.4)	628	(2.5)	127
British Columbia	**377**	**(12.4)**	**416**	**(8.7)**	**475**	**(6.3)**	**602**	**(4.5)**	**651**	**(5.4)**	**678**	**(4.5)**	**127**
Portugal	336	(5.4)	367	(4.3)	423	(4.1)	551	(3.4)	603	(3.7)	632	(4.9)	128
Austria	351	(6.8)	383	(6.7)	443	(4.8)	571	(3.8)	618	(4.1)	644	(4.0)	128
Liechtenstein	366	(11.2)	405	(11.7)	461	(6.6)	589	(7.1)	634	(12.1)	667	(9.1)	129
Norway	333	(7.6)	368	(5.7)	426	(3.6)	555	(3.1)	608	(4.0)	640	(4.1)	129
Manitoba	**350**	**(9.6)**	**390**	**(6.7)**	**456**	**(3.9)**	**585**	**(4.6)**	**642**	**(6.3)**	**674**	**(6.9)**	**129**
Uruguay	271	(7.9)	308	(5.2)	365	(4.2)	494	(3.2)	552	(3.7)	584	(5.1)	129
Nova Scotia	**355**	**(8.0)**	**391**	**(6.2)**	**452**	**(5.2)**	**582**	**(5.4)**	**636**	**(4.5)**	**665**	**(7.2)**	**129**
Canada	**363**	**(4.9)**	**404**	**(4.1)**	**469**	**(2.9)**	**599**	**(2.3)**	**652**	**(2.5)**	**683**	**(2.9)**	**130**
OECD average	**339**	**(1.1)**	**375**	**(0.9)**	**436**	**(0.7)**	**565**	**(0.6)**	**618**	**(0.6)**	**648**	**(0.8)**	**130**
Argentina	219	(13.2)	263	(10.2)	334	(6.9)	464	(5.4)	518	(6.0)	552	(7.3)	130
New Brunswick	**353**	**(6.1)**	**387**	**(4.1)**	**448**	**(3.8)**	**578**	**(3.3)**	**631**	**(4.3)**	**664**	**(6.0)**	**130**
Switzerland	350	(4.9)	387	(4.4)	452	(3.9)	583	(3.1)	633	(3.7)	661	(4.6)	131
Sweden	338	(4.5)	374	(4.2)	435	(3.2)	566	(3.2)	619	(3.1)	653	(3.3)	131
Australia	368	(4.3)	406	(3.1)	471	(2.7)	604	(2.8)	658	(3.2)	689	(3.6)	133
Ireland	357	(5.7)	391	(4.9)	450	(4.0)	584	(3.3)	638	(3.4)	668	(4.4)	133
Prince Edward Island	**346**	**(6.3)**	**381**	**(4.2)**	**439**	**(3.3)**	**572**	**(4.0)**	**627**	**(4.1)**	**659**	**(5.4)**	**134**
Saskatchewan	**353**	**(11.4)**	**390**	**(7.6)**	**450**	**(4.8)**	**584**	**(4.5)**	**634**	**(5.1)**	**661**	**(6.3)**	**134**
Italy	310	(4.7)	347	(3.5)	409	(3.0)	543	(2.8)	600	(2.7)	632	(3.4)	134
Chinese Taipei	344	(5.7)	379	(5.9)	444	(5.5)	578	(3.2)	628	(3.7)	655	(3.8)	135
Germany	341	(8.3)	381	(6.6)	444	(5.0)	579	(3.4)	630	(3.5)	660	(4.0)	135
Newfoundland and Labrador	**369**	**(5.6)**	**401**	**(4.0)**	**458**	**(4.5)**	**594**	**(4.5)**	**647**	**(5.3)**	**675**	**(7.2)**	**135**
Czech Republic	341	(8.2)	376	(5.9)	434	(4.7)	570	(4.5)	625	(5.2)	656	(5.2)	136
Quebec	**348**	**(10.1)**	**393**	**(9.2)**	**465**	**(5.8)**	**602**	**(4.3)**	**660**	**(5.7)**	**694**	**(6.4)**	**136**
Belgium	340	(8.6)	382	(6.6)	449	(3.7)	587	(2.9)	639	(2.9)	668	(3.5)	138
Hong Kong-China	352	(6.6)	393	(5.4)	461	(4.4)	599	(3.8)	652	(4.5)	683	(4.4)	138
Iceland	318	(5.0)	358	(4.8)	426	(2.5)	566	(2.2)	625	(3.1)	656	(3.7)	141
United States	330	(5.8)	362	(5.3)	420	(4.7)	563	(4.2)	621	(4.9)	654	(5.2)	143
United Kingdom	337	(6.1)	377	(4.3)	443	(2.9)	587	(2.8)	648	(2.8)	682	(3.2)	144
Japan	337	(8.2)	381	(6.9)	453	(5.6)	597	(3.9)	652	(4.0)	682	(4.0)	144
Netherlands	360	(7.3)	397	(5.7)	462	(4.5)	606	(3.5)	662	(4.0)	694	(4.5)	144
New Zealand	356	(4.8)	396	(4.8)	465	(4.3)	612	(3.0)	668	(3.0)	701	(3.5)	147
France	319	(7.0)	358	(5.9)	427	(5.5)	576	(3.5)	629	(3.7)	659	(4.5)	148
Bulgaria	251	(8.2)	289	(8.7)	350	(7.3)	504	(7.6)	571	(7.4)	607	(8.4)	155
Israel	272	(6.4)	311	(5.5)	378	(4.2)	538	(4.7)	604	(5.4)	641	(5.6)	161

Note: Countries and provinces in ascending order by the difference in score points between the 75th and 25th percentiles.

Table B.1.7

Variation in performance: Science – explaining phenomena scientifically

Country and province	Percentile												Difference in score points between the 75th and 25th percentile
	5th		10th		25th		75th		90th		95th		
	score	standard error	score	standard error	score	standard error	score	standard error	score	standard error	score	standard error	
Azerbaijan	314	(2.8)	334	(2.9)	368	(2.9)	452	(3.6)	494	(5.3)	523	(8.1)	83
Indonesia	284	(4.1)	307	(4.1)	345	(3.2)	440	(7.7)	492	(9.9)	521	(9.5)	95
Thailand	304	(3.8)	327	(2.7)	368	(2.5)	468	(2.7)	519	(4.0)	551	(4.2)	100
Kyrgyzstan	199	(5.2)	228	(4.2)	279	(3.3)	386	(3.4)	438	(5.0)	475	(5.5)	107
Tunisia	253	(3.4)	281	(3.0)	327	(3.1)	437	(3.8)	491	(6.8)	526	(9.5)	109
Qatar	226	(2.5)	252	(1.8)	296	(2.2)	406	(1.8)	472	(2.5)	515	(2.5)	110
Montenegro	289	(2.3)	314	(2.2)	359	(2.0)	471	(1.8)	526	(2.7)	559	(4.6)	111
Turkey	297	(3.8)	321	(2.9)	363	(2.7)	475	(6.5)	542	(11.2)	584	(12.5)	112
Mexico	274	(4.8)	301	(3.7)	349	(3.2)	462	(2.9)	514	(3.5)	545	(4.1)	113
Romania	297	(5.7)	321	(5.3)	367	(6.0)	481	(4.8)	535	(7.2)	567	(7.2)	114
Macao-China	381	(4.3)	413	(3.1)	464	(2.0)	578	(2.3)	626	(2.5)	652	(2.8)	115
Latvia	340	(4.8)	373	(3.8)	427	(3.6)	546	(4.0)	599	(3.7)	631	(4.1)	119
Brazil	252	(4.5)	280	(3.1)	328	(2.5)	447	(4.2)	512	(5.4)	551	(6.5)	119
Colombia	230	(5.8)	264	(5.2)	319	(4.5)	439	(4.5)	495	(4.6)	528	(4.1)	120
Finland	420	(4.8)	452	(3.3)	506	(2.6)	626	(2.5)	679	(2.8)	709	(4.0)	120
Croatia	351	(4.1)	380	(3.8)	432	(3.5)	552	(3.3)	606	(3.8)	638	(4.1)	121
Portugal	329	(4.7)	357	(4.5)	409	(3.8)	530	(2.7)	581	(2.9)	610	(3.7)	122
Serbia	295	(5.6)	326	(4.7)	380	(3.6)	502	(3.9)	557	(3.8)	589	(4.2)	122
Russian Federation	335	(5.1)	367	(4.3)	422	(4.5)	544	(3.8)	600	(4.2)	634	(4.3)	122
Korea	359	(6.3)	392	(5.0)	450	(3.9)	576	(4.1)	627	(5.1)	656	(5.9)	126
Estonia	393	(5.1)	422	(3.1)	477	(3.2)	604	(3.2)	658	(3.5)	688	(3.7)	127
Greece	321	(6.5)	356	(5.4)	413	(4.1)	541	(3.6)	596	(3.5)	626	(4.2)	127
Hong Kong-China	387	(7.0)	423	(5.0)	488	(3.4)	615	(2.7)	667	(3.3)	695	(3.9)	127
Iceland	335	(4.3)	369	(3.3)	425	(2.3)	553	(2.4)	606	(2.9)	636	(4.3)	128
Chile	284	(4.3)	314	(4.0)	366	(4.0)	495	(5.7)	560	(6.1)	597	(6.7)	129
Hungary	365	(3.8)	398	(4.0)	453	(3.2)	583	(3.4)	639	(4.3)	674	(5.5)	130
Slovak Republic	342	(4.5)	377	(5.5)	435	(3.0)	568	(3.6)	626	(3.8)	660	(5.1)	132
Nova Scotia	**364**	**(8.5)**	**396**	**(6.2)**	**452**	**(5.1)**	**585**	**(4.4)**	**643**	**(6.1)**	**680**	**(7.4)**	**133**
Uruguay	260	(7.0)	295	(4.9)	357	(4.2)	490	(3.3)	550	(3.8)	586	(5.4)	133
Lithuania	338	(4.3)	370	(4.1)	428	(3.5)	561	(3.8)	617	(5.1)	651	(6.3)	134
Denmark	342	(5.1)	376	(5.0)	435	(4.0)	568	(3.6)	627	(3.8)	658	(4.2)	134
Jordan	278	(4.9)	314	(3.7)	371	(3.5)	505	(4.1)	563	(5.3)	597	(5.9)	134
Alberta	**394**	**(8.4)**	**428**	**(6.2)**	**487**	**(5.8)**	**620**	**(4.4)**	**675**	**(5.9)**	**709**	**(6.3)**	**134**
Japan	362	(6.5)	399	(5.3)	462	(4.2)	595	(2.9)	649	(3.6)	680	(3.9)	134
Poland	353	(4.4)	384	(3.8)	438	(2.8)	572	(3.3)	630	(3.2)	664	(3.8)	134
Manitoba	**350**	**(8.6)**	**388**	**(7.5)**	**456**	**(5.1)**	**590**	**(4.6)**	**650**	**(6.5)**	**685**	**(7.2)**	**134**
Sweden	346	(7.2)	382	(5.6)	443	(3.6)	578	(3.3)	636	(3.6)	669	(3.4)	134
Netherlands	360	(5.3)	394	(5.6)	455	(4.7)	589	(2.7)	643	(3.3)	673	(3.5)	134
New Brunswick	**344**	**(5.1)**	**378**	**(5.2)**	**433**	**(3.9)**	**567**	**(3.7)**	**624**	**(4.5)**	**657**	**(6.0)**	**134**
Spain	329	(4.0)	364	(3.2)	423	(2.7)	558	(3.1)	616	(2.6)	649	(2.9)	135
Quebec	**351**	**(9.0)**	**392**	**(7.3)**	**458**	**(4.6)**	**592**	**(4.4)**	**648**	**(5.2)**	**680**	**(5.7)**	**135**
Ontario	**367**	**(8.6)**	**402**	**(7.4)**	**467**	**(6.2)**	**602**	**(5.0)**	**657**	**(4.9)**	**688**	**(4.9)**	**135**
Liechtenstein	357	(10.1)	390	(10.5)	450	(7.3)	586	(7.2)	640	(8.7)	670	(12.2)	136
Luxembourg	321	(2.9)	357	(2.5)	416	(2.2)	552	(1.8)	608	(2.4)	639	(4.2)	136
OECD average	**339**	**(1.0)**	**374**	**(0.8)**	**433**	**(0.7)**	**568**	**(0.6)**	**626**	**(0.7)**	**658**	**(0.9)**	**136**
Italy	315	(3.7)	350	(3.2)	411	(2.8)	548	(2.6)	608	(2.6)	642	(2.6)	137
Canada	**362**	**(4.4)**	**400**	**(3.4)**	**464**	**(2.8)**	**601**	**(2.5)**	**657**	**(2.4)**	**689**	**(2.6)**	**137**
Norway	327	(8.2)	366	(5.1)	427	(3.6)	565	(3.2)	624	(3.3)	656	(4.0)	138
Argentina	207	(12.8)	252	(8.4)	320	(6.3)	459	(6.6)	516	(5.5)	552	(6.9)	139
Ireland	340	(6.1)	377	(5.0)	436	(4.1)	575	(3.9)	635	(3.9)	668	(4.4)	139
France	313	(5.6)	349	(5.5)	412	(4.7)	552	(3.3)	609	(3.9)	640	(3.6)	140
Saskatchewan	**349**	**(8.9)**	**385**	**(8.2)**	**447**	**(5.7)**	**588**	**(4.7)**	**647**	**(4.4)**	**675**	**(6.6)**	**141**
Australia	351	(3.2)	388	(3.0)	450	(2.7)	592	(2.8)	650	(3.1)	683	(3.1)	141

Table B.1.7 (concluded)

Variation in performance: Science – explaining phenomena scientifically

Country and province	5th		10th		25th		75th		90th		95th		Difference in score points between the 75th and 25th percentile
	score	standard error	score	standard error	score	standard error	score	standard error	score	standard error	score	standard error	
Switzerland	333	(5.3)	373	(4.6)	438	(4.1)	580	(3.4)	635	(4.8)	667	(4.7)	142
Czech Republic	360	(6.3)	395	(5.1)	456	(4.5)	598	(3.8)	659	(4.6)	694	(4.7)	142
Austria	343	(7.5)	382	(7.3)	447	(4.9)	590	(4.0)	642	(3.5)	672	(3.9)	142
British Columbia	**366**	**(10.7)**	**406**	**(7.3)**	**467**	**(6.4)**	**610**	**(5.3)**	**666**	**(5.9)**	**698**	**(5.8)**	**143**
Newfoundland and Labrador	**357**	**(4.6)**	**387**	**(5.0)**	**446**	**(5.0)**	**590**	**(4.6)**	**646**	**(5.0)**	**678**	**(6.1)**	**144**
Germany	345	(6.8)	381	(6.2)	448	(5.5)	592	(3.8)	651	(3.6)	684	(4.6)	144
Chinese Taipei	373	(4.5)	407	(5.0)	474	(5.7)	619	(3.9)	673	(3.4)	702	(3.4)	145
Prince Edward Island	**343**	**(6.6)**	**375**	**(4.3)**	**435**	**(3.8)**	**580**	**(5.1)**	**645**	**(4.1)**	**680**	**(7.5)**	**145**
Bulgaria	276	(9.4)	312	(6.1)	370	(5.6)	516	(6.9)	583	(8.0)	618	(8.8)	146
Belgium	328	(6.5)	365	(5.8)	432	(4.0)	578	(2.3)	632	(2.4)	661	(2.5)	146
Slovenia	353	(4.7)	388	(3.9)	449	(2.0)	595	(2.6)	661	(3.3)	698	(5.4)	146
Israel	269	(6.0)	304	(5.6)	366	(4.2)	520	(4.7)	587	(4.2)	625	(4.2)	154
United Kingdom	340	(4.5)	375	(3.4)	439	(3.0)	594	(2.9)	660	(3.4)	696	(3.9)	154
New Zealand	339	(5.9)	378	(4.3)	445	(3.6)	601	(3.2)	664	(3.1)	700	(4.1)	156
United States	311	(5.5)	345	(5.2)	404	(5.5)	565	(4.8)	632	(4.6)	670	(6.0)	160

Note: Countries and provinces in ascending order by the difference in score points between the 75th and 25th percentiles.

Table B.1.8

Variation in performance: Science – using scientific evidence

Country and province	5th		10th		25th		75th		90th		95th		Difference in score points between the 75th and 25th percentile
	score	standard error	score	standard error	score	standard error	score	standard error	score	standard error	score	standard error	
Azerbaijan	226	(5.3)	250	(4.6)	292	(4.2)	391	(5.2)	446	(7.2)	483	(8.2)	100
Indonesia	255	(6.5)	282	(5.8)	328	(5.9)	440	(9.1)	498	(14.3)	532	(13.8)	112
Macao-China	367	(3.8)	401	(2.9)	456	(1.7)	571	(2.0)	618	(2.4)	645	(3.4)	115
Colombia	233	(8.2)	266	(6.3)	324	(5.1)	445	(4.7)	497	(4.3)	529	(4.4)	121
Thailand	280	(4.5)	309	(4.1)	361	(3.2)	483	(3.7)	544	(4.9)	581	(5.1)	122
Latvia	332	(6.7)	370	(5.5)	429	(4.5)	555	(3.5)	606	(3.4)	636	(3.2)	126
Turkey	271	(4.6)	302	(3.7)	352	(3.3)	479	(6.9)	548	(9.2)	589	(10.5)	127
Estonia	374	(5.3)	409	(3.9)	468	(3.3)	595	(3.2)	650	(3.4)	681	(3.8)	128
Montenegro	258	(2.7)	288	(3.1)	342	(1.9)	469	(2.4)	529	(3.0)	565	(4.3)	128
Qatar	174	(2.8)	203	(2.4)	254	(1.9)	382	(1.8)	462	(2.8)	515	(3.0)	128
Mexico	248	(6.0)	280	(5.4)	339	(3.8)	467	(3.3)	523	(3.0)	554	(3.6)	129
Finland	406	(5.4)	442	(4.0)	504	(2.9)	633	(2.7)	690	(2.9)	722	(3.9)	130
Tunisia	227	(4.9)	260	(5.1)	317	(3.9)	447	(4.9)	506	(6.4)	541	(7.7)	130
Manitoba	**356**	**(7.8)**	**395**	**(6.7)**	**467**	**(4.8)**	**598**	**(4.1)**	**652**	**(5.1)**	**685**	**(8.0)**	**131**
Alberta	**394**	**(8.2)**	**431**	**(7.6)**	**488**	**(5.6)**	**619**	**(4.1)**	**673**	**(4.0)**	**703**	**(6.2)**	**131**
Ontario	**377**	**(7.8)**	**415**	**(7.5)**	**482**	**(5.7)**	**614**	**(4.8)**	**664**	**(5.0)**	**695**	**(6.4)**	**132**
Croatia	333	(5.8)	367	(4.3)	424	(3.8)	557	(3.5)	614	(3.8)	645	(3.4)	133
Nova Scotia	**362**	**(7.0)**	**400**	**(5.9)**	**460**	**(5.2)**	**593**	**(4.8)**	**644**	**(4.5)**	**675**	**(6.6)**	**133**
Hong Kong-China	367	(6.0)	408	(4.7)	479	(4.4)	613	(3.1)	663	(3.2)	691	(3.3)	134
British Columbia	**370**	**(11.0)**	**409**	**(9.8)**	**476**	**(6.6)**	**611**	**(4.9)**	**662**	**(5.0)**	**690**	**(4.7)**	**134**
Kyrgyzstan	125	(6.7)	160	(4.9)	218	(4.3)	352	(4.0)	424	(6.8)	473	(9.1)	134
Jordan	235	(6.6)	277	(4.4)	339	(3.6)	474	(4.2)	532	(5.1)	566	(5.8)	135

Table B.1.8 (concluded)

Variation in performance: Science – using scientific evidence

Country and province	Percentile												Difference in score points between the 75th and 25th percentile
	5th		10th		25th		75th		90th		95th		
	score	standard error	score	standard error	score	standard error	score	standard error	score	standard error	score	standard error	
Canada	370	(4.3)	408	(4.3)	477	(2.9)	612	(2.2)	664	(2.5)	695	(3.1)	135
New Brunswick	346	(5.1)	384	(4.5)	443	(4.2)	581	(4.1)	634	(3.9)	666	(5.0)	138
Russian Federation	311	(6.5)	350	(5.6)	413	(4.9)	551	(4.7)	611	(5.1)	647	(4.7)	138
Poland	330	(4.7)	365	(3.7)	425	(3.4)	563	(3.5)	621	(3.5)	652	(4.0)	138
Spain	315	(5.5)	355	(3.6)	418	(3.6)	556	(3.2)	610	(3.2)	641	(3.8)	138
Serbia	260	(5.4)	295	(4.5)	357	(4.8)	495	(4.6)	554	(4.4)	589	(4.8)	138
Saskatchewan	345	(9.4)	386	(8.1)	451	(5.3)	589	(4.3)	641	(5.4)	672	(7.0)	138
Lithuania	321	(5.2)	357	(3.8)	418	(4.0)	557	(3.9)	612	(4.3)	643	(4.9)	139
Korea	359	(9.1)	402	(7.6)	473	(5.4)	611	(4.1)	664	(4.3)	694	(5.0)	139
Hungary	325	(7.6)	362	(6.3)	429	(4.2)	568	(4.4)	628	(4.8)	661	(4.4)	139
Greece	279	(9.9)	325	(7.9)	399	(5.8)	539	(3.8)	596	(4.3)	630	(4.3)	139
Slovenia	351	(4.3)	386	(3.1)	447	(2.0)	586	(2.6)	647	(3.2)	679	(3.1)	139
Brazil	215	(7.5)	250	(5.2)	307	(3.3)	446	(4.6)	518	(6.0)	557	(7.0)	140
Chinese Taipei	356	(5.8)	393	(5.9)	464	(6.0)	605	(3.3)	656	(3.5)	683	(3.2)	141
Quebec	357	(11.9)	401	(8.9)	475	(5.6)	616	(4.4)	672	(5.6)	704	(5.3)	142
Ireland	331	(5.4)	370	(5.0)	437	(4.5)	579	(3.1)	635	(3.8)	666	(4.5)	142
Prince Edward Island	332	(7.5)	373	(5.9)	439	(4.4)	582	(3.3)	637	(5.3)	670	(6.0)	143
Newfoundland and Labrador	365	(5.4)	401	(5.5)	462	(5.1)	605	(4.6)	658	(4.7)	686	(6.4)	144
Chile	275	(5.2)	309	(5.3)	367	(5.4)	511	(6.7)	576	(5.9)	613	(6.5)	144
Romania	239	(7.5)	273	(6.8)	335	(7.9)	480	(6.8)	541	(7.0)	576	(8.2)	145
Sweden	318	(6.4)	359	(4.9)	425	(3.5)	570	(3.0)	630	(3.3)	664	(3.2)	146
Portugal	297	(6.9)	337	(6.0)	401	(5.2)	547	(3.4)	602	(3.5)	634	(4.3)	147
Slovak Republic	294	(8.1)	336	(5.8)	407	(4.6)	554	(4.2)	615	(4.1)	647	(4.1)	148
Australia	348	(3.8)	390	(3.3)	459	(2.8)	607	(2.7)	665	(2.7)	698	(3.5)	148
Denmark	310	(6.6)	349	(4.8)	416	(4.3)	564	(3.9)	624	(4.6)	658	(5.3)	148
Uruguay	249	(5.2)	287	(5.1)	355	(4.6)	504	(2.9)	566	(3.8)	602	(4.0)	149
OECD average	316	(1.3)	357	(1.1)	427	(0.8)	576	(0.7)	635	(0.8)	668	(0.9)	149
Norway	294	(7.9)	334	(5.8)	398	(4.5)	549	(3.8)	613	(3.4)	649	(4.7)	151
Italy	279	(5.0)	323	(3.5)	393	(3.0)	545	(2.8)	606	(2.8)	642	(2.9)	151
Switzerland	325	(6.4)	368	(5.0)	445	(4.4)	597	(3.5)	656	(4.5)	691	(5.5)	152
Iceland	303	(5.3)	345	(4.1)	414	(3.1)	570	(2.4)	632	(3.3)	666	(3.3)	155
Argentina	181	(12.3)	229	(12.3)	311	(8.2)	467	(6.4)	533	(6.9)	571	(6.9)	156
Belgium	312	(9.8)	360	(7.2)	442	(4.5)	599	(2.4)	652	(2.6)	680	(3.3)	157
Luxembourg	296	(4.3)	341	(3.1)	415	(2.5)	572	(1.9)	635	(2.8)	668	(3.0)	157
Czech Republic	312	(8.6)	353	(6.6)	423	(5.1)	581	(4.7)	644	(5.4)	681	(5.9)	157
Germany	317	(11.2)	361	(8.1)	440	(6.8)	597	(3.9)	658	(4.2)	691	(4.4)	158
Japan	340	(8.6)	388	(7.9)	468	(5.9)	627	(3.6)	685	(3.4)	719	(4.8)	159
Netherlands	346	(6.5)	382	(6.5)	446	(5.3)	606	(3.4)	662	(2.9)	691	(3.0)	159
Liechtenstein	354	(19.1)	388	(11.3)	458	(10.1)	619	(7.6)	681	(12.4)	710	(12.4)	161
Austria	305	(11.2)	350	(9.0)	428	(6.2)	589	(4.6)	649	(4.7)	680	(4.7)	162
United Kingdom	316	(6.2)	361	(4.3)	434	(3.6)	597	(2.9)	661	(3.2)	699	(3.8)	163
France	311	(7.9)	359	(6.7)	432	(5.9)	595	(4.2)	654	(4.1)	685	(4.3)	164
United States	296	(10.1)	335	(8.8)	405	(7.0)	573	(5.1)	640	(5.2)	677	(5.9)	168
New Zealand	331	(7.1)	377	(5.2)	453	(4.4)	624	(3.4)	687	(4.5)	725	(4.9)	171
Bulgaria	216	(10.2)	256	(8.8)	325	(8.1)	506	(8.7)	585	(9.3)	624	(8.7)	182
Israel	241	(7.4)	286	(6.5)	366	(6.0)	558	(5.5)	635	(4.6)	676	(5.2)	192

Note: Countries and provinces in ascending order by the difference in score points between the 75th and 25th percentiles.

Table B.1.9

Percent of students at each level for provinces and countries: Combined science

Country and province	Below level 1 %	(SE)	Level 1 %	(SE)	Level 2 %	(SE)	Level 3 %	(SE)	Level 4 %	(SE)	Level 5 %	(SE)	Level 6 %	(SE)
Finland	0.5	(0.1)	3.5	(0.4)	13.5	(0.7)	29.1	(1.1)	32.4	(0.9)	17.0	(0.7)	4.0	(0.4)
Alberta	**0.8**	**(0.4)**	**5.3**	**(0.7)**	**17.2**	**(1.3)**	**29.2**	**(1.3)**	**29.1**	**(1.5)**	**14.8**	**(1.0)**	**3.6**	**(0.5)**
Estonia	0.9	(0.2)	6.6	(0.6)	20.9	(0.9)	33.6	(1.0)	26.3	(0.9)	10.2	(0.7)	1.4	(0.3)
Hong Kong-China	1.7	(0.4)	7.0	(0.7)	16.9	(0.8)	28.6	(0.9)	29.8	(1.0)	13.9	(0.8)	2.1	(0.3)
British Columbia	**1.9**	**(0.5)**	**7.1**	**(0.9)**	**18.5**	**(1.2)**	**28.1**	**(1.4)**	**28.3**	**(1.6)**	**13.7**	**(1.4)**	**2.3**	**(0.5)**
Ontario	**1.8**	**(0.5)**	**7.6**	**(1.0)**	**18.4**	**(1.3)**	**28.4**	**(1.1)**	**29.4**	**(1.4)**	**12.0**	**(1.0)**	**2.4**	**(0.4)**
Canada	**2.2**	**(0.3)**	**7.8**	**(0.5)**	**19.0**	**(0.6)**	**28.8**	**(0.6)**	**27.8**	**(0.6)**	**12.1**	**(0.5)**	**2.4**	**(0.2)**
Macao-China	1.4	(0.2)	8.7	(0.5)	25.9	(1.0)	35.7	(1.2)	22.9	(0.8)	5.1	(0.3)	0.3	(0.1)
Korea	2.5	(0.5)	8.6	(0.7)	21.2	(1.0)	31.7	(1.2)	25.6	(0.9)	9.3	(0.8)	1.1	(0.3)
Quebec	**3.1**	**(0.7)**	**8.0**	**(0.9)**	**19.2**	**(1.2)**	**28.8**	**(1.3)**	**26.4**	**(1.1)**	**11.9**	**(1.0)**	**2.5**	**(0.5)**
Chinese Taipei	1.9	(0.3)	9.6	(0.8)	18.5	(0.9)	27.3	(0.8)	28.0	(1.0)	13.0	(0.8)	1.7	(0.2)
Nova Scotia	**1.9**	**(0.6)**	**9.7**	**(1.1)**	**22.7**	**(1.1)**	**30.7**	**(1.4)**	**24.8**	**(1.5)**	**8.6**	**(0.9)**	**1.6**	**(0.4)**
Japan	3.1	(0.4)	8.8	(0.7)	18.4	(0.8)	27.4	(0.9)	27.1	(1.1)	12.5	(0.6)	2.7	(0.3)
Newfoundland and Labrador	**2.1**	**(0.6)**	**9.7**	**(0.9)**	**21.2**	**(1.3)**	**28.9**	**(1.4)**	**24.5**	**(1.5)**	**11.6**	**(1.2)**	**1.9**	**(0.5)**
Manitoba	**2.8**	**(0.5)**	**9.6**	**(1.1)**	**19.2**	**(1.4)**	**32.0**	**(1.7)**	**23.8**	**(1.5)**	**10.6**	**(0.9)**	**1.9**	**(0.4)**
Australia	3.0	(0.3)	9.8	(0.5)	20.2	(0.6)	27.7	(0.5)	24.7	(0.5)	11.8	(0.5)	2.9	(0.3)
Netherlands	2.3	(0.4)	10.6	(0.9)	21.1	(1.0)	26.9	(0.9)	26.0	(1.0)	11.6	(0.8)	1.7	(0.2)
Liechtenstein	2.6	(1.0)	10.3	(2.1)	20.9	(2.8)	28.5	(2.7)	25.4	(2.6)	9.9	(1.7)	2.3	(0.8)
New Zealand	4.0	(0.4)	9.6	(0.6)	19.7	(0.8)	25.1	(0.7)	24.0	(0.8)	13.7	(0.7)	4.0	(0.4)
Saskatchewan	**3.2**	**(0.7)**	**10.3**	**(1.0)**	**22.0**	**(1.4)**	**29.6**	**(1.3)**	**24.0**	**(1.5)**	**9.3**	**(1.0)**	**1.5**	**(0.4)**
Slovenia	2.8	(0.3)	11.0	(0.7)	23.1	(0.7)	27.6	(1.1)	22.6	(1.2)	10.8	(0.6)	2.2	(0.3)
Hungary	2.7	(0.3)	12.2	(0.9)	26.0	(1.2)	31.1	(1.1)	21.1	(0.9)	6.3	(0.6)	0.6	(0.2)
New Brunswick	**3.1**	**(0.4)**	**12.0**	**(1.0)**	**26.0**	**(1.3)**	**29.1**	**(1.6)**	**21.8**	**(1.3)**	**6.8**	**(0.7)**	**1.2**	**(0.3)**
Germany	4.0	(0.7)	11.2	(1.0)	21.3	(1.1)	27.9	(1.1)	23.6	(0.9)	10.1	(0.6)	1.8	(0.2)
Ireland	3.5	(0.5)	11.8	(0.8)	24.0	(0.9)	29.7	(0.9)	21.5	(0.9)	8.3	(0.6)	1.1	(0.2)
Czech Republic	3.4	(0.6)	11.9	(0.8)	23.4	(1.1)	27.7	(1.1)	21.8	(0.9)	9.8	(0.9)	1.8	(0.3)
Switzerland	4.5	(0.5)	11.4	(0.6)	21.8	(0.9)	28.2	(0.8)	23.6	(1.1)	9.1	(0.8)	1.4	(0.3)
Prince Edward Island	**3.8**	**(0.7)**	**12.1**	**(1.2)**	**23.7**	**(1.3)**	**29.1**	**(1.7)**	**21.5**	**(1.6)**	**8.2**	**(1.0)**	**1.6**	**(0.5)**
Austria	4.2	(0.9)	11.9	(1.0)	21.8	(1.0)	28.2	(1.1)	23.8	(1.1)	8.8	(0.7)	1.2	(0.2)
Sweden	3.7	(0.4)	12.5	(0.6)	25.1	(0.9)	29.5	(0.8)	21.2	(0.8)	6.9	(0.5)	1.1	(0.2)
United Kingdom	4.8	(0.5)	11.8	(0.6)	21.8	(0.7)	26.0	(0.7)	21.8	(0.6)	10.9	(0.5)	2.9	(0.3)
Belgium	4.8	(0.7)	12.1	(0.6)	20.8	(0.9)	27.6	(0.9)	24.6	(0.8)	9.2	(0.5)	1.0	(0.2)
Poland	3.2	(0.4)	13.7	(0.6)	27.4	(1.0)	29.5	(1.1)	19.5	(0.8)	6.1	(0.4)	0.7	(0.1)
Croatia	2.9	(0.4)	13.9	(0.7)	29.2	(0.9)	31.0	(1.0)	17.8	(0.8)	4.6	(0.4)	0.5	(0.1)
Latvia	3.5	(0.5)	13.7	(1.0)	29.0	(1.2)	32.9	(0.9)	16.8	(0.9)	3.9	(0.4)	0.3	(0.1)
Denmark	4.3	(0.6)	14.0	(0.8)	25.9	(1.0)	29.3	(1.0)	19.6	(0.9)	6.1	(0.7)	0.7	(0.2)
OECD average	**5.2**	**(0.1)**	**14.0**	**(0.1)**	**24.0**	**(0.2)**	**27.4**	**(0.2)**	**20.4**	**(0.2)**	**7.7**	**(0.1)**	**1.3**	**(0.0)**
Spain	4.7	(0.4)	14.8	(0.7)	27.3	(0.8)	30.2	(0.7)	18.0	(0.8)	4.6	(0.4)	0.3	(0.1)
Slovak Republic	5.1	(0.6)	14.9	(0.9)	28.0	(1.0)	28.2	(1.0)	18.0	(1.0)	5.3	(0.5)	0.6	(0.1)
Lithuania	4.3	(0.4)	15.9	(0.8)	27.3	(0.9)	29.9	(0.9)	17.6	(0.9)	4.6	(0.6)	0.4	(0.2)
Iceland	5.8	(0.5)	14.6	(0.8)	25.9	(0.7)	28.2	(0.9)	19.1	(0.7)	5.6	(0.5)	0.7	(0.2)
Norway	5.8	(0.8)	15.1	(0.8)	27.3	(0.8)	28.5	(1.0)	17.2	(0.7)	5.5	(0.4)	0.6	(0.1)
France	6.5	(0.7)	14.5	(1.0)	22.8	(1.1)	27.2	(1.1)	20.9	(1.0)	7.3	(0.6)	0.8	(0.2)
Luxembourg	6.4	(0.4)	15.6	(0.6)	25.3	(0.6)	28.6	(0.9)	18.3	(0.7)	5.4	(0.3)	0.5	(0.1)
Russian Federation	5.2	(0.6)	16.8	(1.1)	30.2	(0.9)	28.4	(1.3)	15.1	(1.1)	3.7	(0.5)	0.5	(0.1)
Greece	7.1	(0.9)	16.8	(0.9)	28.9	(1.1)	29.5	(1.0)	14.3	(0.8)	3.2	(0.3)	0.2	(0.1)
Portugal	5.7	(0.8)	18.6	(1.0)	28.8	(0.9)	28.9	(1.2)	14.9	(0.9)	3.1	(0.4)	0.1	(0.1)
United States	7.4	(0.9)	16.8	(0.9)	24.2	(1.0)	24.1	(0.8)	18.3	(0.9)	7.6	(0.6)	1.6	(0.2)
Italy	7.2	(0.5)	17.9	(0.6)	27.6	(0.8)	27.5	(0.6)	15.2	(0.6)	4.2	(0.3)	0.4	(0.1)
Israel	14.8	(1.2)	21.1	(1.0)	24.1	(1.0)	20.8	(0.9)	13.9	(0.8)	4.4	(0.5)	0.8	(0.2)
Serbia	11.7	(0.9)	26.6	(1.2)	32.3	(1.3)	21.9	(1.2)	6.7	(0.6)	0.8	(0.2)	0.0	(0.0)
Chile	12.9	(1.1)	26.5	(1.5)	30.0	(1.1)	20.2	(1.5)	8.5	(1.0)	1.8	(0.3)	0.1	(0.1)
Uruguay	16.6	(1.2)	25.3	(1.1)	29.9	(1.6)	19.8	(1.1)	7.0	(0.5)	1.3	(0.2)	0.1	(0.1)
Bulgaria	18.2	(1.7)	24.3	(1.3)	25.2	(1.2)	18.9	(1.1)	10.4	(1.1)	2.6	(0.5)	0.4	(0.2)

Statistics Canada – Catalogue no. 81-590 no. 3

Table B.1.9 (concluded)

Percent of students at each level for provinces and countries: Combined science

Country and province	Below level 1 %	(SE)	Level 1 %	(SE)	Level 2 %	(SE)	Level 3 %	(SE)	Level 4 %	(SE)	Level 5 %	(SE)	Level 6 %	(SE)
Jordan	16.0	(0.9)	28.1	(0.9)	30.8	(0.8)	18.8	(0.8)	5.6	(0.7)	0.6	(0.2)	0.0	(0.0)
Thailand	12.4	(0.8)	33.4	(1.0)	33.3	(0.9)	16.4	(0.8)	4.1	(0.4)	0.4	(0.1)	0.0	(0.0)
Turkey	12.7	(0.8)	33.6	(1.3)	31.4	(1.4)	15.1	(1.0)	6.2	(1.1)	0.9	(0.3)	0.0	(0.0)
Romania	15.8	(1.5)	30.8	(1.5)	31.9	(1.6)	16.7	(1.2)	4.3	(0.8)	0.5	(0.1)	0.0	(0.0)
Montenegro	17.0	(0.8)	32.9	(1.2)	31.1	(0.9)	15.0	(0.7)	3.7	(0.4)	0.3	(0.1)	0.0	(0.0)
Mexico	18.0	(1.2)	32.7	(0.9)	30.8	(1.0)	14.9	(0.7)	3.2	(0.3)	0.3	(0.1)	0.0	(0.0)
Argentina	28.2	(2.3)	27.8	(1.4)	25.7	(1.3)	13.7	(1.3)	4.1	(0.6)	0.4	(0.1)	0.0	(0.0)
Colombia	25.9	(1.7)	34.0	(1.4)	27.4	(1.5)	10.6	(1.0)	1.9	(0.3)	0.2	(0.1)	0.0	(0.0)
Brazil	27.7	(1.0)	33.2	(0.9)	23.9	(0.9)	11.3	(0.9)	3.4	(0.4)	0.5	(0.2)	0.0	(0.0)
Indonesia	20.1	(1.7)	41.3	(2.2)	27.7	(1.4)	9.6	(2.0)	1.4	(0.5)	0.0	(0.0)	0.0	(0.0)
Tunisia	27.4	(1.1)	35.1	(0.9)	25.1	(1.0)	10.3	(1.0)	2.0	(0.5)	0.1	(0.1)	0.0	(0.0)
Azerbaijan	19.0	(1.5)	53.2	(1.5)	22.7	(1.4)	4.7	(0.9)	0.4	(0.2)	0.0	(0.0)	0.0	(0.0)
Qatar	47.3	(0.6)	31.7	(0.6)	13.9	(0.5)	5.1	(0.3)	1.7	(0.2)	0.3	(0.1)	0.0	(0.0)
Kyrgyzstan	57.9	(1.6)	28.2	(1.2)	10.2	(0.8)	2.9	(0.4)	0.7	(0.2)	0.0	(0.0)	0.0	(0.0)

0   true zero or a value rounded to zero

(SE)   Standard error

Note: Countries and provinces have been sorted by the total percentage of students who attained level 2 or higher.

Table B.1.10

Percent of students at each level for provinces and countries: Science – identifying scientific issues

Country and province	Below level 1 %	(SE)	Level 1 %	(SE)	Level 2 %	(SE)	Level 3 %	(SE)	Level 4 %	(SE)	Level 5 %	(SE)	Level 6 %	(SE)
Finland	0.9	(0.2)	4.0	(0.4)	14.4	(0.7)	30.5	(0.9)	33.0	(1.1)	14.7	(0.7)	2.6	(0.3)
Alberta	**1.6**	**(0.5)**	**5.7**	**(0.9)**	**17.7**	**(1.3)**	**29.7**	**(1.5)**	**27.6**	**(1.8)**	**14.2**	**(1.3)**	**3.6**	**(0.6)**
Estonia	1.1	(0.2)	7.7	(0.8)	24.5	(0.9)	36.8	(0.9)	24.1	(1.0)	5.6	(0.6)	0.3	(0.1)
British Columbia	**2.2**	**(0.7)**	**6.6**	**(0.9)**	**19.3**	**(1.2)**	**29.4**	**(1.2)**	**27.9**	**(1.6)**	**12.6**	**(1.4)**	**2.1**	**(0.5)**
Liechtenstein	2.6	(0.8)	7.8	(1.5)	23.1	(2.7)	30.5	(2.7)	25.7	(3.0)	8.7	(1.9)	1.6	(0.8)
Ontario	**2.7**	**(0.6)**	**7.8**	**(0.9)**	**18.0**	**(1.4)**	**29.4**	**(1.2)**	**28.4**	**(1.3)**	**11.3**	**(1.1)**	**2.4**	**(0.6)**
Australia	2.5	(0.2)	8.0	(0.4)	18.6	(0.5)	28.4	(0.6)	26.7	(0.6)	12.6	(0.5)	3.1	(0.4)
Canada	**2.8**	**(0.3)**	**7.9**	**(0.5)**	**18.8**	**(0.7)**	**29.2**	**(0.7)**	**26.8**	**(0.7)**	**11.7**	**(0.6)**	**2.7**	**(0.3)**
Slovenia	2.0	(0.2)	9.4	(0.7)	23.4	(0.7)	31.8	(1.0)	24.9	(1.1)	7.6	(0.6)	0.9	(0.2)
Korea	3.0	(0.5)	8.7	(0.8)	21.2	(0.9)	32.1	(1.1)	25.6	(1.1)	8.2	(0.8)	1.1	(0.3)
Newfoundland and Labrador	**2.1**	**(0.5)**	**9.9**	**(0.8)**	**21.2**	**(1.4)**	**29.0**	**(1.6)**	**24.5**	**(1.5)**	**11.3**	**(1.1)**	**2.1**	**(0.4)**
Netherlands	3.2	(0.6)	9.0	(0.8)	19.4	(1.1)	26.0	(1.2)	25.5	(1.1)	13.6	(0.8)	3.5	(0.4)
New Zealand	3.4	(0.4)	8.8	(0.6)	18.5	(0.8)	25.5	(0.9)	25.2	(0.9)	14.3	(0.8)	4.3	(0.4)
Quebec	**3.8**	**(0.8)**	**8.5**	**(1.0)**	**18.5**	**(1.0)**	**28.2**	**(1.2)**	**25.0**	**(1.5)**	**12.2**	**(0.9)**	**3.7**	**(0.6)**
Hong Kong-China	3.7	(0.5)	9.2	(0.6)	18.6	(0.8)	28.2	(1.0)	25.8	(0.9)	12.0	(0.8)	2.5	(0.4)
Manitoba	**3.8**	**(0.7)**	**9.3**	**(0.8)**	**21.1**	**(1.4)**	**30.6**	**(1.4)**	**23.5**	**(1.5)**	**9.6**	**(1.0)**	**2.0**	**(0.4)**
Nova Scotia	**3.1**	**(0.7)**	**10.3**	**(1.1)**	**21.9**	**(1.6)**	**31.2**	**(2.0)**	**22.8**	**(1.3)**	**9.1**	**(1.0)**	**1.7**	**(0.4)**
Ireland	3.0	(0.4)	10.6	(0.8)	23.1	(1.1)	29.3	(0.9)	23.0	(0.9)	9.3	(0.7)	1.8	(0.3)
Saskatchewan	**3.3**	**(0.8)**	**10.3**	**(1.0)**	**23.0**	**(1.3)**	**28.9**	**(1.5)**	**24.4**	**(1.2)**	**8.7**	**(0.9)**	**1.3**	**(0.3)**
Switzerland	3.6	(0.4)	10.5	(0.6)	21.4	(0.9)	29.8	(0.8)	24.6	(1.0)	9.0	(0.7)	1.0	(0.2)
Japan	4.8	(0.8)	9.7	(0.7)	19.4	(0.9)	27.0	(1.0)	25.1	(1.0)	11.5	(0.8)	2.6	(0.3)
New Brunswick	**3.3**	**(0.5)**	**11.0**	**(0.8)**	**23.1**	**(1.3)**	**30.0**	**(1.3)**	**22.9**	**(1.3)**	**8.0**	**(1.0)**	**1.6**	**(0.3)**
Belgium	4.5	(0.8)	10.5	(0.7)	21.1	(0.8)	28.5	(0.8)	24.1	(0.7)	9.8	(0.5)	1.5	(0.2)
Austria	3.3	(0.6)	12.1	(0.9)	23.9	(1.2)	30.7	(1.2)	23.2	(1.1)	6.5	(0.8)	0.4	(0.1)

Table B.1.10 (concluded)

Percent of students at each level for provinces and countries:
Science – identifying scientific issues

Country and province	Below level 1 %	(SE)	Level 1 %	(SE)	Level 2 %	(SE)	Level 3 %	(SE)	Level 4 %	(SE)	Level 5 %	(SE)	Level 6 %	(SE)
Macao-China	2.7	(0.3)	12.9	(0.8)	30.3	(0.9)	34.0	(0.9)	17.3	(0.7)	2.7	(0.4)	0.1	(0.1)
Germany	4.4	(0.8)	11.2	(0.8)	22.2	(0.8)	29.1	(1.0)	23.8	(1.0)	7.9	(0.6)	1.3	(0.2)
United Kingdom	4.7	(0.5)	11.2	(0.6)	22.4	(0.6)	26.6	(0.8)	22.1	(0.7)	10.2	(0.6)	2.7	(0.3)
Chinese Taipei	4.1	(0.6)	12.1	(0.9)	21.8	(0.8)	29.5	(1.0)	23.6	(0.9)	8.0	(0.6)	0.9	(0.2)
Prince Edward Island	**3.8**	**(0.6)**	**12.6**	**(1.2)**	**24.8**	**(1.3)**	**28.5**	**(1.3)**	**21.6**	**(1.2)**	**7.6**	**(0.7)**	**1.1**	**(0.3)**
Croatia	3.0	(0.4)	13.3	(0.8)	29.0	(0.9)	31.7	(1.0)	17.8	(0.8)	4.5	(0.5)	0.6	(0.1)
Latvia	3.8	(0.6)	13.5	(1.0)	29.1	(1.0)	33.0	(1.2)	17.3	(1.0)	3.1	(0.4)	0.2	(0.1)
Czech Republic	4.4	(0.8)	13.2	(0.9)	24.8	(1.2)	28.4	(1.2)	20.6	(1.0)	7.3	(0.7)	1.2	(0.3)
Sweden	4.6	(0.4)	13.0	(0.8)	25.3	(1.1)	29.6	(1.1)	19.8	(0.9)	6.6	(0.5)	1.0	(0.2)
Hungary	3.8	(0.6)	14.1	(0.8)	31.1	(1.0)	33.7	(1.0)	14.9	(0.8)	2.3	(0.4)	0.1	(0.1)
Denmark	4.3	(0.5)	13.6	(0.9)	26.2	(1.0)	31.5	(0.9)	18.8	(0.8)	5.1	(0.6)	0.4	(0.2)
Spain	4.4	(0.3)	13.7	(0.7)	27.9	(0.7)	32.1	(0.6)	17.6	(0.7)	4.0	(0.4)	0.3	(0.1)
OECD average	5.2	(0.1)	13.5	(0.1)	24.6	(0.2)	28.3	(0.2)	20.0	(0.2)	7.1	(0.1)	1.3	(0.0)
Poland	3.9	(0.4)	15.6	(0.9)	30.4	(0.8)	30.8	(0.9)	15.8	(0.8)	3.2	(0.4)	0.2	(0.1)
Norway	5.2	(0.7)	14.4	(0.8)	27.1	(0.9)	29.6	(1.0)	17.8	(0.9)	5.3	(0.6)	0.6	(0.2)
France	6.7	(0.7)	13.6	(0.9)	21.9	(1.0)	27.1	(1.2)	21.5	(0.9)	8.0	(0.7)	1.2	(0.3)
Portugal	4.8	(0.6)	15.6	(0.9)	27.6	(1.0)	29.5	(1.1)	17.7	(1.0)	4.6	(0.5)	0.3	(0.1)
Iceland	6.5	(0.6)	13.9	(0.8)	24.6	(0.8)	27.1	(0.8)	19.4	(0.7)	7.3	(0.5)	1.1	(0.2)
Luxembourg	5.7	(0.4)	15.7	(0.6)	27.6	(0.7)	29.5	(0.9)	17.1	(0.7)	4.1	(0.3)	0.3	(0.1)
United States	5.6	(0.7)	15.9	(1.1)	25.2	(0.9)	26.7	(0.9)	18.5	(0.9)	6.9	(0.6)	1.2	(0.3)
Lithuania	4.8	(0.5)	16.9	(1.0)	30.6	(1.0)	31.1	(1.0)	14.2	(1.0)	2.3	(0.3)	0.1	(0.1)
Slovak Republic	6.9	(0.7)	15.7	(1.1)	29.5	(1.2)	29.0	(1.1)	15.3	(1.2)	3.5	(0.4)	0.2	(0.1)
Greece	8.1	(0.8)	16.4	(0.8)	29.3	(0.9)	30.0	(0.9)	13.8	(0.9)	2.2	(0.3)	0.1	(0.1)
Italy	8.0	(0.5)	17.0	(0.6)	27.8	(0.7)	27.0	(0.7)	15.4	(0.7)	4.4	(0.4)	0.5	(0.1)
Russian Federation	7.5	(0.8)	19.9	(1.2)	31.4	(0.8)	26.9	(1.1)	11.8	(1.0)	2.3	(0.3)	0.2	(0.1)
Israel	14.7	(1.0)	19.9	(0.7)	24.3	(0.8)	21.5	(0.9)	13.8	(0.9)	4.7	(0.5)	1.1	(0.2)
Chile	11.0	(0.9)	24.2	(1.2)	32.3	(0.9)	22.0	(1.1)	8.8	(0.9)	1.6	(0.4)	0.1	(0.1)
Serbia	12.4	(1.0)	25.6	(1.0)	35.5	(1.0)	21.2	(1.2)	5.0	(0.5)	0.3	(0.1)	0.0	(0.0)
Uruguay	15.8	(1.2)	26.2	(1.0)	29.5	(1.2)	19.7	(0.9)	7.5	(0.6)	1.2	(0.3)	0.1	(0.1)
Turkey	11.0	(0.9)	31.1	(1.2)	34.4	(1.3)	18.1	(1.2)	4.9	(0.9)	0.5	(0.2)	0.0	(0.0)
Mexico	15.0	(1.0)	28.9	(0.8)	32.9	(0.9)	18.2	(0.7)	4.6	(0.4)	0.5	(0.1)	0.0	(0.0)
Bulgaria	20.6	(2.0)	23.8	(1.3)	24.5	(1.2)	18.8	(1.2)	9.4	(1.0)	2.5	(0.6)	0.3	(0.1)
Thailand	16.9	(0.9)	31.4	(1.0)	31.7	(1.0)	15.9	(0.9)	3.8	(0.5)	0.3	(0.1)	0.0	(0.0)
Jordan	19.6	(0.9)	29.5	(1.0)	30.8	(1.2)	16.1	(1.0)	3.7	(0.5)	0.3	(0.1)	0.0	(0.0)
Romania	16.5	(1.4)	33.8	(1.6)	32.8	(1.4)	14.2	(1.4)	2.6	(0.6)	0.1	(0.1)	0.0	(0.0)
Colombia	22.2	(1.4)	28.2	(1.1)	30.3	(1.2)	15.2	(1.1)	3.6	(0.5)	0.5	(0.2)	0.0	(0.0)
Argentina	25.2	(2.0)	28.4	(1.2)	27.8	(1.3)	14.2	(1.2)	4.0	(0.6)	0.4	(0.2)	0.0	(0.0)
Montenegro	21.4	(0.8)	32.6	(1.1)	29.3	(0.9)	14.0	(0.7)	2.6	(0.4)	0.2	(0.1)	0.0	(0.0)
Brazil	25.1	(1.1)	30.1	(1.3)	27.2	(1.2)	13.0	(0.9)	4.0	(0.5)	0.6	(0.2)	0.0	(0.0)
Indonesia	22.0	(1.7)	37.0	(1.7)	28.7	(1.3)	10.5	(1.8)	1.5	(0.5)	0.2	(0.2)	0.0	(0.0)
Tunisia	28.7	(1.5)	33.6	(1.1)	24.8	(1.0)	10.3	(0.9)	2.4	(0.5)	0.2	(0.1)	0.0	(0.0)
Qatar	43.5	(0.6)	35.5	(1.1)	14.9	(0.7)	4.6	(0.3)	1.2	(0.2)	0.2	(0.1)	0.0	(0.0)
Azerbaijan	38.5	(2.1)	42.9	(1.6)	15.9	(1.2)	2.4	(0.4)	0.2	(0.1)	0.0	(0.0)	0.0	(0.0)
Kyrgyzstan	55.1	(1.5)	28.8	(1.1)	12.2	(0.7)	3.3	(0.5)	0.6	(0.2)	0.1	(0.0)	0.0	(0.0)

0   true zero or a value rounded to zero

(SE)   Standard error

Note: Countries and provinces have been sorted by the total percentage of students who attained level 2 or higher.

Table B.1.11

Percent of students at each level for provinces and countries:
Science – explaining phenomena scientifically

Country and province	Below level 1 %	(SE)	Level 1 %	(SE)	Level 2 %	(SE)	Level 3 %	(SE)	Level 4 %	(SE)	Level 5 %	(SE)	Level 6 %	(SE)
Finland	0.5	(0.1)	3.4	(0.3)	13.8	(0.6)	28.1	(0.9)	31.5	(1.0)	17.5	(0.8)	5.1	(0.5)
Alberta	**1.2**	**(0.4)**	**5.5**	**(0.9)**	**17.4**	**(1.3)**	**27.2**	**(1.5)**	**27.8**	**(1.4)**	**15.6**	**(1.0)**	**5.2**	**(0.7)**
Estonia	1.0	(0.2)	6.5	(0.6)	20.0	(0.9)	29.4	(1.2)	27.2	(1.2)	12.9	(0.8)	2.9	(0.3)
Hong Kong-China	1.5	(0.4)	6.3	(0.6)	16.0	(0.8)	28.2	(1.0)	29.1	(0.8)	15.5	(0.7)	3.5	(0.4)
Macao-China	1.5	(0.3)	7.9	(0.5)	23.3	(1.0)	33.9	(0.9)	25.1	(0.9)	7.5	(0.6)	0.8	(0.2)
Chinese Taipei	1.7	(0.3)	8.7	(0.7)	17.1	(0.9)	25.3	(0.9)	26.8	(1.0)	16.1	(0.9)	4.3	(0.4)
British Columbia	**2.5**	**(0.6)**	**8.1**	**(1.1)**	**19.6**	**(1.3)**	**25.6**	**(1.5)**	**26.5**	**(1.5)**	**14.0**	**(1.1)**	**3.8**	**(0.6)**
Ontario	**2.4**	**(0.6)**	**8.9**	**(1.2)**	**19.1**	**(1.3)**	**28.0**	**(1.3)**	**26.4**	**(1.7)**	**12.3**	**(1.2)**	**3.0**	**(0.5)**
Canada	**2.7**	**(0.3)**	**8.9**	**(0.5)**	**19.8**	**(0.7)**	**27.9**	**(0.7)**	**25.4**	**(0.8)**	**12.2**	**(0.6)**	**3.1**	**(0.2)**
Japan	2.8	(0.4)	8.9	(0.7)	20.4	(1.0)	28.5	(0.8)	25.9	(1.0)	11.1	(0.9)	2.4	(0.3)
Hungary	2.5	(0.3)	9.9	(1.0)	23.6	(1.0)	30.2	(1.0)	22.8	(1.0)	9.0	(0.6)	2.1	(0.3)
Nova Scotia	**2.6**	**(0.5)**	**10.0**	**(1.1)**	**23.1**	**(1.4)**	**29.3**	**(1.9)**	**22.9**	**(1.7)**	**9.5**	**(0.8)**	**2.5**	**(0.5)**
Czech Republic	2.8	(0.5)	10.1	(0.8)	20.9	(1.0)	27.4	(1.0)	23.2	(1.0)	12.1	(0.9)	3.5	(0.4)
Quebec	**3.6**	**(0.7)**	**9.4**	**(0.8)**	**20.7**	**(1.1)**	**28.7**	**(1.3)**	**24.2**	**(1.2)**	**11.0**	**(0.9)**	**2.4**	**(0.5)**
Netherlands	2.6	(0.4)	10.4	(0.8)	21.2	(1.0)	28.6	(1.2)	25.0	(0.9)	10.3	(0.6)	1.9	(0.3)
Korea	2.7	(0.4)	10.8	(0.7)	24.0	(0.9)	30.9	(1.2)	22.8	(0.8)	7.6	(0.9)	1.2	(0.4)
Manitoba	**3.7**	**(0.6)**	**10.2**	**(1.0)**	**19.5**	**(1.3)**	**30.4**	**(1.3)**	**22.7**	**(1.6)**	**10.4**	**(0.9)**	**3.0**	**(0.6)**
Australia	3.5	(0.3)	10.6	(0.4)	21.8	(0.5)	27.6	(0.6)	23.0	(0.7)	10.8	(0.5)	2.7	(0.3)
Slovenia	3.5	(0.4)	10.6	(0.6)	22.0	(1.1)	27.0	(0.9)	21.5	(0.7)	11.5	(0.7)	3.9	(0.4)
Liechtenstein	3.2	(1.0)	10.8	(1.9)	22.5	(3.4)	28.9	(4.3)	23.3	(3.1)	9.4	(1.8)	1.8	(0.9)
Newfoundland and Labrador	**2.5**	**(0.5)**	**12.0**	**(1.0)**	**22.3**	**(1.6)**	**27.2**	**(1.5)**	**23.1**	**(2.0)**	**10.7**	**(1.3)**	**2.2**	**(0.6)**
Saskatchewan	**3.6**	**(0.8)**	**11.2**	**(1.3)**	**22.6**	**(1.5)**	**27.9**	**(1.6)**	**22.0**	**(1.3)**	**10.5**	**(1.1)**	**2.2**	**(0.4)**
Austria	4.1	(0.7)	11.0	(0.9)	21.4	(1.0)	27.5	(1.0)	23.9	(1.0)	10.3	(0.8)	1.8	(0.2)
Germany	3.9	(0.6)	11.4	(0.9)	20.6	(0.9)	27.6	(1.0)	22.6	(1.0)	11.1	(0.9)	2.8	(0.3)
Sweden	4.0	(0.6)	11.5	(0.8)	23.4	(1.0)	29.2	(0.9)	21.4	(0.8)	8.7	(0.6)	1.8	(0.3)
New Zealand	4.6	(0.5)	11.3	(0.7)	21.0	(0.8)	24.7	(1.1)	22.0	(0.9)	12.2	(0.6)	4.2	(0.4)
Poland	3.1	(0.4)	12.9	(0.7)	25.6	(1.0)	28.8	(1.0)	20.1	(0.8)	7.9	(0.5)	1.6	(0.3)
Ireland	4.5	(0.5)	12.5	(0.7)	24.6	(1.0)	28.0	(1.1)	19.9	(0.9)	8.6	(0.7)	1.9	(0.3)
Slovak Republic	4.1	(0.6)	12.9	(0.8)	26.0	(1.3)	28.7	(1.0)	19.6	(0.9)	7.2	(0.6)	1.4	(0.3)
United Kingdom	4.5	(0.4)	12.6	(0.6)	21.7	(0.7)	25.2	(0.7)	20.8	(0.6)	11.4	(0.6)	3.8	(0.3)
Switzerland	5.1	(0.6)	12.2	(0.6)	21.8	(0.9)	28.0	(0.9)	22.6	(0.8)	8.6	(0.7)	1.8	(0.3)
Denmark	4.1	(0.5)	13.4	(0.8)	25.2	(0.8)	29.0	(0.9)	19.6	(0.8)	7.5	(0.7)	1.3	(0.3)
Croatia	3.1	(0.4)	14.3	(0.8)	29.4	(1.1)	30.1	(1.2)	17.5	(0.9)	4.8	(0.4)	0.7	(0.1)
New Brunswick	**4.1**	**(0.5)**	**13.7**	**(0.9)**	**25.5**	**(1.4)**	**28.3**	**(1.5)**	**20.0**	**(1.1)**	**7.0**	**(0.7)**	**1.4**	**(0.3)**
Prince Edward Island	**4.2**	**(0.5)**	**13.6**	**(1.0)**	**22.5**	**(1.2)**	**27.0**	**(1.3)**	**20.5**	**(1.2)**	**9.5**	**(1.0)**	**2.6**	**(0.6)**
Latvia	4.3	(0.6)	14.9	(0.9)	29.5	(1.1)	30.6	(0.9)	16.0	(0.9)	4.2	(0.4)	0.5	(0.1)
Lithuania	4.5	(0.5)	14.9	(0.7)	26.1	(0.9)	28.4	(1.0)	18.8	(0.8)	6.2	(0.6)	1.2	(0.3)
Belgium	5.8	(0.8)	13.5	(0.7)	21.9	(0.7)	27.2	(0.7)	21.8	(0.7)	8.5	(0.4)	1.2	(0.2)
Norway	5.7	(0.7)	13.7	(0.7)	25.4	(0.9)	27.9	(0.8)	18.9	(0.9)	7.2	(0.6)	1.2	(0.2)
OECD average	**5.4**	**(0.1)**	**14.2**	**(0.1)**	**24.0**	**(0.2)**	**27.0**	**(0.2)**	**19.7**	**(0.2)**	**8.0**	**(0.1)**	**1.7**	**(0.0)**
Iceland	4.9	(0.5)	14.9	(0.8)	27.5	(0.9)	29.7	(0.8)	17.5	(0.7)	4.9	(0.5)	0.5	(0.1)
Spain	5.6	(0.4)	15.1	(0.7)	26.1	(0.7)	28.2	(0.7)	17.9	(0.7)	6.2	(0.4)	0.9	(0.1)
Russian Federation	4.9	(0.5)	15.7	(1.0)	29.6	(0.9)	29.2	(1.1)	15.4	(0.9)	4.5	(0.4)	0.6	(0.1)
Luxembourg	6.7	(0.4)	16.3	(0.7)	26.3	(1.0)	27.7	(0.9)	17.3	(0.7)	5.0	(0.4)	0.6	(0.2)
Greece	6.6	(0.8)	17.0	(0.9)	28.8	(1.0)	28.4	(1.1)	15.1	(0.9)	3.6	(0.4)	0.5	(0.1)
France	7.6	(0.7)	16.6	(1.0)	25.5	(0.9)	27.4	(0.9)	17.0	(0.8)	5.4	(0.5)	0.6	(0.2)
Italy	7.4	(0.5)	16.8	(0.6)	27.0	(0.7)	26.9	(0.6)	15.8	(0.6)	5.2	(0.3)	0.8	(0.1)
Portugal	5.7	(0.7)	19.4	(1.1)	31.0	(0.8)	28.0	(1.1)	13.3	(0.7)	2.5	(0.3)	0.1	(0.1)
United States	8.3	(0.8)	17.9	(1.0)	23.6	(0.9)	23.5	(0.9)	17.0	(0.9)	7.8	(0.6)	2.0	(0.3)
Serbia	11.7	(0.9)	25.1	(1.0)	31.3	(1.0)	22.1	(1.1)	8.2	(0.6)	1.5	(0.2)	0.1	(0.0)
Bulgaria	14.9	(1.5)	23.3	(1.3)	26.4	(1.2)	20.8	(1.2)	10.9	(1.1)	3.1	(0.6)	0.6	(0.3)
Jordan	14.3	(0.8)	24.3	(0.9)	29.1	(0.9)	21.3	(0.8)	8.9	(0.7)	1.9	(0.3)	0.2	(0.1)
Israel	16.2	(1.2)	23.2	(0.8)	24.7	(1.0)	20.2	(0.9)	11.5	(0.8)	3.6	(0.3)	0.6	(0.2)
Chile	14.7	(1.0)	27.7	(1.3)	29.1	(0.9)	18.3	(1.1)	8.1	(0.8)	1.9	(0.4)	0.1	(0.1)

Table B.1.11 (concluded)

Percent of students at each level for provinces and countries: Science – explaining phenomena scientifically

Country and province	Below level 1 %	(SE)	Level 1 %	(SE)	Level 2 %	(SE)	Level 3 %	(SE)	Level 4 %	(SE)	Level 5 %	(SE)	Level 6 %	(SE)
Romania	13.7	(1.5)	29.9	(1.5)	32.5	(1.3)	17.7	(1.2)	5.3	(0.8)	0.8	(0.2)	0.0	(0.0)
Uruguay	18.7	(1.1)	26.3	(1.0)	27.9	(1.2)	18.4	(0.8)	7.0	(0.5)	1.5	(0.3)	0.2	(0.1)
Thailand	12.2	(0.9)	34.4	(1.3)	34.0	(1.2)	15.2	(0.9)	3.8	(0.4)	0.4	(0.1)	0.0	(0.0)
Turkey	14.1	(0.8)	33.3	(1.2)	30.0	(1.3)	14.9	(0.9)	6.2	(1.1)	1.4	(0.5)	0.1	(0.0)
Montenegro	15.7	(0.7)	32.2	(0.8)	31.2	(0.8)	15.7	(0.8)	4.7	(0.5)	0.4	(0.1)	0.0	(0.0)
Azerbaijan	10.3	(0.9)	39.7	(1.6)	37.2	(1.7)	10.8	(1.1)	1.8	(0.5)	0.1	(0.1)	0.0	(0.0)
Mexico	19.3	(1.2)	33.2	(0.9)	29.8	(1.0)	14.0	(0.7)	3.3	(0.4)	0.4	(0.1)	0.0	(0.0)
Argentina	29.7	(2.1)	28.0	(1.2)	24.6	(1.3)	13.3	(1.2)	3.8	(0.6)	0.5	(0.2)	0.0	(0.0)
Indonesia	20.0	(1.4)	40.5	(2.3)	27.5	(1.5)	10.4	(2.0)	1.5	(0.5)	0.0	(0.0)	0.0	(0.0)
Brazil	27.8	(1.0)	33.3	(0.9)	23.7	(0.8)	11.0	(0.8)	3.5	(0.4)	0.7	(0.2)	0.1	(0.1)
Tunisia	28.1	(1.3)	35.4	(1.1)	25.2	(1.1)	9.1	(0.8)	2.1	(0.5)	0.1	(0.1)	0.0	(0.0)
Colombia	30.5	(1.7)	33.1	(1.4)	24.2	(1.3)	10.0	(0.9)	1.9	(0.3)	0.2	(0.1)	0.0	(0.0)
Qatar	43.2	(0.6)	32.7	(0.7)	15.8	(0.5)	5.9	(0.3)	1.8	(0.2)	0.5	(0.1)	0.1	(0.0)
Kyrgyzstan	51.0	(1.7)	32.0	(1.2)	12.9	(0.8)	3.3	(0.4)	0.8	(0.2)	0.1	(0.1)	0.0	(0.0)

0   true zero or a value rounded to zero

(SE)   Standard error

Note: Countries and provinces have been sorted by the total percentage of students who attained level 2 or higher.

Table B.1.12

Percent of students at each level for provinces and countries: Science – using scientific evidence

Country and province	Below level 1 %	(SE)	Level 1 %	(SE)	Level 2 %	(SE)	Level 3 %	(SE)	Level 4 %	(SE)	Level 5 %	(SE)	Level 6 %	(SE)
Finland	1.0	(0.2)	4.3	(0.4)	13.9	(0.7)	25.9	(0.7)	29.8	(0.8)	18.3	(0.7)	6.8	(0.5)
Alberta	1.4	(0.6)	5.4	(0.9)	16.7	(1.4)	27.3	(1.3)	28.9	(1.6)	15.8	(1.1)	4.4	(0.6)
Ontario	1.9	(0.5)	7.2	(1.0)	16.3	(1.4)	26.8	(1.6)	29.5	(1.5)	14.7	(1.3)	3.6	(0.6)
British Columbia	2.5	(0.7)	7.5	(1.0)	17.3	(1.2)	27.0	(1.2)	28.5	(1.4)	14.3	(1.3)	3.0	(0.6)
Estonia	1.9	(0.3)	8.1	(0.6)	20.2	(0.8)	30.5	(1.1)	25.3	(1.1)	11.7	(0.7)	2.3	(0.3)
Canada	2.5	(0.3)	7.6	(0.5)	17.1	(0.7)	27.0	(0.8)	27.9	(0.7)	14.3	(0.6)	3.6	(0.3)
Hong Kong-China	2.6	(0.4)	7.6	(0.6)	16.1	(0.7)	26.7	(1.0)	29.0	(0.9)	15.0	(0.8)	3.0	(0.3)
Korea	3.1	(0.6)	7.9	(0.8)	17.0	(0.6)	27.3	(1.2)	26.8	(0.9)	14.4	(1.0)	3.4	(0.5)
Quebec	3.4	(0.7)	8.0	(0.9)	16.4	(1.0)	26.3	(1.0)	26.3	(1.1)	15.0	(1.0)	4.6	(0.6)
Newfoundland and Labrador	2.5	(0.4)	9.0	(0.9)	19.8	(1.6)	26.2	(1.4)	26.1	(1.4)	13.7	(1.2)	2.7	(0.6)
Macao-China	2.3	(0.3)	9.3	(0.5)	24.7	(0.8)	33.6	(0.9)	23.2	(1.0)	6.4	(0.5)	0.5	(0.2)
Nova Scotia	2.8	(0.5)	8.8	(1.1)	21.1	(1.4)	29.8	(1.9)	24.9	(1.4)	10.4	(0.9)	2.1	(0.4)
Manitoba	3.1	(0.6)	8.9	(0.8)	17.8	(1.2)	29.4	(1.7)	26.2	(1.6)	11.8	(1.2)	2.8	(0.6)
Chinese Taipei	3.1	(0.5)	9.8	(0.8)	17.5	(0.8)	26.6	(0.9)	27.2	(1.0)	13.5	(0.7)	2.3	(0.3)
Australia	3.9	(0.3)	9.4	(0.6)	18.8	(0.7)	26.2	(0.6)	24.5	(0.6)	13.4	(0.6)	4.0	(0.4)
Japan	4.6	(0.6)	8.6	(0.7)	15.5	(0.8)	22.8	(0.8)	25.5	(1.0)	16.8	(0.9)	6.2	(0.5)
Liechtenstein	3.9	(1.1)	9.7	(1.7)	19.2	(3.1)	24.5	(2.5)	22.0	(2.7)	15.3	(2.1)	5.4	(1.4)
Saskatchewan	4.1	(0.7)	10.1	(1.0)	21.5	(1.2)	27.9	(1.3)	24.6	(1.7)	9.9	(1.2)	1.8	(0.4)
Slovenia	3.4	(0.3)	11.5	(0.5)	22.7	(0.7)	27.5	(0.7)	22.4	(0.7)	10.2	(0.5)	2.2	(0.4)
New Zealand	5.3	(0.7)	10.0	(0.7)	17.7	(0.7)	22.0	(0.8)	22.5	(0.8)	15.5	(0.8)	6.9	(0.6)
New Brunswick	3.8	(0.5)	11.7	(0.9)	23.1	(1.4)	28.1	(1.1)	23.2	(1.1)	8.6	(0.8)	1.5	(0.4)
Netherlands	3.7	(0.6)	12.0	(1.0)	19.5	(0.8)	23.9	(1.2)	23.9	(1.4)	13.8	(1.0)	3.2	(0.3)
Switzerland	5.9	(0.6)	11.0	(0.5)	19.2	(0.8)	25.7	(0.7)	23.3	(0.8)	11.5	(0.6)	3.4	(0.4)

Table B.1.12 (concluded)

Percent of students at each level for provinces and countries:
Science – using scientific evidence

Country and province	Below level 1 %	(SE)	Level 1 %	(SE)	Level 2 %	(SE)	Level 3 %	(SE)	Level 4 %	(SE)	Level 5 %	(SE)	Level 6 %	(SE)
Prince Edward Island	5.1	(0.6)	11.8	(0.9)	21.8	(1.3)	28.3	(1.4)	22.1	(1.2)	9.2	(0.9)	1.7	(0.4)
Ireland	5.4	(0.6)	12.4	(0.7)	22.5	(0.8)	27.6	(1.0)	21.7	(1.1)	8.8	(0.7)	1.6	(0.3)
Belgium	7.0	(0.8)	10.8	(0.6)	18.0	(0.7)	24.6	(0.7)	24.8	(0.7)	12.6	(0.6)	2.1	(0.2)
Germany	6.7	(1.0)	11.5	(0.9)	18.8	(0.9)	25.3	(0.9)	22.8	(1.0)	11.6	(0.8)	3.3	(0.4)
Latvia	5.2	(0.7)	13.9	(1.0)	26.2	(1.0)	30.9	(1.0)	18.5	(1.0)	5.0	(0.5)	0.4	(0.1)
United Kingdom	6.7	(0.5)	12.4	(0.6)	20.1	(0.6)	23.9	(0.8)	21.2	(0.8)	11.7	(0.5)	4.0	(0.4)
Hungary	6.0	(0.7)	13.7	(0.9)	24.2	(1.1)	28.0	(1.1)	19.0	(0.9)	7.8	(0.7)	1.4	(0.3)
France	7.1	(0.8)	12.5	(0.8)	19.5	(1.0)	23.5	(1.1)	22.7	(1.0)	12.0	(0.8)	2.6	(0.5)
Croatia	5.2	(0.6)	15.0	(0.8)	26.8	(1.0)	28.4	(1.0)	17.9	(0.9)	5.9	(0.5)	0.9	(0.2)
Poland	5.5	(0.6)	14.8	(0.8)	25.4	(0.7)	27.7	(0.9)	18.9	(1.0)	6.6	(0.6)	1.0	(0.2)
Austria	8.0	(1.2)	12.5	(1.1)	20.5	(1.0)	24.0	(0.9)	21.9	(0.9)	10.7	(0.9)	2.4	(0.4)
Sweden	6.6	(0.6)	14.0	(0.8)	23.4	(1.0)	27.1	(0.8)	19.6	(0.8)	7.8	(0.5)	1.6	(0.2)
Czech Republic	7.4	(0.9)	13.5	(0.9)	22.4	(1.1)	24.8	(1.1)	19.8	(1.0)	9.3	(0.8)	2.8	(0.4)
OECD average	7.9	(0.1)	14.1	(0.1)	21.7	(0.2)	24.8	(0.2)	19.8	(0.2)	9.3	(0.1)	2.4	(0.1)
Lithuania	6.6	(0.6)	15.6	(0.9)	25.2	(0.9)	28.0	(0.9)	18.2	(0.9)	5.6	(0.6)	0.8	(0.2)
Spain	7.1	(0.5)	15.2	(0.7)	25.5	(0.6)	28.0	(0.6)	18.2	(0.7)	5.3	(0.4)	0.7	(0.1)
Denmark	7.7	(0.7)	15.4	(0.7)	23.9	(0.9)	26.1	(0.9)	18.3	(0.8)	7.1	(0.6)	1.4	(0.3)
Iceland	8.5	(0.6)	15.0	(0.7)	22.3	(0.8)	25.6	(0.9)	18.9	(0.7)	7.8	(0.6)	1.9	(0.3)
Luxembourg	9.2	(0.4)	14.4	(0.7)	21.7	(0.7)	25.4	(0.7)	19.1	(0.7)	8.5	(0.5)	1.8	(0.3)
Russian Federation	7.6	(0.8)	16.2	(1.0)	27.2	(1.1)	26.4	(0.9)	15.9	(1.0)	5.5	(0.5)	1.1	(0.2)
Slovak Republic	9.7	(0.9)	15.9	(1.1)	25.4	(1.1)	25.2	(1.0)	16.9	(0.9)	6.1	(0.6)	0.9	(0.2)
United States	9.9	(1.4)	16.0	(0.8)	22.0	(1.2)	22.9	(0.9)	17.9	(0.8)	8.7	(0.8)	2.5	(0.4)
Portugal	9.6	(0.9)	17.9	(0.9)	25.4	(1.1)	25.7	(1.1)	16.3	(0.9)	4.6	(0.4)	0.5	(0.2)
Greece	11.2	(1.1)	16.5	(0.9)	26.3	(1.1)	27.2	(1.1)	14.2	(0.9)	4.1	(0.5)	0.5	(0.1)
Norway	10.0	(0.9)	18.3	(0.9)	25.5	(1.0)	23.8	(1.2)	15.6	(0.9)	5.6	(0.5)	1.2	(0.2)
Italy	11.8	(0.6)	17.7	(0.6)	24.9	(0.6)	24.6	(0.6)	15.0	(0.6)	5.2	(0.3)	0.8	(0.1)
Israel	18.1	(1.3)	18.1	(0.9)	20.3	(0.8)	18.6	(0.8)	14.6	(0.9)	7.7	(0.6)	2.6	(0.3)
Chile	15.8	(1.3)	23.9	(1.3)	26.9	(1.3)	20.1	(1.3)	10.1	(0.9)	2.8	(0.4)	0.3	(0.1)
Uruguay	19.7	(1.1)	22.2	(1.0)	26.4	(0.9)	20.1	(0.9)	9.2	(0.6)	2.1	(0.4)	0.3	(0.1)
Serbia	18.6	(1.2)	25.4	(1.0)	27.5	(1.0)	19.4	(1.2)	7.6	(0.7)	1.5	(0.3)	0.1	(0.1)
Thailand	16.2	(0.9)	29.2	(1.0)	30.0	(0.9)	16.9	(0.7)	6.5	(0.7)	1.1	(0.2)	0.1	(0.1)
Bulgaria	27.5	(2.3)	20.7	(1.2)	21.0	(1.2)	16.6	(1.2)	10.0	(1.0)	3.2	(0.7)	0.9	(0.3)
Turkey	18.9	(1.1)	30.3	(1.4)	27.1	(1.4)	15.3	(1.0)	6.8	(1.0)	1.6	(0.5)	0.1	(0.1)
Romania	24.9	(2.4)	25.6	(1.4)	25.7	(1.8)	16.6	(1.9)	5.9	(0.8)	1.2	(0.3)	0.1	(0.1)
Jordan	23.4	(1.2)	27.3	(1.2)	27.5	(1.2)	15.9	(0.9)	5.2	(0.6)	0.8	(0.3)	0.0	(0.0)
Montenegro	22.5	(0.6)	29.5	(0.9)	27.3	(0.8)	15.0	(0.7)	5.0	(0.5)	0.7	(0.2)	0.0	(0.0)
Mexico	23.5	(1.4)	29.1	(0.9)	27.6	(0.9)	15.3	(0.7)	4.1	(0.4)	0.5	(0.1)	0.0	(0.0)
Argentina	31.7	(2.4)	24.5	(1.2)	23.5	(1.2)	13.8	(1.1)	5.5	(0.7)	0.9	(0.3)	0.1	(0.1)
Colombia	28.9	(2.0)	31.9	(1.3)	26.2	(1.3)	10.5	(0.9)	2.3	(0.3)	0.2	(0.1)	0.0	(0.0)
Tunisia	31.5	(1.4)	29.8	(1.0)	24.2	(1.0)	11.3	(0.9)	3.0	(0.6)	0.3	(0.1)	0.0	(0.0)
Indonesia	27.7	(2.6)	35.1	(1.7)	24.5	(1.5)	10.2	(1.9)	2.4	(1.0)	0.1	(0.1)	0.0	(0.0)
Brazil	34.7	(1.3)	28.4	(1.1)	21.0	(0.9)	11.0	(0.8)	4.0	(0.5)	0.8	(0.3)	0.1	(0.1)
Azerbaijan	47.6	(2.1)	33.4	(1.4)	14.1	(1.2)	4.2	(0.8)	0.7	(0.2)	0.0	(0.0)	0.0	(0.0)
Qatar	59.1	(0.6)	22.5	(0.6)	10.9	(0.6)	4.8	(0.3)	1.9	(0.2)	0.6	(0.1)	0.1	(0.1)
Kyrgyzstan	69.6	(1.3)	18.2	(0.8)	7.9	(0.6)	3.0	(0.5)	1.1	(0.3)	0.1	(0.1)	0.0	(0.0)

0   true zero or a value rounded to zero

(SE)   Standard error

Note: Countries and provinces have been sorted by the total percentage of students who attained level 2 or higher.

Table B.2.1

Estimated average scores and confidence intervals for provinces and countries: Reading

Country and province	estimated average score	standard error	confidence interval – 95% lower limit	confidence interval – 95% upper limit
Korea	556	(3.8)	549	563
Finland	547	(2.1)	543	551
Hong Kong-China	536	(2.4)	531	541
Alberta	535	(4.2)	527	543
Ontario	534	(4.6)	525	543
British Columbia	528	(5.7)	517	539
Canada	527	(2.4)	522	532
Quebec	522	(5.0)	512	532
New Zealand	521	(3.0)	515	527
Ireland	517	(3.5)	510	524
Manitoba	516	(3.5)	510	523
Newfoundland and Labrador	514	(3.2)	507	520
Australia	513	(2.1)	509	517
Liechtenstein	510	(3.9)	503	518
Poland	508	(2.8)	502	513
Netherlands	507	(2.9)	501	512
Saskatchewan	507	(4.2)	498	515
Sweden	507	(3.4)	501	514
Nova Scotia	505	(3.5)	498	512
Belgium	501	(3.0)	495	507
Estonia	501	(2.9)	495	506
Switzerland	499	(3.1)	493	505
Japan	498	(3.6)	491	505
New Brunswick	497	(2.3)	493	502
Prince Edward Island	497	(2.8)	492	502
Chinese Taipei	496	(3.4)	490	503
Germany	495	(4.4)	486	504
United Kingdom	495	(2.3)	491	500
Denmark	494	(3.2)	488	501
Slovenia	494	(1.0)	492	496
Macao-China	492	(1.1)	490	494
OECD average	491	(0.6)	490	492
Austria	490	(4.1)	482	498
France	488	(4.1)	480	496
Iceland	484	(1.9)	481	488
Norway	484	(3.2)	478	491
Czech Republic	483	(4.2)	475	491
Hungary	482	(3.3)	476	489
Latvia	479	(3.7)	472	487
Luxembourg	479	(1.3)	477	482
Croatia	477	(2.8)	472	483
Portugal	472	(3.6)	465	479
Lithuania	470	(3.0)	464	476
Italy	469	(2.4)	464	473
Slovak Republic	466	(3.1)	460	472
Spain	461	(2.2)	456	465
Greece	460	(4.0)	452	468
Turkey	447	(4.2)	439	455
Chile	442	(5.0)	432	452
Russian Federation	440	(4.3)	431	448
Israel	439	(4.6)	430	448

Table B.2.1 (concluded)

Estimated average scores and confidence intervals for provinces and countries: Reading

Country and province	estimated average score	standard error	confidence interval – 95% lower limit	confidence interval – 95% upper limit
Thailand	417	(2.6)	412	422
Uruguay	413	(3.4)	406	419
Mexico	410	(3.1)	404	416
Bulgaria	402	(6.9)	388	415
Jordan	401	(3.3)	394	407
Serbia	401	(3.5)	394	408
Romania	396	(4.7)	387	405
Brazil	393	(3.7)	386	400
Indonesia	393	(5.9)	381	405
Montenegro	392	(1.2)	390	394
Colombia	385	(5.1)	375	395
Tunisia	380	(4.0)	372	388
Argentina	374	(7.2)	360	388
Azerbaijan	353	(3.1)	347	359
Qatar	312	(1.2)	310	315
Kyrgyzstan	285	(3.5)	278	292

Note: Data for the United States are not available for reading.

Table B.2.2

Estimated average scores and confidence intervals for provinces and countries: Mathematics

Country and province	estimated average score	standard error	confidence interval – 95% lower limit	confidence interval – 95% upper limit
Chinese Taipei	549	(4.1)	541	557
Finland	548	(2.3)	544	553
Hong Kong-China	547	(2.7)	542	553
Korea	547	(3.8)	540	555
Quebec	540	(4.2)	532	548
Netherlands	531	(2.6)	526	536
Alberta	530	(3.8)	522	537
Switzerland	530	(3.2)	523	536
Canada	527	(2.0)	523	531
Ontario	526	(3.7)	519	533
Macao-China	525	(1.3)	522	528
Liechtenstein	525	(4.2)	517	533
British Columbia	523	(4.4)	514	531
Japan	523	(3.3)	517	530
New Zealand	522	(2.4)	517	527
Manitoba	521	(3.3)	514	527
Belgium	520	(3.0)	515	526
Australia	520	(2.2)	516	524
Estonia	515	(2.7)	509	520
Denmark	513	(2.6)	508	518
Czech Republic	510	(3.6)	503	517
Newfoundland and Labrador	507	(2.5)	502	512
Saskatchewan	507	(3.3)	500	513
Iceland	506	(1.8)	502	509
New Brunswick	506	(2.1)	502	510
Nova Scotia	506	(2.3)	502	511
Austria	505	(3.7)	498	513
Germany	504	(3.9)	496	511
Slovenia	504	(1.0)	502	506
Sweden	502	(2.4)	498	507
Ireland	501	(2.8)	496	507
Prince Edward Island	501	(2.3)	496	505
OECD average	498	(0.5)	497	499
France	496	(3.2)	489	502
Poland	495	(2.4)	491	500
United Kingdom	495	(2.1)	491	500
Slovak Republic	492	(2.8)	487	498
Hungary	491	(2.9)	485	497
Luxembourg	490	(1.1)	488	492
Norway	490	(2.6)	485	495
Latvia	486	(3.0)	480	492
Lithuania	486	(2.9)	481	492
Spain	480	(2.3)	475	485
Azerbaijan	476	(2.3)	472	480
Russian Federation	476	(3.9)	468	483
United States	474	(4.0)	466	482
Croatia	467	(2.4)	463	472
Portugal	466	(3.1)	460	472
Italy	462	(2.3)	457	466
Greece	459	(3.0)	453	465
Israel	442	(4.3)	433	450

Table B.2.2 (concluded)

Estimated average scores and confidence intervals for provinces and countries: Mathematics

Country and province	estimated average score	standard error	confidence interval – 95% lower limit	confidence interval – 95% upper limit
Serbia	435	(3.5)	428	442
Uruguay	427	(2.6)	422	432
Turkey	424	(4.9)	414	434
Thailand	417	(2.3)	412	422
Romania	415	(4.2)	407	423
Bulgaria	413	(6.1)	401	425
Chile	411	(4.6)	402	420
Mexico	406	(2.9)	400	411
Montenegro	399	(1.4)	397	402
Indonesia	391	(5.6)	380	402
Jordan	384	(3.3)	378	391
Argentina	381	(6.2)	369	393
Brazil	370	(2.9)	364	375
Colombia	370	(3.8)	363	377
Tunisia	365	(4.0)	358	373
Qatar	318	(1.0)	316	320
Kyrgyzstan	311	(3.4)	304	317

Table B.2.3

Variation in performance: Reading

	Percentile												Difference in score points between the 75th and 25th percentile
	5th		10th		25th		75th		90th		95th		
Country and province	score	standard error	score	standard error	score	standard error	score	standard error	score	standard error	score	standard error	
Azerbaijan	243	(4.4)	266	(3.9)	305	(3.6)	397	(3.7)	441	(5.0)	472	(6.0)	92
Macao-China	359	(4.3)	394	(2.5)	445	(1.9)	545	(1.6)	587	(1.8)	610	(2.4)	100
Indonesia	270	(5.3)	298	(5.0)	342	(5.3)	444	(8.4)	490	(8.6)	517	(8.6)	101
Finland	410	(4.8)	441	(3.8)	494	(2.9)	603	(2.2)	649	(2.5)	675	(2.8)	109
Hong Kong-China	390	(6.2)	426	(5.8)	484	(3.7)	594	(2.4)	636	(2.9)	660	(2.7)	110
Thailand	280	(5.9)	312	(3.9)	363	(3.3)	472	(2.9)	522	(3.7)	549	(3.6)	110
Estonia	353	(7.2)	389	(5.4)	448	(3.8)	560	(2.8)	606	(3.2)	632	(3.8)	112
Chinese Taipei	346	(5.8)	381	(5.9)	442	(4.9)	556	(3.0)	598	(3.0)	624	(4.0)	114
Korea	399	(9.7)	440	(7.9)	503	(4.8)	617	(3.4)	663	(4.3)	688	(5.0)	115
Ontario	**375**	**(9.5)**	**418**	**(8.3)**	**479**	**(5.2)**	**596**	**(5.1)**	**644**	**(5.2)**	**671**	**(6.5)**	**116**
Spain	304	(4.6)	343	(4.1)	405	(2.9)	523	(2.3)	569	(2.7)	594	(2.8)	118
Denmark	339	(6.4)	378	(5.0)	437	(3.9)	557	(2.9)	604	(3.7)	633	(5.1)	119
Slovenia	340	(4.2)	377	(2.6)	437	(1.8)	558	(2.2)	603	(2.1)	627	(2.7)	121
Turkey	291	(5.9)	330	(6.4)	388	(4.4)	510	(5.2)	564	(6.5)	594	(7.8)	122
Croatia	324	(6.6)	359	(5.4)	418	(4.1)	540	(3.0)	589	(3.4)	615	(3.3)	122
Montenegro	243	(3.7)	276	(3.2)	331	(2.1)	454	(1.9)	506	(2.6)	536	(3.7)	123
Alberta	**380**	**(9.3)**	**416**	**(8.0)**	**476**	**(5.6)**	**599**	**(4.7)**	**647**	**(4.2)**	**674**	**(5.1)**	**123**
Latvia	325	(6.7)	361	(5.4)	419	(4.9)	543	(4.2)	593	(4.0)	622	(4.8)	124
Jordan	233	(7.3)	277	(6.1)	342	(3.7)	467	(3.8)	514	(4.5)	541	(4.9)	124
New Brunswick	**335**	**(5.9)**	**376**	**(4.5)**	**437**	**(3.5)**	**562**	**(3.4)**	**612**	**(3.3)**	**639**	**(4.1)**	**124**
Ireland	358	(6.3)	395	(5.5)	457	(4.7)	582	(3.9)	633	(3.5)	661	(4.3)	125
Canada	**357**	**(4.8)**	**402**	**(3.9)**	**468**	**(3.0)**	**593**	**(2.6)**	**644**	**(2.7)**	**674**	**(3.9)**	**125**
Liechtenstein	337	(14.0)	379	(10.6)	452	(9.9)	578	(6.5)	623	(10.5)	658	(11.5)	126
Australia	349	(3.4)	388	(3.4)	453	(2.4)	579	(2.3)	628	(2.9)	656	(2.6)	126
Switzerland	331	(6.5)	373	(5.1)	440	(3.5)	566	(3.1)	615	(3.6)	642	(4.3)	126
Hungary	318	(9.1)	359	(5.0)	422	(4.8)	549	(3.6)	595	(4.4)	623	(4.6)	127
Manitoba	**350**	**(7.2)**	**391**	**(7.6)**	**456**	**(4.4)**	**583**	**(4.4)**	**633**	**(5.8)**	**662**	**(6.7)**	**127**
Serbia	246	(5.7)	282	(4.6)	339	(4.5)	466	(3.9)	518	(3.7)	546	(3.9)	127
Nova Scotia	**353**	**(7.5)**	**385**	**(5.3)**	**443**	**(5.4)**	**570**	**(4.3)**	**619**	**(5.2)**	**647**	**(5.3)**	**127**
Russian Federation	281	(7.3)	316	(6.0)	377	(5.7)	505	(4.2)	556	(3.6)	586	(4.9)	128
Romania	243	(6.6)	274	(7.2)	333	(7.3)	461	(5.2)	512	(5.6)	541	(6.1)	128
Iceland	314	(4.7)	356	(4.1)	423	(3.0)	552	(2.8)	603	(3.2)	633	(3.9)	129
Mexico	247	(7.5)	285	(6.2)	348	(4.2)	478	(2.8)	530	(3.1)	559	(3.0)	130
Sweden	335	(7.7)	378	(5.6)	445	(3.8)	575	(3.3)	629	(4.0)	658	(4.9)	130
Netherlands	332	(10.0)	379	(6.4)	446	(4.3)	578	(2.5)	622	(2.4)	649	(3.5)	132
Lithuania	309	(4.4)	343	(3.9)	405	(4.0)	538	(3.9)	591	(3.9)	621	(4.0)	133
Greece	272	(11.6)	321	(8.5)	398	(5.2)	531	(3.8)	583	(4.2)	613	(4.5)	133
Quebec	**339**	**(13.4)**	**386**	**(10.1)**	**460**	**(6.8)**	**593**	**(4.8)**	**647**	**(5.9)**	**678**	**(5.6)**	**133**
Kyrgyzstan	123	(7.2)	159	(5.3)	216	(3.8)	349	(4.1)	419	(5.9)	462	(7.6)	133
OECD average	**317**	**(1.4)**	**360**	**(1.1)**	**428**	**(0.8)**	**561**	**(0.6)**	**613**	**(0.7)**	**642**	**(0.7)**	**133**
Brazil	224	(10.1)	264	(6.0)	326	(4.2)	460	(4.0)	523	(5.3)	562	(6.8)	134
British Columbia	**346**	**(10.3)**	**394**	**(8.9)**	**464**	**(7.9)**	**598**	**(5.9)**	**651**	**(7.4)**	**684**	**(6.2)**	**134**
Tunisia	217	(7.3)	252	(5.3)	315	(4.4)	450	(5.0)	502	(5.3)	532	(6.8)	135
United Kingdom	318	(5.2)	359	(4.0)	431	(2.8)	566	(2.5)	621	(3.1)	653	(3.6)	135
Portugal	299	(7.6)	339	(6.3)	408	(5.3)	543	(3.6)	594	(3.7)	622	(4.5)	135
Prince Edward Island	**315**	**(7.8)**	**358**	**(7.1)**	**434**	**(5.1)**	**569**	**(3.2)**	**626**	**(5.0)**	**657**	**(8.4)**	**136**
Japan	317	(6.8)	361	(6.6)	433	(6.1)	569	(3.4)	623	(3.5)	654	(3.8)	136
Luxembourg	302	(5.1)	344	(3.3)	415	(2.3)	552	(1.8)	602	(2.5)	630	(2.8)	136
Newfoundland and Labrador	**335**	**(9.2)**	**376**	**(7.2)**	**448**	**(5.6)**	**585**	**(4.9)**	**642**	**(4.7)**	**673**	**(8.5)**	**137**
Saskatchewan	**324**	**(10.7)**	**370**	**(7.4)**	**442**	**(5.7)**	**579**	**(4.5)**	**634**	**(5.4)**	**665**	**(9.3)**	**137**
Poland	335	(4.8)	374	(4.6)	441	(3.5)	579	(3.2)	633	(3.4)	663	(4.0)	138
Chile	271	(7.5)	310	(5.8)	373	(5.4)	513	(6.4)	575	(6.7)	609	(6.6)	140
Norway	301	(7.3)	346	(5.5)	416	(4.6)	558	(3.0)	613	(4.1)	643	(3.6)	142

Table B.2.3 (concluded)

Variation in performance: Reading

Country and province	5th		10th		25th		75th		90th		95th		Difference in score points between the 75th and 25th percentile
	score	standard error	score	standard error	score	standard error	score	standard error	score	standard error	score	standard error	
New Zealand	339	(5.8)	381	(4.6)	453	(4.5)	595	(2.9)	651	(2.8)	683	(4.5)	142
France	298	(9.7)	346	(7.5)	421	(6.1)	564	(3.8)	614	(4.0)	639	(4.1)	143
Qatar	148	(3.7)	181	(2.7)	237	(1.8)	380	(1.9)	456	(3.6)	506	(3.7)	144
Italy	276	(5.9)	325	(4.8)	402	(3.6)	546	(2.3)	599	(2.9)	627	(2.8)	144
Germany	299	(9.7)	350	(8.0)	429	(5.9)	573	(3.4)	625	(3.7)	657	(3.7)	144
Slovak Republic	281	(7.1)	326	(6.6)	398	(4.3)	542	(3.4)	597	(3.8)	628	(3.3)	144
Colombia	200	(9.1)	243	(7.0)	316	(7.2)	462	(5.6)	518	(5.2)	550	(5.9)	146
Austria	298	(11.9)	348	(9.4)	421	(5.5)	568	(3.7)	621	(3.1)	651	(3.7)	147
Belgium	297	(10.1)	347	(8.3)	433	(4.7)	581	(2.3)	631	(2.2)	657	(2.8)	148
Czech Republic	290	(10.5)	335	(7.0)	408	(6.2)	564	(3.8)	621	(4.2)	653	(4.3)	156
Uruguay	204	(7.8)	253	(5.8)	333	(5.0)	497	(3.8)	565	(4.3)	604	(5.7)	164
Bulgaria	210	(11.4)	251	(9.0)	321	(8.5)	486	(7.6)	554	(7.8)	589	(8.5)	165
Israel	237	(10.1)	280	(8.0)	356	(6.2)	526	(4.8)	588	(4.9)	626	(5.0)	170
Argentina	155	(14.8)	209	(10.7)	291	(9.0)	464	(7.1)	527	(7.0)	560	(5.9)	172

Notes: Countries and provinces in ascending order by the difference in score points between the 75th and 25th percentiles.

Data for the United States are not available for reading.

Table B.2.4

Variation in performance: Mathematics

Country and province	5th		10th		25th		75th		90th		95th		Difference in score points between the 75th and 25th percentile
	score	standard error	score	standard error	score	standard error	score	standard error	score	standard error	score	standard error	
Azerbaijan	403	(2.4)	419	(2.2)	443	(2.5)	505	(3.0)	536	(3.6)	556	(5.2)	62
Indonesia	265	(5.6)	293	(3.9)	336	(4.2)	444	(9.3)	498	(9.4)	528	(10.3)	107
Thailand	289	(4.8)	317	(3.5)	362	(3.3)	470	(2.9)	524	(3.7)	558	(4.6)	107
Estonia	381	(5.9)	411	(4.3)	461	(3.5)	570	(3.3)	618	(3.2)	646	(4.1)	109
Latvia	347	(5.6)	378	(5.2)	432	(3.6)	542	(3.2)	590	(3.4)	619	(4.2)	110
Qatar	187	(2.9)	212	(2.2)	257	(1.3)	368	(1.7)	438	(2.7)	486	(3.0)	111
Nova Scotia	371	(5.5)	400	(5.2)	451	(3.9)	561	(2.8)	611	(5.2)	641	(7.5)	111
Kyrgyzstan	175	(5.1)	204	(5.0)	253	(3.6)	363	(4.2)	423	(5.9)	465	(7.6)	111
Finland	411	(5.0)	444	(3.4)	494	(2.6)	605	(2.6)	652	(2.8)	678	(3.0)	111
Jordan	244	(5.7)	279	(4.3)	330	(3.4)	441	(3.9)	489	(5.0)	519	(5.8)	112
Romania	278	(6.5)	307	(7.4)	358	(5.5)	470	(4.9)	523	(7.1)	557	(7.7)	112
Ontario	387	(8.9)	419	(6.8)	471	(5.0)	583	(4.1)	629	(4.4)	656	(4.0)	113
Alberta	392	(8.6)	424	(6.2)	475	(4.8)	588	(4.7)	637	(3.8)	665	(5.4)	113
New Brunswick	369	(4.7)	399	(3.7)	451	(3.7)	564	(3.6)	611	(2.9)	638	(3.8)	113
Montenegro	261	(3.3)	291	(3.0)	342	(2.0)	456	(2.4)	510	(2.4)	543	(3.6)	114
Croatia	332	(4.3)	361	(3.3)	410	(3.0)	524	(3.3)	576	(3.6)	605	(3.8)	114
Mexico	268	(6.6)	299	(4.9)	349	(3.7)	463	(2.8)	514	(3.3)	546	(4.2)	114
Ireland	366	(4.6)	396	(4.4)	445	(4.1)	559	(3.1)	608	(3.2)	634	(2.9)	114
Saskatchewan	359	(9.7)	395	(7.2)	453	(4.4)	567	(3.5)	613	(5.2)	641	(6.6)	114
British Columbia	387	(6.0)	416	(6.3)	466	(5.3)	581	(5.6)	629	(5.4)	656	(5.6)	115
Denmark	371	(5.0)	404	(4.3)	456	(3.4)	572	(2.8)	621	(3.4)	649	(4.3)	115
Manitoba	374	(6.8)	405	(5.2)	464	(4.9)	580	(4.5)	629	(5.8)	658	(6.7)	116
Canada	383	(4.0)	416	(3.3)	470	(2.4)	587	(2.3)	635	(2.3)	664	(3.3)	116

Table B.2.4 (concluded)

Variation in performance: Mathematics

Country and province	5th score	5th standard error	10th score	10th standard error	25th score	25th standard error	75th score	75th standard error	90th score	90th standard error	95th score	95th standard error	Difference in score points between the 75th and 25th percentile
Newfoundland and Labrador	**373**	**(5.9)**	**401**	**(4.9)**	**449**	**(3.9)**	**566**	**(3.9)**	**614**	**(5.3)**	**640**	**(5.9)**	**117**
Colombia	226	(8.4)	258	(5.6)	311	(4.9)	428	(4.6)	482	(3.8)	515	(6.1)	117
Prince Edward Island	**362**	**(4.4)**	**393**	**(3.8)**	**442**	**(3.9)**	**559**	**(2.9)**	**609**	**(4.3)**	**636**	**(5.4)**	**117**
Turkey	287	(6.1)	316	(4.0)	360	(3.3)	477	(7.2)	550	(12.4)	595	(15.8)	117
Macao-China	384	(3.6)	416	(3.1)	467	(2.1)	585	(2.0)	632	(2.4)	660	(3.3)	118
Russian Federation	331	(5.4)	363	(4.8)	416	(4.2)	535	(5.1)	592	(5.3)	625	(5.5)	119
Brazil	225	(6.4)	255	(4.5)	308	(3.0)	427	(3.7)	487	(5.8)	530	(8.3)	119
Hungary	343	(5.6)	377	(3.9)	431	(2.9)	551	(4.1)	609	(5.0)	643	(5.8)	120
Chile	273	(5.6)	302	(4.3)	350	(4.4)	470	(5.1)	527	(6.6)	561	(7.7)	120
Australia	375	(3.2)	406	(2.7)	460	(2.3)	581	(2.5)	633	(3.3)	663	(4.0)	121
Spain	332	(4.4)	366	(2.8)	421	(3.2)	542	(2.5)	593	(2.9)	622	(3.3)	121
Iceland	357	(3.5)	391	(3.6)	446	(2.4)	567	(2.4)	618	(3.2)	646	(4.4)	121
Poland	353	(3.3)	384	(3.4)	435	(2.8)	557	(3.3)	610	(3.7)	638	(3.5)	122
United Kingdom	351	(5.0)	381	(3.3)	434	(2.7)	557	(2.5)	612	(3.2)	643	(3.8)	122
Greece	304	(7.3)	341	(5.6)	399	(3.9)	522	(4.0)	575	(4.1)	607	(4.5)	123
Quebec	**380**	**(9.3)**	**418**	**(8.7)**	**482**	**(4.9)**	**604**	**(4.2)**	**656**	**(5.5)**	**686**	**(6.1)**	**123**
Serbia	282	(6.2)	318	(5.0)	375	(4.4)	498	(3.8)	553	(3.9)	584	(4.4)	123
Sweden	354	(5.6)	387	(4.2)	442	(3.5)	565	(3.2)	617	(2.8)	649	(4.2)	123
Lithuania	338	(4.9)	369	(4.3)	426	(3.3)	549	(3.6)	602	(4.9)	632	(4.6)	123
Liechtenstein	367	(9.7)	402	(11.1)	464	(10.0)	588	(5.2)	643	(9.5)	677	(10.6)	124
Norway	339	(6.0)	373	(3.8)	428	(3.9)	552	(2.8)	609	(3.3)	638	(2.8)	124
Japan	370	(6.4)	404	(5.5)	463	(4.6)	587	(3.0)	638	(3.6)	668	(4.2)	124
Slovenia	361	(2.7)	390	(2.1)	441	(2.4)	566	(2.1)	623	(2.7)	654	(3.8)	125
Slovak Republic	333	(7.0)	370	(5.1)	433	(3.6)	558	(3.5)	611	(4.4)	640	(4.8)	125
OECD average	**346**	**(1.1)**	**380**	**(0.8)**	**436**	**(0.7)**	**561**	**(0.6)**	**615**	**(0.8)**	**646**	**(0.9)**	**125**
Portugal	315	(6.5)	348	(5.2)	404	(4.2)	530	(3.0)	583	(2.8)	612	(3.8)	126
Tunisia	219	(4.9)	250	(3.9)	301	(3.7)	427	(5.5)	488	(7.8)	522	(7.7)	126
United States	328	(7.6)	358	(5.8)	411	(4.8)	537	(5.0)	593	(4.8)	625	(4.8)	126
Korea	392	(7.1)	426	(6.1)	485	(4.3)	612	(4.4)	664	(6.9)	694	(8.2)	127
Hong Kong-China	386	(6.1)	423	(6.4)	486	(4.5)	614	(3.1)	665	(3.5)	692	(4.8)	128
Luxembourg	332	(4.4)	368	(3.5)	426	(1.9)	555	(1.9)	610	(2.7)	641	(3.6)	129
Italy	305	(4.4)	341	(3.3)	398	(2.7)	527	(2.8)	584	(4.2)	616	(3.8)	129
Netherlands	382	(6.0)	412	(5.0)	467	(4.6)	596	(2.7)	645	(3.3)	672	(4.3)	129
New Zealand	368	(3.6)	401	(4.1)	458	(3.2)	587	(3.0)	643	(4.0)	674	(3.6)	129
Argentina	209	(11.2)	249	(9.8)	316	(7.9)	451	(6.9)	508	(7.6)	543	(9.2)	135
Uruguay	261	(4.1)	296	(4.4)	360	(3.5)	495	(3.5)	551	(5.5)	587	(5.6)	135
Switzerland	362	(5.5)	401	(4.7)	464	(4.1)	600	(3.7)	652	(3.7)	682	(4.2)	136
France	334	(5.5)	369	(5.4)	429	(4.7)	565	(3.8)	617	(3.8)	646	(4.0)	136
Bulgaria	251	(8.3)	287	(7.2)	345	(6.1)	481	(6.8)	543	(8.4)	583	(11.0)	136
Germany	339	(8.5)	375	(6.8)	437	(4.9)	574	(3.9)	632	(3.8)	664	(4.6)	136
Austria	338	(6.8)	373	(6.3)	438	(5.5)	577	(4.0)	630	(3.8)	657	(4.0)	139
Czech Republic	340	(5.2)	376	(4.7)	441	(4.3)	582	(4.7)	644	(4.8)	677	(6.0)	141
Belgium	337	(8.9)	381	(6.6)	451	(4.0)	598	(2.5)	650	(2.4)	678	(2.7)	148
Chinese Taipei	373	(7.2)	409	(6.2)	477	(6.1)	625	(3.3)	677	(3.4)	707	(3.9)	148
Israel	266	(11.2)	304	(6.9)	368	(5.4)	518	(4.7)	581	(5.0)	615	(4.7)	149

Note: Countries and provinces in ascending order by the difference in score points between the 75th and 25th percentiles.

Table B.3.1

Mean score and gender differences in student performance: Science combined and subscales

| | All students | | Gender differences | | | | | |
| | Mean score | | Females | | Males | | Difference (Female – Male) | |
	mean	standard error	mean score	standard error	mean score	standard error	score difference	standard error
Combined science								
Newfoundland and Labrador	526	(2.5)	531	(3.1)	519	(3.8)	12	(4.9)
Prince Edward Island	509	(2.7)	510	(3.4)	507	(4.0)	3	(5.0)
Nova Scotia	520	(2.5)	519	(3.0)	521	(3.9)	-1	(4.9)
New Brunswick	506	(2.3)	505	(3.2)	507	(2.9)	-1	(4.1)
Quebec	531	(4.2)	527	(4.3)	534	(5.1)	-8	(4.2)
Ontario	537	(4.2)	535	(4.6)	539	(4.8)	-4	(4.1)
Manitoba	523	(3.2)	522	(4.0)	525	(4.4)	-4	(5.3)
Saskatchewan	517	(3.6)	519	(4.4)	514	(4.8)	5	(5.7)
Alberta	550	(3.8)	548	(3.9)	552	(4.9)	-4	(4.7)
British Columbia	539	(4.7)	536	(4.9)	541	(5.8)	-5	(5.4)
Canada	534	(2.0)	532	(2.1)	536	(2.5)	-4	(2.2)
OECD average	500	(0.5)	499	(0.6)	501	(0.7)	-2	(0.7)
Science – identifying scientific issues								
Newfoundland and Labrador	525	(3.2)	541	(3.8)	508	(4.0)	33	(4.8)
Prince Edward Island	505	(2.5)	516	(3.3)	494	(3.6)	22	(4.9)
Nova Scotia	516	(3.5)	523	(3.5)	509	(4.8)	15	(4.9)
New Brunswick	512	(2.3)	519	(3.1)	505	(3.0)	14	(4.0)
Quebec	531	(4.6)	537	(4.7)	524	(5.5)	12	(4.4)
Ontario	533	(4.9)	540	(5.8)	527	(5.0)	13	(4.7)
Manitoba	519	(3.3)	526	(4.3)	511	(4.0)	15	(5.1)
Saskatchewan	515	(4.1)	528	(4.6)	503	(5.0)	25	(5.3)
Alberta	546	(3.9)	552	(4.2)	539	(4.9)	13	(4.7)
British Columbia	536	(5.2)	543	(4.7)	529	(6.8)	15	(5.3)
Canada	532	(2.3)	539	(2.4)	525	(2.7)	14	(2.4)
OECD average	500	(0.5)	508	(0.6)	491	(0.7)	17	(0.7)
Science – explaining phenomena scientifically								
Newfoundland and Labrador	519	(3.0)	517	(3.7)	520	(4.4)	-3	(5.5)
Prince Edward Island	509	(2.7)	504	(3.7)	515	(4.2)	-11	(5.7)
Nova Scotia	520	(3.4)	512	(3.5)	527	(4.7)	-16	(5.1)
New Brunswick	501	(2.6)	493	(3.2)	509	(3.5)	-15	(4.4)
Quebec	523	(4.0)	512	(4.2)	533	(5.0)	-21	(4.4)
Ontario	533	(4.4)	525	(5.1)	541	(5.0)	-16	(4.7)
Manitoba	522	(3.5)	515	(4.3)	530	(4.4)	-15	(5.3)
Saskatchewan	516	(4.4)	511	(5.2)	521	(5.4)	-10	(5.9)
Alberta	553	(4.1)	547	(4.4)	559	(5.2)	-13	(5.0)
British Columbia	538	(4.9)	528	(5.3)	548	(5.9)	-21	(5.8)
Canada	531	(2.1)	522	(2.3)	539	(2.6)	-17	(2.5)
OECD average	500	(0.5)	492	(0.6)	507	(0.7)	-15	(0.7)

Table B.3.1 (concluded)

Mean score and gender differences in student performance: Science combined and subscales

	All students		Gender differences					
	Mean score		Females		Males		Difference (Female − Male)	
	mean	standard error	mean score	standard error	mean score	standard error	score difference	standard error
Science – using scientific evidence								
Newfoundland and Labrador	533	(2.9)	540	(3.5)	524	(4.4)	16	(5.4)
Prince Edward Island	509	(2.7)	514	(3.5)	504	(4.1)	10	(5.5)
Nova Scotia	524	(2.4)	524	(3.0)	524	(3.7)	0	(4.8)
New Brunswick	511	(2.4)	513	(3.5)	509	(3.3)	4	(4.9)
Quebec	542	(4.7)	541	(4.8)	542	(5.6)	-2	(4.6)
Ontario	546	(4.4)	546	(4.9)	545	(4.8)	0	(4.2)
Manitoba	530	(3.4)	531	(4.0)	528	(4.6)	3	(5.3)
Saskatchewan	517	(3.7)	523	(4.3)	511	(4.9)	12	(5.6)
Alberta	552	(4.1)	553	(4.1)	551	(5.3)	2	(4.7)
British Columbia	541	(5.1)	542	(5.4)	540	(6.3)	2	(5.7)
Canada	542	(2.2)	542	(2.3)	541	(2.7)	1	(2.3)
OECD average	499	(0.6)	500	(0.7)	498	(0.8)	3	(0.8)

Table B.3.2

Mean score and gender differences in student performance: Reading and mathematics

	All students		Gender differences					
	Mean score		Females		Males		Difference (Female – Male)	
	mean	standard error	mean score	standard error	mean score	standard error	score difference	standard error
Reading								
Newfoundland and Labrador	514	(3.2)	542	(3.6)	483	(4.4)	59	(5.4)
Prince Edward Island	497	(2.8)	522	(3.3)	471	(4.3)	51	(5.4)
Nova Scotia	505	(3.5)	522	(3.4)	489	(4.6)	33	(5.1)
New Brunswick	497	(2.3)	516	(3.3)	477	(2.9)	39	(4.1)
Quebec	522	(5.0)	536	(4.9)	508	(6.1)	28	(4.8)
Ontario	534	(4.6)	549	(5.2)	520	(4.8)	29	(4.3)
Manitoba	516	(3.5)	533	(4.2)	499	(4.5)	34	(5.3)
Saskatchewan	507	(4.2)	534	(4.7)	482	(5.2)	52	(6.0)
Alberta	535	(4.2)	549	(4.4)	521	(5.2)	27	(4.7)
British Columbia	528	(5.7)	549	(5.6)	506	(7.2)	42	(5.7)
Canada	527	(2.4)	543	(2.5)	511	(2.8)	32	(2.3)
OECD average	492	(0.6)	511	(0.7)	473	(0.7)	38	(0.8)
Mathematics								
Newfoundland and Labrador	507	(2.5)	505	(3.1)	509	(3.8)	-4	(4.7)
Prince Edward Island	501	(2.3)	497	(3.0)	505	(3.5)	-7	(4.7)
Nova Scotia	506	(2.3)	500	(2.8)	511	(3.2)	-11	(4.0)
New Brunswick	506	(2.1)	502	(3.1)	510	(2.8)	-8	(4.2)
Quebec	540	(4.2)	533	(4.5)	547	(4.8)	-13	(3.8)
Ontario	526	(3.7)	517	(3.9)	534	(4.3)	-17	(3.5)
Manitoba	521	(3.3)	515	(3.8)	526	(4.4)	-11	(4.9)
Saskatchewan	507	(3.3)	503	(3.7)	510	(4.7)	-7	(5.2)
Alberta	530	(3.8)	523	(4.0)	537	(4.8)	-14	(4.4)
British Columbia	523	(4.4)	516	(4.4)	530	(5.3)	-14	(4.2)
Canada	527	(2.0)	520	(2.0)	534	(2.4)	-14	(1.9)
OECD average	498	(0.5)	492	(0.6)	504	(0.7)	-11	(0.7)

Table B.3.3

Differences in student performance in science by immigrant status

Province	Non-immigrants		Second-generation immigrants		First-generation immigrants	
	percentage of students	standard error	percentage of students	standard error	percentage of students	standard error
Percentage of students by immigrant status						
Quebec	87.0	(1.7)	7.4	(1.0)	5.7	(0.9)
Ontario	69.4	(2.6)	15.8	(1.3)	14.9	(1.8)
Manitoba	87.6	(0.9)	7.1	(0.7)	5.3	(0.6)
Alberta	83.2	(1.9)	10.4	(1.5)	6.3	(0.8)
British Columbia	71.5	(2.9)	14.7	(1.8)	13.7	(1.9)
Canada	78.9	(1.2)	11.2	(0.7)	9.9	(0.7)
OECD average	90.7	(0.1)	4.6	(0.1)	4.8	(0.1)

Province	Non-immigrants		Second-generation immigrants		First-generation immigrants	
	mean score	standard error	mean score	standard error	mean score	standard error
Performance on the science scale						
Quebec	540	(4.1)	501	(7.8)	483	(11.4)
Ontario	546	(3.9)	538	(8.4)	520	(7.8)
Manitoba	529	(3.4)	509	(9.2)	496	(11.5)
Alberta	553	(3.9)	543	(7.8)	548	(13.1)
British Columbia	544	(4.8)	519	(8.5)	536	(11.2)
Canada	541	(1.8)	528	(4.8)	519	(5.2)
OECD average	506	(0.5)	468	(3.7)	450	(3.4)

Province	Second-generation immigrants minus non-immigrants		First-generation immigrants minus non-immigrants		First-generation immigrants minus second-generation immigrants	
	difference	standard error	difference	standard error	difference	standard error
Difference in the science score						
Quebec	-39	(8.4)	-57	(11.5)	-18	(11.1)
Ontario	-8	(8.6)	-26	(8.2)	-18	(6.3)
Manitoba	-20	(10.1)	-33	(11.7)	-14	(13.6)
Alberta	-11	(7.6)	-5	(13.2)	6	(14.2)
British Columbia	-25	(8.9)	-8	(11.2)	17	(10.8)
Canada	-12	(4.9)	-22	(5.3)	-9	(4.6)
OECD average	-39	(3.7)	-56	(3.2)	-14	(4.7)

Table B.3.4

Differences in student performance by highest level of parental education attainment

| | percentage of students | standard error | Performance | | | | | |
| | | | Science | | Reading | | Mathematics | |
			mean score	standard error	mean score	standard error	mean score	standard error
Parents with high school or below								
Newfoundland and Labrador	44	(1.2)	502	(3.2)	493	(4.1)	490	(3.6)
Prince Edward Island	30	(1.0)	490	(4.0)	479	(4.4)	486	(3.8)
Nova Scotia	38	(1.3)	498	(4.5)	482	(4.7)	486	(4.6)
New Brunswick	35	(1.0)	483	(4.2)	475	(4.1)	487	(3.7)
Quebec	36	(1.3)	505	(4.9)	500	(6.4)	518	(5.0)
Ontario	23	(1.3)	520	(7.1)	513	(7.4)	514	(6.3)
Manitoba	36	(1.5)	510	(4.7)	500	(4.6)	509	(4.9)
Saskatchewan	41	(1.3)	499	(4.6)	490	(5.2)	492	(4.0)
Alberta	32	(2.1)	529	(6.2)	512	(6.7)	510	(6.3)
British Columbia	31	(1.8)	525	(6.3)	513	(6.5)	512	(5.4)
Canada	30	(0.6)	514	(2.7)	505	(3.2)	511	(2.5)
OECD average	52	(0.4)	468	(1.0)	462	(1.1)	463	(1.1)
Parents with post-secondary education								
Newfoundland and Labrador	56	(1.2)	545	(3.5)	532	(4.2)	522	(3.7)
Prince Edward Island	70	(1.0)	518	(3.4)	507	(3.3)	508	(2.8)
Nova Scotia	62	(1.3)	534	(3.2)	519	(3.7)	519	(2.9)
New Brunswick	65	(1.0)	519	(2.6)	510	(2.8)	517	(2.5)
Quebec	64	(1.3)	547	(4.6)	536	(5.4)	554	(4.5)
Ontario	77	(1.3)	546	(4.0)	543	(4.3)	532	(3.6)
Manitoba	64	(1.5)	533	(3.7)	527	(3.8)	529	(3.5)
Saskatchewan	59	(1.3)	531	(4.3)	522	(4.9)	519	(3.9)
Alberta	68	(2.1)	562	(3.9)	547	(4.5)	541	(3.7)
British Columbia	69	(1.8)	546	(4.8)	536	(6.0)	529	(4.6)
Canada	70	(0.6)	546	(2.0)	539	(2.4)	536	(2.0)
OECD average	48	(0.4)	521	(1.6)	507	(1.7)	511	(1.5)

| | Difference in performance | | | | | |
| | Science | | Reading | | Mathematics | |
	mean score	standard error	mean score	standard error	mean score	standard error
Difference in scores: Parents with high school or less - parents with post-secondary education						
Newfoundland and Labrador	-43	(4.6)	-39	(5.5)	-33	(5.2)
Prince Edward Island	-27	(5.2)	-27	(5.5)	-22	(4.8)
Nova Scotia	-35	(5.9)	-38	(4.7)	-33	(5.9)
New Brunswick	-36	(5.0)	-35	(5.0)	-30	(4.4)
Quebec	-41	(5.0)	-36	(6.4)	-36	(4.8)
Ontario	-26	(6.9)	-30	(6.7)	-18	(5.9)
Manitoba	-22	(5.3)	-27	(4.8)	-20	(5.1)
Saskatchewan	-33	(5.6)	-32	(6.1)	-27	(4.6)
Alberta	-32	(7.0)	-35	(7.7)	-31	(7.0)
British Columbia	-22	(6.2)	-23	(6.2)	-17	(5.2)
Canada	-32	(2.7)	-34	(2.9)	-25	(2.4)
OECD average	-53	(1.6)	-44	(1.4)	-48	(1.4)

Table B.3.5

Index of economic, social and cultural status, by national and provincial quarters of the index

| | Index of economic, social and cultural status | | | | | | | | | |
| | All students | | Bottom quarter | | Second quarter | | Third quarter | | Top quarter | |
	mean index	standard error	mean index	standard error	mean index	standard error	mean index	standard error	mean index	standard error
Newfoundland and Labrador	0.11	(0.02)	-0.95	(0.01)	-0.19	(0.01)	0.41	(0.01)	1.20	(0.02)
Prince Edward Island	0.21	(0.02)	-0.77	(0.02)	-0.04	(0.01)	0.49	(0.01)	1.16	(0.01)
Nova Scotia	0.24	(0.03)	-0.78	(0.02)	-0.06	(0.01)	0.52	(0.01)	1.29	(0.02)
New Brunswick	0.2	(0.02)	-0.83	(0.02)	-0.06	(0.01)	0.48	(0.01)	1.20	(0.02)
Quebec	0.21	(0.03)	-0.83	(0.02)	-0.06	(0.01)	0.51	(0.01)	1.24	(0.02)
Ontario	0.48	(0.04)	-0.57	(0.03)	0.26	(0.01)	0.79	(0.01)	1.44	(0.02)
Manitoba	0.34	(0.03)	-0.71	(0.02)	0.08	(0.01)	0.65	(0.01)	1.33	(0.02)
Saskatchewan	0.28	(0.03)	-0.75	(0.02)	0.04	(0.01)	0.57	(0.01)	1.25	(0.02)
Alberta	0.43	(0.05)	-0.58	(0.03)	0.18	(0.01)	0.72	(0.01)	1.40	(0.02)
British Columbia	0.40	(0.04)	-0.62	(0.03)	0.17	(0.01)	0.69	(0.01)	1.37	(0.02)
Canada	0.37	(0.02)	-0.69	(0.01)	0.12	(0.00)	0.68	(0.00)	1.36	(0.01)
OECD average	0.00	(0.00)	-1.45	(0.01)	-0.36	(0.00)	0.30	(0.00)	1.17	(0.01)

| | Performance on the science scale, by national and provincial quarters of this index | | | | | | | | Change in the science score per unit of this index | |
| | Bottom quarter | | Second quarter | | Third quarter | | Top quarter | | | |
	mean score	standard error	mean score	standard error	mean score	standard error	mean score	standard error	effect	standard error
Newfoundland and Labrador	480	(4.3)	511	(4.0)	538	(5.5)	576	(5.0)	43.8	(2.7)
Prince Edward Island	480	(4.6)	499	(5.3)	523	(4.9)	535	(5.1)	29.5	(3.2)
Nova Scotia	484	(4.8)	509	(5.0)	532	(4.7)	559	(4.8)	35.5	(3.2)
New Brunswick	472	(4.8)	494	(4.2)	516	(4.2)	544	(4.0)	37.1	(2.7)
Quebec	495	(5.5)	522	(4.9)	537	(5.7)	574	(5.7)	36.8	(3.4)
Ontario	506	(5.9)	531	(5.7)	557	(4.7)	568	(5.1)	30.6	(3.0)
Manitoba	494	(5.7)	517	(5.3)	534	(5.1)	556	(4.9)	30.0	(3.3)
Saskatchewan	480	(5.4)	509	(5.5)	531	(5.1)	550	(5.7)	34.9	(3.5)
Alberta	519	(7.3)	541	(4.6)	560	(4.7)	584	(4.4)	33.2	(4.1)
British Columbia	508	(6.4)	539	(5.7)	545	(6.4)	564	(5.3)	27.5	(4.0)
Canada	501	(2.7)	527	(2.4)	548	(2.3)	569	(2.5)	33.1	(1.4)
OECD average	430	(1.3)	481	(1.7)	512	(1.4)	549	(1.3)	45.0	(0.6)

Note: Results based on students' self-reports.

Table B.4.1

Index of science self efficacy, by national and provincial quarters of the index

| | Index of science self efficacy | | | | | | | | | |
| | All students | | Bottom quarter | | Second quarter | | Third quarter | | Top quarter | |
	mean index	standard error	mean index	standard error	mean index	standard error	mean index	standard error	mean index	standard error
Newfoundland and Labrador	0.30	(0.03)	-0.95	(0.03)	-0.01	(0.01)	0.57	(0.01)	1.57	(0.04)
Prince Edward Island	0.15	(0.03)	-1.24	(0.04)	-0.16	(0.01)	0.42	(0.01)	1.58	(0.04)
Nova Scotia	0.17	(0.03)	-1.16	(0.04)	-0.16	(0.01)	0.46	(0.01)	1.54	(0.04)
New Brunswick	0.00	(0.03)	-1.39	(0.04)	-0.27	(0.01)	0.32	(0.01)	1.33	(0.03)
Quebec	0.08	(0.03)	-1.16	(0.03)	-0.25	(0.01)	0.37	(0.01)	1.37	(0.03)
Ontario	0.26	(0.03)	-1.00	(0.04)	-0.07	(0.01)	0.50	(0.01)	1.60	(0.03)
Manitoba	0.16	(0.02)	-1.15	(0.03)	-0.19	(0.01)	0.42	(0.01)	1.56	(0.04)
Saskatchewan	0.07	(0.03)	-1.20	(0.04)	-0.26	(0.01)	0.35	(0.01)	1.39	(0.04)
Alberta	0.39	(0.03)	-0.79	(0.02)	0.03	(0.01)	0.59	(0.01)	1.73	(0.03)
British Columbia	0.27	(0.04)	-0.97	(0.04)	-0.09	(0.01)	0.53	(0.01)	1.63	(0.04)
Canada	0.21	(0.01)	-1.05	(0.02)	-0.12	(0.00)	0.47	(0.00)	1.55	(0.02)
OECD average	0.00	(0.00)	-1.17	(0.00)	-0.29	(0.00)	0.26	(0.00)	1.21	(0.00)

| | Performance on the science scale, by national and provincial quarters of this index | | | | | | | | Change in the science score per unit of this index | |
| | Bottom quarter | | Second quarter | | Third quarter | | Top quarter | | | |
	mean score	standard error	mean score	standard error	mean score	standard error	mean score	standard error	effect	standard error
Newfoundland and Labrador	468	(4.0)	509	(4.4)	548	(5.3)	582	(5.0)	42.2	(2.2)
Prince Edward Island	453	(4.9)	493	(4.3)	523	(4.9)	569	(4.9)	38.3	(2.3)
Nova Scotia	465	(4.7)	512	(4.4)	536	(5.2)	570	(5.1)	36.9	(2.3)
New Brunswick	450	(3.7)	492	(3.9)	519	(3.6)	565	(3.9)	39.3	(1.5)
Quebec	478	(4.6)	518	(4.2)	550	(4.8)	581	(6.2)	37.2	(2.0)
Ontario	484	(5.6)	527	(4.9)	556	(5.1)	594	(4.8)	39.7	(2.6)
Manitoba	468	(5.2)	517	(4.5)	539	(5.2)	578	(5.6)	36.9	(2.4)
Saskatchewan	462	(5.5)	495	(5.3)	535	(5.0)	575	(5.6)	39.4	(2.5)
Alberta	502	(5.6)	537	(4.8)	560	(4.8)	603	(4.9)	35.9	(2.1)
British Columbia	485	(6.8)	519	(4.5)	560	(5.8)	592	(5.3)	40.6	(1.8)
Canada	480	(2.8)	523	(2.3)	552	(2.5)	589	(2.9)	39.0	(1.1)
OECD average	452	(0.7)	489	(0.6)	513	(0.7)	551	(0.7)	37.7	(0.3)

Note: Results based on students' self-reports.

Table B.4.2

Index of science self concept,
by national and provincial quarters of the index

| | Index of science self concept | | | | | | | | | |
| | All students | | Bottom quarter | | Second quarter | | Third quarter | | Top quarter | |
	mean index	standard error	mean index	standard error	mean index	standard error	mean index	standard error	mean index	standard error
Newfoundland and Labrador	0.27	(0.03)	-1.05	(0.04)	0.00	(0.01)	0.58	(0.01)	1.54	(0.03)
Prince Edward Island	0.34	(0.04)	-1.12	(0.03)	0.03	(0.01)	0.66	(0.01)	1.80	(0.03)
Nova Scotia	0.23	(0.03)	-1.23	(0.03)	-0.10	(0.01)	0.57	(0.01)	1.66	(0.03)
New Brunswick	0.28	(0.03)	-1.14	(0.03)	-0.04	(0.01)	0.59	(0.01)	1.70	(0.03)
Quebec	0.33	(0.03)	-1.27	(0.03)	0.00	(0.01)	0.73	(0.01)	1.85	(0.01)
Ontario	0.24	(0.03)	-1.10	(0.03)	-0.08	(0.01)	0.56	(0.01)	1.59	(0.03)
Manitoba	0.17	(0.03)	-1.20	(0.03)	-0.15	(0.01)	0.55	(0.01)	1.48	(0.03)
Saskatchewan	0.15	(0.03)	-1.21	(0.04)	-0.15	(0.01)	0.54	(0.01)	1.42	(0.03)
Alberta	0.28	(0.03)	-1.04	(0.03)	-0.01	(0.01)	0.57	(0.01)	1.59	(0.02)
British Columbia	0.28	(0.04)	-1.09	(0.03)	-0.05	(0.01)	0.58	(0.01)	1.67	(0.03)
Canada	0.27	(0.02)	-1.15	(0.02)	-0.05	(0.01)	0.59	(0.00)	1.68	(0.01)
OECD average	0.00	(0.00)	-1.19	(0.00)	-0.28	(0.00)	0.29	(0.00)	1.20	(0.00)

| | Performance on the science scale, by national and provincial quarters of this index | | | | | | | | Change in the science score per unit of this index | |
| | Bottom quarter | | Second quarter | | Third quarter | | Top quarter | | | |
	mean score	standard error	mean score	standard error	mean score	standard error	mean score	standard error	effect	standard error
Newfoundland and Labrador	471	(3.6)	501	(5.5)	550	(5.5)	589	(4.5)	45.1	(2.0)
Prince Edward Island	453	(4.8)	487	(5.1)	521	(4.3)	574	(6.3)	40.2	(2.4)
Nova Scotia	478	(4.3)	501	(4.9)	533	(5.2)	577	(5.2)	32.9	(2.4)
New Brunswick	452	(4.7)	482	(4.6)	525	(4.5)	564	(5.1)	39.0	(2.3)
Quebec	490	(4.8)	521	(5.7)	551	(4.8)	594	(5.9)	32.7	(1.8)
Ontario	502	(6.8)	517	(6.3)	559	(5.7)	593	(5.3)	33.1	(2.5)
Manitoba	474	(5.7)	512	(6.3)	547	(6.3)	572	(6.3)	36.1	(2.7)
Saskatchewan	467	(6.2)	496	(5.4)	538	(6.1)	568	(7.8)	38.7	(2.9)
Alberta	513	(5.1)	534	(5.4)	562	(6.4)	603	(5.7)	33.9	(2.7)
British Columbia	494	(5.4)	514	(6.7)	564	(6.1)	597	(6.8)	37.4	(2.2)
Canada	494	(2.9)	519	(3.0)	553	(2.6)	592	(2.9)	34.3	(1.0)
OECD average	471	(0.6)	492	(0.7)	514	(0.7)	537	(0.8)	26.8	(0.3)

Note: Results based on students' self-reports.

Table B.4.3

Index of general value of science, by national and provincial quarters of the index

	Index of general value of science									
	All students		Bottom quarter		Second quarter		Third quarter		Top quarter	
	mean index	standard error	mean index	standard error	mean index	standard error	mean index	standard error	index	standard error
Newfoundland and Labrador	0.18	(0.03)	-1.04	(0.03)	-0.25	(0.01)	0.43	(0.01)	1.57	(0.03)
Prince Edward Island	0.09	(0.03)	-1.17	(0.03)	-0.35	(0.01)	0.34	(0.01)	1.54	(0.03)
Nova Scotia	0.06	(0.03)	-1.15	(0.03)	-0.37	(0.01)	0.28	(0.01)	1.48	(0.03)
New Brunswick	0.07	(0.02)	-1.15	(0.02)	-0.35	(0.01)	0.31	(0.01)	1.47	(0.03)
Quebec	0.13	(0.03)	-1.15	(0.02)	-0.26	(0.01)	0.42	(0.01)	1.53	(0.02)
Ontario	0.15	(0.03)	-1.03	(0.02)	-0.29	(0.01)	0.41	(0.01)	1.51	(0.02)
Manitoba	0.10	(0.03)	-1.15	(0.03)	-0.34	(0.00)	0.35	(0.01)	1.55	(0.03)
Saskatchewan	0.02	(0.03)	-1.13	(0.03)	-0.36	(0.00)	0.26	(0.01)	1.33	(0.03)
Alberta	0.20	(0.03)	-0.91	(0.02)	-0.26	(0.01)	0.41	(0.01)	1.54	(0.03)
British Columbia	0.18	(0.03)	-0.97	(0.02)	-0.24	(0.01)	0.42	(0.01)	1.52	(0.03)
Canada	0.14	(0.01)	-1.06	(0.01)	-0.28	(0.00)	0.40	(0.01)	1.51	(0.01)
OECD average	0.00	(0.00)	-1.15	(0.00)	-0.37	(0.00)	0.24	(0.00)	1.28	(0.00)

	Performance on the science scale, by national and provincial quarters of this index								Change in the science score per unit of this index	
	Bottom quarter		Second quarter		Third quarter		Top quarter			
	mean score	standard error	mean score	standard error	mean score	standard error	mean score	standard error	effect	standard error
Newfoundland and Labrador	482	(5.3)	514	(5.1)	546	(4.7)	562	(5.2)	30.6	(2.6)
Prince Edward Island	467	(5.2)	489	(4.6)	533	(5.3)	549	(5.3)	32.2	(2.4)
Nova Scotia	484	(4.5)	510	(4.8)	536	(4.6)	554	(4.3)	26.0	(2.3)
New Brunswick	467	(4.4)	495	(4.0)	521	(4.3)	544	(4.1)	29.4	(1.7)
Quebec	492	(6.1)	522	(4.8)	549	(4.9)	566	(5.0)	29.1	(2.3)
Ontario	508	(6.2)	535	(5.2)	552	(5.6)	567	(5.1)	22.4	(2.3)
Manitoba	493	(6.2)	519	(5.2)	542	(5.0)	550	(5.2)	22.0	(2.2)
Saskatchewan	485	(4.9)	509	(4.9)	529	(5.0)	544	(6.2)	26.5	(2.5)
Alberta	526	(5.1)	536	(5.7)	564	(6.1)	577	(5.6)	21.3	(2.3)
British Columbia	506	(6.6)	525	(5.0)	554	(5.8)	571	(5.3)	26.1	(2.0)
Canada	502	(2.9)	526	(2.6)	552	(2.2)	565	(2.7)	25.3	(1.1)
OECD average	464	(0.7)	495	(0.7)	515	(0.7)	533	(0.7)	28.1	(0.3)

Note: Results based on students' self-reports.

Table B.4.4

Index of personal value of science,
by national and provincial quarters of the index

	Index of personal value of science									
	All students		Bottom quarter		Second quarter		Third quarter		Top quarter	
	mean index	standard error	mean index	standard error	mean index	standard error	mean index	standard error	index	standard error
Newfoundland and Labrador	0.36	(0.03)	-0.87	(0.03)	0.04	(0.01)	0.62	(0.01)	1.68	(0.03)
Prince Edward Island	0.33	(0.03)	-1.02	(0.03)	0.01	(0.01)	0.61	(0.01)	1.71	(0.03)
Nova Scotia	0.26	(0.03)	-1.04	(0.03)	-0.05	(0.02)	0.51	(0.01)	1.63	(0.03)
New Brunswick	0.24	(0.03)	-1.12	(0.03)	-0.11	(0.01)	0.55	(0.01)	1.65	(0.02)
Quebec	0.03	(0.02)	-1.30	(0.02)	-0.30	(0.01)	0.36	(0.01)	1.36	(0.02)
Ontario	0.22	(0.03)	-1.12	(0.02)	-0.17	(0.01)	0.51	(0.01)	1.65	(0.02)
Manitoba	0.21	(0.03)	-1.13	(0.03)	-0.14	(0.01)	0.48	(0.01)	1.63	(0.03)
Saskatchewan	0.20	(0.03)	-1.02	(0.03)	-0.09	(0.01)	0.47	(0.01)	1.43	(0.03)
Alberta	0.34	(0.03)	-0.89	(0.02)	0.04	(0.01)	0.56	(0.01)	1.67	(0.03)
British Columbia	0.27	(0.03)	-0.97	(0.02)	-0.09	(0.01)	0.54	(0.01)	1.61	(0.03)
Canada	0.20	(0.01)	-1.11	(0.01)	-0.16	(0.00)	0.49	(0.00)	1.57	(0.01)
OECD average	0.00	(0.00)	-1.18	(0.00)	-0.32	(0.00)	0.26	(0.00)	1.23	(0.00)

	Performance on the science scale, by national and provincial quarters of this index								Change in the science score per unit of this index	
	Bottom quarter		Second quarter		Third quarter		Top quarter			
	mean score	standard error	mean score	standard error	mean score	standard error	mean score	standard error	effect	standard error
Newfoundland and Labrador	482	(4.6)	507	(6.4)	544	(4.9)	572	(4.7)	35.8	(2.3)
Prince Edward Island	468	(4.9)	496	(5.5)	517	(4.6)	557	(5.6)	31.5	(2.3)
Nova Scotia	481	(4.3)	513	(5.8)	524	(4.3)	565	(4.1)	28.4	(2.3)
New Brunswick	464	(4.1)	496	(4.3)	513	(4.2)	554	(4.4)	29.9	(1.8)
Quebec	498	(5.0)	524	(5.5)	537	(5.3)	569	(5.3)	25.0	(1.9)
Ontario	511	(4.7)	533	(5.1)	538	(6.1)	580	(5.8)	22.9	(2.1)
Manitoba	491	(5.5)	520	(5.6)	527	(5.5)	565	(5.1)	24.0	(2.3)
Saskatchewan	479	(5.0)	513	(4.1)	527	(5.1)	548	(6.8)	28.5	(2.9)
Alberta	523	(5.0)	542	(4.7)	555	(6.3)	583	(5.5)	22.5	(2.4)
British Columbia	501	(5.9)	532	(5.4)	544	(6.6)	579	(5.7)	27.8	(1.9)
Canada	504	(2.5)	529	(2.4)	538	(2.9)	575	(2.9)	24.8	(1.0)
OECD average	477	(0.7)	495	(0.7)	506	(0.7)	528	(0.8)	20.4	(0.3)

Note: Results based on students' self-reports.

Table B.4.5

Index of general interest in science, by national and provincial quarters of the index

| | Index of general interest in science | | | | | | | | | |
| | All students | | Bottom quarter | | Second quarter | | Third quarter | | Top quarter | |
	mean index	standard error	mean index	standard error	mean index	standard error	mean index	standard error	mean index	standard error
Newfoundland and Labrador	0.17	(0.03)	-1.00	(0.05)	0.02	(0.01)	0.48	(0.01)	1.17	(0.02)
Prince Edward Island	0.09	(0.03)	-1.31	(0.05)	-0.05	(0.01)	0.47	(0.01)	1.25	(0.03)
Nova Scotia	0.08	(0.02)	-1.21	(0.05)	-0.07	(0.01)	0.44	(0.01)	1.17	(0.03)
New Brunswick	0.18	(0.02)	-1.16	(0.04)	0.01	(0.01)	0.54	(0.01)	1.32	(0.02)
Quebec	0.13	(0.02)	-1.14	(0.03)	-0.07	(0.01)	0.47	(0.01)	1.25	(0.02)
Ontario	0.09	(0.02)	-1.12	(0.04)	-0.09	(0.01)	0.42	(0.01)	1.15	(0.03)
Manitoba	0.00	(0.02)	-1.34	(0.05)	-0.12	(0.01)	0.36	(0.01)	1.10	(0.03)
Saskatchewan	0.03	(0.03)	-1.22	(0.04)	-0.13	(0.01)	0.37	(0.01)	1.10	(0.03)
Alberta	0.14	(0.03)	-1.00	(0.04)	-0.02	(0.01)	0.44	(0.01)	1.13	(0.02)
British Columbia	0.13	(0.03)	-1.01	(0.04)	-0.05	(0.01)	0.42	(0.01)	1.14	(0.02)
Canada	0.11	(0.01)	-1.11	(0.02)	-0.07	(0.00)	0.44	(0.00)	1.17	(0.01)
OECD average	0.00	(0.00)	-1.23	(0.00)	-0.17	(0.00)	0.32	(0.00)	1.08	(0.00)

| | Performance on the science scale, by national and provincial quarters of this index | | | | | | | | Change in the science score per unit of this index | |
| | Bottom quarter | | Second quarter | | Third quarter | | Top quarter | | | |
	mean score	standard error	mean score	standard error	mean score	standard error	mean score	standard error	effect	standard error
Newfoundland and Labrador	478	(4.9)	527	(5.5)	544	(4.6)	556	(4.6)	32.5	(2.0)
Prince Edward Island	459	(4.5)	505	(4.6)	524	(5.0)	549	(5.1)	31.8	(1.9)
Nova Scotia	484	(4.6)	508	(4.5)	542	(5.4)	549	(4.8)	24.9	(2.0)
New Brunswick	461	(3.4)	502	(4.2)	524	(4.2)	540	(4.6)	27.7	(2.0)
Quebec	495	(4.6)	526	(5.1)	549	(5.0)	559	(6.3)	24.2	(2.2)
Ontario	510	(5.3)	533	(5.4)	552	(5.9)	566	(6.2)	23.0	(2.4)
Manitoba	488	(5.6)	526	(5.8)	541	(5.3)	544	(5.0)	22.2	(2.5)
Saskatchewan	482	(4.6)	517	(6.6)	531	(4.6)	537	(6.8)	22.7	(2.5)
Alberta	513	(4.9)	554	(4.7)	565	(5.2)	571	(5.7)	23.8	(2.2)
British Columbia	510	(8.1)	534	(5.1)	551	(6.1)	561	(5.9)	22.0	(3.0)
Canada	502	(2.7)	532	(2.3)	551	(2.8)	560	(3.2)	23.6	(1.1)
OECD average	466	(0.7)	494	(0.7)	514	(0.7)	529	(0.8)	25.0	(0.3)

Note: Results based on students' self-reports.

Table B.4.6

Index of enjoyment of science, by national and provincial quarters of the index

| | Index of enjoyment of science | | | | | | | | | |
| | All students | | Bottom quarter | | Second quarter | | Third quarter | | Top quarter | |
	mean index	standard error	mean index	standard error	mean index	standard error	mean index	standard error	mean index	standard error
Newfoundland and Labrador	0.27	(0.03)	-0.95	(0.03)	-0.01	(0.01)	0.55	(0.01)	1.49	(0.02)
Prince Edward Island	0.10	(0.03)	-1.32	(0.03)	-0.19	(0.01)	0.43	(0.01)	1.48	(0.02)
Nova Scotia	0.18	(0.03)	-1.23	(0.03)	-0.08	(0.01)	0.54	(0.01)	1.50	(0.02)
New Brunswick	0.22	(0.03)	-1.17	(0.03)	-0.06	(0.01)	0.54	(0.01)	1.56	(0.02)
Quebec	0.19	(0.03)	-1.15	(0.02)	-0.13	(0.01)	0.50	(0.01)	1.54	(0.01)
Ontario	0.14	(0.03)	-1.20	(0.02)	-0.13	(0.01)	0.43	(0.01)	1.49	(0.02)
Manitoba	0.04	(0.03)	-1.30	(0.03)	-0.27	(0.01)	0.37	(0.01)	1.37	(0.03)
Saskatchewan	-0.01	(0.03)	-1.28	(0.03)	-0.29	(0.01)	0.32	(0.01)	1.21	(0.03)
Alberta	0.22	(0.03)	-1.04	(0.03)	-0.02	(0.01)	0.48	(0.01)	1.46	(0.02)
British Columbia	0.25	(0.03)	-1.08	(0.03)	-0.03	(0.01)	0.55	(0.01)	1.57	(0.02)
Canada	0.17	(0.01)	-1.17	(0.01)	-0.11	(0.01)	0.46	(0.00)	1.50	(0.01)
OECD average	0.00	(0.00)	-1.22	(0.00)	-0.32	(0.00)	0.30	(0.00)	1.25	(0.00)

| | Performance on the science scale, by national and provincial quarters of this index | | | | | | | | Change in the science score per unit of this index | |
| | Bottom quarter | | Second quarter | | Third quarter | | Top quarter | | | |
	mean score	standard error	mean score	standard error	mean score	standard error	mean score	standard error	effect	standard error
Newfoundland and Labrador	476	(4.4)	508	(5.6)	537	(4.6)	585	(4.3)	42.8	(2.3)
Prince Edward Island	449	(4.0)	494	(5.0)	524	(5.2)	570	(4.9)	42.7	(2.0)
Nova Scotia	470	(3.7)	511	(4.2)	536	(5.0)	567	(4.3)	33.8	(1.8)
New Brunswick	457	(3.6)	490	(3.7)	521	(5.0)	558	(4.3)	37.1	(1.9)
Quebec	490	(5.1)	519	(4.6)	545	(5.5)	574	(5.5)	31.2	(1.9)
Ontario	499	(5.5)	526	(5.1)	553	(5.8)	584	(6.7)	31.4	(2.3)
Manitoba	483	(5.5)	510	(4.9)	541	(5.1)	566	(6.0)	30.6	(2.5)
Saskatchewan	472	(4.6)	503	(5.8)	529	(4.9)	563	(6.5)	34.6	(2.4)
Alberta	511	(4.8)	542	(4.6)	555	(5.7)	595	(5.9)	32.2	(2.5)
British Columbia	490	(5.8)	525	(5.6)	551	(6.2)	589	(5.2)	36.3	(1.8)
Canada	493	(2.9)	523	(2.4)	548	(2.9)	581	(3.1)	32.6	(1.0)
OECD average	465	(0.7)	488	(0.7)	511	(0.7)	539	(0.8)	29.5	(0.3)

Note: Results based on students' self-reports.

Table B.4.7

Index of instrumental motivation to learn science, by national and provincial quarters of the index

	Index of instrumental motivation to learn science									
	All students		Bottom quarter		Second quarter		Third quarter		Top quarter	
	mean index	standard error	mean index	standard error	mean index	standard error	mean index	standard error	mean index	standard error
Newfoundland and Labrador	0.59	(0.03)	-0.64	(0.03)	0.27	(0.01)	0.92	(0.02)	1.80	(0.00)
Prince Edward Island	0.57	(0.03)	-0.75	(0.03)	0.27	(0.01)	0.93	(0.02)	1.82	(0.00)
Nova Scotia	0.45	(0.03)	-0.83	(0.03)	0.16	(0.02)	0.73	(0.02)	1.76	(0.01)
New Brunswick	0.50	(0.03)	-0.83	(0.03)	0.21	(0.01)	0.84	(0.02)	1.78	(0.01)
Quebec	0.11	(0.03)	-1.30	(0.02)	-0.30	(0.01)	0.48	(0.01)	1.57	(0.01)
Ontario	0.34	(0.03)	-0.98	(0.03)	-0.02	(0.02)	0.63	(0.02)	1.75	(0.01)
Manitoba	0.39	(0.03)	-0.88	(0.03)	0.10	(0.01)	0.64	(0.02)	1.72	(0.01)
Saskatchewan	0.38	(0.04)	-0.79	(0.03)	0.16	(0.01)	0.57	(0.02)	1.60	(0.02)
Alberta	0.48	(0.03)	-0.75	(0.03)	0.20	(0.01)	0.75	(0.02)	1.75	(0.01)
British Columbia	0.39	(0.03)	-0.86	(0.03)	0.07	(0.01)	0.65	(0.01)	1.71	(0.01)
Canada	0.32	(0.02)	-1.01	(0.01)	-0.02	(0.01)	0.62	(0.01)	1.70	(0.00)
OECD average	0.00	(0.00)	-1.20	(0.00)	-0.33	(0.00)	0.27	(0.00)	1.27	(0.00)

	Performance on the science scale, by national and provincial quarters of this index								Change in the science score per unit of this index	
	Bottom quarter		Second quarter		Third quarter		Top quarter			
	mean score	standard error	mean score	standard error	mean score	standard error	mean score	standard error	effect	standard error
Newfoundland and Labrador	489	(5.0)	508	(5.4)	537	(5.8)	577	(5.0)	35.5	(2.8)
Prince Edward Island	471	(5.1)	492	(5.3)	511	(5.2)	562	(6.2)	33.7	(2.9)
Nova Scotia	488	(4.9)	526	(4.2)	527	(4.9)	548	(5.3)	23.2	(2.6)
New Brunswick	475	(5.3)	487	(4.6)	515	(5.4)	545	(4.3)	27.8	(2.7)
Quebec	507	(4.9)	533	(5.5)	542	(5.7)	578	(5.8)	23.4	(1.8)
Ontario	517	(5.9)	531	(6.8)	541	(6.4)	583	(5.1)	22.2	(2.5)
Manitoba	506	(6.7)	512	(7.2)	523	(5.9)	565	(6.0)	23.8	(3.3)
Saskatchewan	485	(4.6)	512	(6.5)	523	(6.5)	551	(9.3)	29.6	(4.3)
Alberta	523	(6.1)	543	(5.5)	554	(6.9)	594	(5.6)	26.4	(2.4)
British Columbia	520	(7.1)	534	(7.1)	542	(7.8)	573	(6.5)	19.5	(2.9)
Canada	514	(2.8)	527	(2.9)	540	(3.1)	578	(2.5)	22.8	(1.1)
OECD average	485	(0.7)	498	(0.7)	502	(0.7)	529	(0.8)	17.6	(0.3)

Note: Results based on students' self-reports.

Table B.4.8

Index of future-oriented science motivation, by national and provincial quarters of the index

	Index of future-oriented science motivation									
	All students		Bottom quarter		Second quarter		Third quarter		Top quarter	
	mean index	standard error	mean index	standard error	mean index	standard error	mean index	standard error	mean index	standard error
Newfoundland and Labrador	0.43	(0.03)	-0.85	(0.03)	0.14	(0.01)	0.77	(0.01)	1.68	(0.02)
Prince Edward Island	0.45	(0.03)	-0.98	(0.02)	0.13	(0.01)	0.83	(0.01)	1.80	(0.02)
Nova Scotia	0.32	(0.03)	-1.08	(0.02)	0.00	(0.01)	0.69	(0.01)	1.67	(0.03)
New Brunswick	0.33	(0.03)	-1.08	(0.02)	0.03	(0.01)	0.71	(0.01)	1.64	(0.02)
Quebec	-0.01	(0.02)	-1.38	(0.00)	-0.40	(0.01)	0.32	(0.01)	1.45	(0.01)
Ontario	0.26	(0.03)	-1.20	(0.01)	-0.08	(0.01)	0.65	(0.01)	1.66	(0.02)
Manitoba	0.22	(0.02)	-1.15	(0.02)	-0.09	(0.01)	0.57	(0.01)	1.55	(0.02)
Saskatchewan	0.15	(0.03)	-1.15	(0.02)	-0.11	(0.01)	0.49	(0.01)	1.36	(0.02)
Alberta	0.33	(0.03)	-1.03	(0.02)	0.06	(0.01)	0.71	(0.01)	1.59	(0.03)
British Columbia	0.24	(0.03)	-1.10	(0.02)	-0.06	(0.01)	0.55	(0.01)	1.57	(0.02)
Canada	0.20	(0.01)	-1.22	(0.01)	-0.14	(0.00)	0.58	(0.01)	1.59	(0.01)
OECD average	0.00	(0.00)	-1.24	(0.00)	-0.30	(0.00)	0.27	(0.00)	1.27	(0.00)

	Performance on the science scale, by national and provincial quarters of this index								Change in the science score per unit of this index	
	Bottom quarter		Second quarter		Third quarter		Top quarter			
	mean score	standard error	mean score	standard error	mean score	standard error	mean score	standard error	effect	standard error
Newfoundland and Labrador	484	(4.9)	498	(3.9)	542	(5.0)	582	(4.9)	39.4	(2.4)
Prince Edward Island	479	(4.1)	489	(5.0)	514	(5.5)	558	(5.4)	29.5	(2.2)
Nova Scotia	496	(4.5)	503	(4.8)	525	(5.1)	561	(4.2)	24.5	(2.1)
New Brunswick	470	(3.8)	487	(4.1)	518	(4.3)	551	(4.2)	30.0	(1.7)
Quebec	500	(4.7)	525	(4.2)	528	(5.3)	578	(6.1)	27.0	(1.7)
Ontario	516	(6.4)	520	(5.1)	551	(5.6)	576	(5.9)	22.5	(2.2)
Manitoba	501	(5.5)	506	(4.8)	538	(5.7)	558	(5.4)	24.1	(2.7)
Saskatchewan	488	(4.6)	497	(5.1)	526	(5.5)	558	(6.5)	29.1	(2.7)
Alberta	524	(5.4)	533	(4.3)	567	(4.9)	580	(6.8)	24.0	(2.3)
British Columbia	511	(6.3)	523	(5.7)	548	(5.6)	575	(6.0)	26.9	(2.5)
Canada	508	(2.8)	518	(2.3)	547	(2.6)	573	(3.1)	25.0	(1.1)
OECD average	482	(0.6)	494	(0.7)	499	(0.7)	533	(0.9)	19.6	(0.3)

Note: Results based on students' self-reports.

Table B.4.9

Index of science activities,
by national and provincial quarters of the index

	Index of science activities									
	All students		Bottom quarter		Second quarter		Third quarter		Top quarter	
	mean index	standard error	mean index	standard error	mean index	standard error	mean index	standard error	mean index	standard error
Newfoundland and Labrador	-0.10	(0.03)	-1.35	(0.02)	-0.39	(0.01)	0.31	(0.01)	1.05	(0.02)
Prince Edward Island	-0.24	(0.03)	-1.53	(0.02)	-0.58	(0.01)	0.16	(0.01)	1.02	(0.02)
Nova Scotia	-0.15	(0.03)	-1.41	(0.02)	-0.50	(0.01)	0.26	(0.01)	1.04	(0.02)
New Brunswick	-0.09	(0.02)	-1.41	(0.02)	-0.44	(0.01)	0.34	(0.01)	1.13	(0.02)
Quebec	-0.09	(0.02)	-1.4	(0.01)	-0.41	(0.01)	0.35	(0.01)	1.09	(0.01)
Ontario	-0.16	(0.03)	-1.5	(0.02)	-0.51	(0.01)	0.27	(0.01)	1.12	(0.02)
Manitoba	-0.29	(0.03)	-1.61	(0.01)	-0.62	(0.01)	0.06	(0.01)	1.00	(0.02)
Saskatchewan	-0.29	(0.03)	-1.56	(0.02)	-0.61	(0.01)	0.08	(0.02)	0.93	(0.02)
Alberta	-0.16	(0.03)	-1.46	(0.02)	-0.48	(0.02)	0.28	(0.01)	1.05	(0.02)
British Columbia	-0.17	(0.03)	-1.48	(0.02)	-0.50	(0.01)	0.25	(0.01)	1.04	(0.02)
Canada	-0.15	(0.01)	-1.47	(0.01)	-0.50	(0.01)	0.29	(0.01)	1.08	(0.01)
OECD average	0.00	(0.00)	-1.25	(0.00)	-0.28	(0.00)	0.37	(0.00)	1.16	(0.00)

	Performance on the science scale, by national and provincial quarters of this index								Change in the science score per unit of this index	
	Bottom quarter		Second quarter		Third quarter		Top quarter			
	mean score	standard error	mean score	standard error	mean score	standard error	mean score	standard error	effect	standard error
Newfoundland and Labrador	496	(4.8)	511	(4.6)	536	(5.7)	562	(5.1)	27.5	(2.6)
Prince Edward Island	471	(4.5)	497	(4.2)	520	(5.6)	550	(5.3)	29.5	(2.5)
Nova Scotia	489	(4.0)	509	(4.6)	530	(5.1)	555	(4.5)	26.8	(2.3)
New Brunswick	470	(4.1)	500	(4.3)	520	(4.2)	536	(4.7)	25.1	(2.4)
Quebec	499	(4.5)	526	(4.9)	547	(5.2)	556	(5.9)	22.1	(2.1)
Ontario	511	(5.3)	534	(5.9)	555	(4.6)	562	(6.4)	19.2	(2.8)
Manitoba	497	(5.6)	514	(4.7)	542	(5.1)	548	(6.0)	20.8	(2.7)
Saskatchewan	487	(4.8)	513	(5.0)	522	(5.9)	546	(5.7)	22.3	(2.6)
Alberta	521	(5.5)	545	(5.3)	562	(4.9)	574	(6.5)	21.3	(2.7)
British Columbia	507	(6.4)	536	(5.2)	545	(6.0)	568	(6.6)	22.5	(2.4)
Canada	507	(2.5)	528	(2.5)	548	(2.6)	561	(3.1)	21.1	(1.3)
OECD average	472	(0.7)	497	(0.6)	513	(0.7)	521	(0.9)	19.3	(0.4)

Note: Results based on students' self-reports.

Table B.4.10

School reports on the teaching of environmental topics

| | Percentage of students whose principals report where topics on the environment sit in the curriculum received by students | | | | | | | |
| | In a specific environmental studies course | | In the natural sciences courses | | As part of a geography course | | As part of another course | |
	percentage	standard error	percentage	standard error	percentage	standard error	percentage	standard error
Newfoundland and Labrador	53.9	(2.90)	98.1	(1.40)	86.1	(1.90)	50.4	(3.20)
Prince Edward Island	71.1	(0.30)	96.2	(0.20)	74.0	(0.40)	50.0	(0.30)
Nova Scotia	10.0	(1.80)	92.3	(1.50)	77.7	(2.20)	51.5	(3.40)
New Brunswick	44.2	(0.80)	93.8	(0.20)	34.8	(0.90)	30.2	(0.60)
Quebec	26.0	(3.90)	81.5	(2.30)	59.9	(4.30)	55.8	(4.40)
Ontario	32.3	(4.20)	95.4	(1.90)	82.5	(4.20)	59.6	(5.50)
Manitoba	15.8	(2.00)	97.0	(0.60)	94.8	(1.20)	53.1	(3.40)
Saskatchewan	14.6	(3.00)	97.2	(1.10)	13.5	(4.10)	48.8	(4.10)
Alberta	11.6	(2.80)	99.8	(0.20)	16.4	(4.30)	50.0	(5.30)
British Columbia	22.0	(4.80)	92.2	(3.80)	79.0	(5.10)	56.1	(5.10)
Canada	26.5	(2.00)	92.2	(1.00)	67.0	(2.10)	55.6	(2.60)
OECD average	20.9	(0.51)	94.0	(0.30)	74.7	(0.50)	63.4	(0.61)

Note: Results based on reports from school principals and reported proportionate to the number of 15-year-olds enrolled in the school.

Table B.4.11

Percentage of students participating in school activities to promote the learning of environmental topics

| | Percentage of students whose principals report the following school activities to promote the learning of environmental topics | | | | | | | | | |
| | Outdoor education | | Trips to museums | | Trips to science and/or technology centers | | Extracurricular environmental projects | | Lectures and/or seminars | |
	percentage	standard error	percentage	standard error	percentage	standard error	percentage	standard error	percentage	standard error
Newfoundland and Labrador	75.8	(1.50)	57.9	(2.60)	70.4	(1.90)	72.8	(2.50)	81.1	(2.70)
Prince Edward Island	63.0	(0.30)	72.6	(0.30)	66.0	(0.30)	67.6	(0.40)	84.3	(0.20)
Nova Scotia	64.1	(2.60)	70.7	(2.30)	58.1	(2.70)	60.8	(2.70)	80.4	(2.70)
New Brunswick	53.3	(0.90)	43.0	(0.90)	48.9	(1.20)	50.4	(0.90)	76.1	(1.00)
Quebec	42.2	(5.00)	53.9	(3.90)	65.1	(3.60)	56.1	(4.20)	51.4	(4.40)
Ontario	74.1	(4.60)	77.1	(4.40)	84.6	(3.80)	73.5	(4.00)	83.7	(3.30)
Manitoba	62.8	(3.60)	76.1	(3.10)	76.9	(2.40)	71.6	(3.30)	75.9	(2.60)
Saskatchewan	74.7	(4.00)	66.4	(3.60)	74.6	(4.00)	36.1	(4.30)	65.6	(3.70)
Alberta	51.7	(5.40)	69.0	(4.30)	84.3	(3.40)	64.0	(5.20)	76.1	(4.30)
British Columbia	55.4	(5.50)	67.5	(4.80)	75.4	(4.40)	60.7	(5.80)	74.1	(5.70)
Canada	60.9	(2.40)	68.0	(2.10)	76.4	(1.90)	64.7	(2.00)	73.0	(1.90)
OECD average	77.0	(0.49)	74.8	(0.53)	66.7	(0.6)	44.8	(0.62)	52.5	(0.60)

Note: Results based on reports from school principals and reported proportionate to the number of 15-year-olds enrolled in the school.

Table B.4.12

Index of awareness of environmental issues,
by national and provincial quarters of the index

	Index of awareness of environmental issues									
	All students		Bottom quarter		Second quarter		Third quarter		Top quarter	
	mean index	standard error	mean index	standard error	mean index	standard error	mean index	standard error	mean index	standard error
Newfoundland and Labrador	0.31	(0.03)	-0.76	(0.03)	0.04	(0.01)	0.54	(0.01)	1.42	(0.03)
Prince Edward Island	0.08	(0.02)	-1.14	(0.03)	-0.26	(0.01)	0.34	(0.01)	1.37	(0.03)
Nova Scotia	0.13	(0.02)	-1.06	(0.03)	-0.17	(0.01)	0.40	(0.01)	1.36	(0.03)
New Brunswick	0.00	(0.02)	-1.16	(0.02)	-0.31	(0.01)	0.25	(0.01)	1.21	(0.03)
Quebec	0.19	(0.03)	-0.98	(0.02)	-0.14	(0.01)	0.43	(0.01)	1.45	(0.03)
Ontario	0.37	(0.03)	-0.84	(0.03)	0.04	(0.01)	0.63	(0.01)	1.67	(0.04)
Manitoba	0.29	(0.03)	-1.06	(0.05)	-0.01	(0.01)	0.58	(0.01)	1.67	(0.05)
Saskatchewan	0.07	(0.03)	-1.08	(0.02)	-0.24	(0.01)	0.32	(0.01)	1.26	(0.04)
Alberta	0.48	(0.03)	-0.70	(0.03)	0.16	(0.01)	0.71	(0.01)	1.75	(0.03)
British Columbia	0.08	(0.03)	-1.08	(0.03)	-0.23	(0.01)	0.31	(0.01)	1.31	(0.03)
Canada	0.27	(0.01)	-0.93	(0.01)	-0.05	(0.00)	0.52	(0.00)	1.55	(0.02)
OECD average	0.00	(0.00)	-1.19	(0.00)	-0.29	(0.00)	0.27	(0.00)	1.21	(0.00)

	Performance on the science scale, by national and provincial quarters of this index								Change in the science score per unit of this index	
	Bottom quarter		Second quarter		Third quarter		Top quarter			
	mean score	standard error	mean score	standard error	mean score	standard error	mean score	standard error	effect	standard error
Newfoundland and Labrador	473	(4.2)	526	(4.4)	546	(5.0)	561	(5.4)	35.3	(2.6)
Prince Edward Island	449	(4.7)	509	(4.4)	526	(5.0)	553	(5.3)	34.6	(2.4)
Nova Scotia	477	(5.2)	512	(4.5)	536	(4.5)	559	(4.6)	30.1	(2.9)
New Brunswick	449	(3.9)	504	(3.8)	524	(4.0)	550	(4.5)	37.1	(2.3)
Quebec	471	(4.4)	526	(4.5)	551	(4.5)	581	(5.4)	40.4	(2.4)
Ontario	486	(5.3)	536	(5.1)	558	(6.2)	583	(4.8)	34.5	(2.3)
Manitoba	462	(6.0)	526	(5.5)	544	(4.8)	570	(5.6)	37.0	(2.4)
Saskatchewan	463	(5.1)	509	(5.9)	538	(3.9)	558	(5.0)	38.0	(3.0)
Alberta	502	(7.0)	541	(4.7)	572	(4.1)	589	(5.0)	30.7	(2.7)
British Columbia	484	(5.8)	536	(6.1)	555	(5.3)	582	(5.9)	37.6	(2.2)
Canada	482	(2.6)	530	(2.2)	554	(2.5)	580	(2.7)	36.2	(1.2)
OECD average	439	(0.7)	492	(0.6)	522	(0.6)	553	(0.7)	43.8	(0.3)

Note: Results based on students' self-reports.

Table B.4.13

Index of perception of environmental issues, by national and provincial quarters of the index

	Index of perception of environmental issues									
	All students		Bottom quarter		Second quarter		Third quarter		Top quarter	
	mean index	standard error	mean index	standard error	mean index	standard error	mean index	standard error	mean index	standard error
Newfoundland and Labrador	-0.28	(0.03)	-1.43	(0.04)	-0.59	(0.01)	-0.07	(0.01)	0.98	(0.03)
Prince Edward Island	-0.17	(0.03)	-1.49	(0.05)	-0.53	(0.01)	0.08	(0.01)	1.25	(0.02)
Nova Scotia	-0.17	(0.05)	-1.46	(0.05)	-0.52	(0.01)	0.08	(0.01)	1.21	(0.02)
New Brunswick	-0.07	(0.02)	-1.24	(0.03)	-0.44	(0.01)	0.15	(0.01)	1.24	(0.01)
Quebec	0.06	(0.02)	-0.98	(0.02)	-0.29	(0.01)	0.25	(0.01)	1.24	(0.01)
Ontario	-0.08	(0.03)	-1.30	(0.05)	-0.43	(0.01)	0.16	(0.01)	1.25	(0.01)
Manitoba	-0.27	(0.03)	-1.53	(0.04)	-0.60	(0.01)	-0.06	(0.01)	1.11	(0.02)
Saskatchewan	-0.25	(0.03)	-1.41	(0.03)	-0.60	(0.01)	-0.06	(0.01)	1.08	(0.02)
Alberta	-0.21	(0.03)	-1.48	(0.05)	-0.51	(0.01)	0.03	(0.01)	1.13	(0.02)
British Columbia	-0.25	(0.03)	-1.49	(0.04)	-0.55	(0.01)	-0.05	(0.01)	1.09	(0.02)
Canada	-0.10	(0.01)	-1.29	(0.02)	-0.45	(0.00)	0.13	(0.01)	1.20	(0.01)
OECD average	0.00	(0.00)	-1.14	(0.00)	-0.32	(0.00)	0.26	(0.00)	1.20	(0.00)

	Performance on the science scale, by national and provincial quarters of this index								Change in the science score per unit of this index	
	Bottom quarter		Second quarter		Third quarter		Top quarter			
	mean score	standard error	mean score	standard error	mean score	standard error	mean score	standard error	effect	standard error
Newfoundland and Labrador	516	(5.2)	538	(4.7)	527	(5.9)	526	(4.5)	5.9	(2.4)
Prince Edward Island	492	(5.5)	518	(6.0)	521	(4.1)	507	(5.4)	7.6	(2.5)
Nova Scotia	518	(5.4)	523	(4.6)	527	(5.4)	516	(4.4)	3.6	(2.3)
New Brunswick	490	(4.0)	514	(4.8)	518	(3.6)	504	(3.9)	7.9	(1.9)
Quebec	522	(5.6)	540	(4.4)	539	(4.3)	530	(5.4)	5.0	(2.1)
Ontario	531	(6.9)	546	(5.0)	550	(5.9)	538	(4.5)	5.4	(2.5)
Manitoba	521	(5.2)	533	(6.0)	531	(4.8)	518	(4.4)	2.4	(2.1)
Saskatchewan	510	(6.0)	519	(5.2)	526	(6.3)	513	(6.1)	4.3	(2.7)
Alberta	549	(6.4)	551	(5.2)	555	(5.8)	548	(4.8)	2.6	(2.2)
British Columbia	531	(7.3)	539	(5.6)	549	(5.2)	537	(5.8)	5.1	(2.7)
Canada	527	(2.8)	541	(2.3)	545	(2.6)	533	(2.5)	4.6	(1.2)
OECD average	490	(0.8)	509	(0.7)	509	(0.7)	500	(0.7)	5.9	(0.3)

Note: Results based on students' self-reports.

Table B.4.14

Index of environmental optimism, by national and provincial quarters of the index

	Index of environmental optimism									
	All students		Bottom quarter		Second quarter		Third quarter		Top quarter	
	mean index	standard error	mean index	standard error	mean index	standard error	mean index	standard error	mean index	standard error
Newfoundland and Labrador	-0.03	(0.03)	-1.33	(0.02)	-0.28	(0.01)	0.31	(0.01)	1.19	(0.04)
Prince Edward Island	-0.15	(0.03)	-1.59	(0.01)	-0.46	(0.01)	0.24	(0.01)	1.21	(0.03)
Nova Scotia	-0.17	(0.02)	-1.57	(0.01)	-0.45	(0.01)	0.20	(0.01)	1.13	(0.04)
New Brunswick	-0.17	(0.02)	-1.50	(0.01)	-0.40	(0.01)	0.18	(0.01)	1.06	(0.03)
Quebec	-0.31	(0.02)	-1.55	(0.01)	-0.54	(0.01)	0.03	(0.01)	0.84	(0.02)
Ontario	-0.23	(0.03)	-1.59	(0.01)	-0.50	(0.01)	0.15	(0.01)	1.03	(0.03)
Manitoba	-0.11	(0.03)	-1.51	(0.01)	-0.39	(0.01)	0.25	(0.01)	1.23	(0.04)
Saskatchewan	-0.14	(0.03)	-1.49	(0.01)	-0.39	(0.01)	0.23	(0.01)	1.10	(0.03)
Alberta	-0.17	(0.03)	-1.50	(0.01)	-0.47	(0.01)	0.18	(0.01)	1.09	(0.04)
British Columbia	-0.15	(0.02)	-1.46	(0.02)	-0.42	(0.01)	0.20	(0.01)	1.07	(0.04)
Canada	-0.22	(0.01)	-1.54	(0.00)	-0.49	(0.00)	0.15	(0.00)	1.02	(0.01)
OECD average	0.00	(0.00)	-1.27	(0.00)	-0.25	(0.00)	0.31	(0.00)	1.20	(0.00)

	Performance on the science scale, by national and provincial quarters of this index								Change in the science score per unit of this index	
	Bottom quarter		Second quarter		Third quarter		Top quarter			
	mean score	standard error	mean score	standard error	mean score	standard error	mean score	standard error	effect	standard error
Newfoundland and Labrador	538	(4.4)	533	(4.9)	531	(4.8)	503	(5.7)	-14.4	(2.5)
Prince Edward Island	519	(5.0)	524	(5.0)	516	(5.0)	479	(5.1)	-13.9	(2.5)
Nova Scotia	525	(4.5)	532	(4.7)	521	(5.8)	506	(6.2)	-9.6	(2.8)
New Brunswick	510	(4.7)	515	(4.1)	512	(4.8)	491	(4.6)	-7.5	(2.3)
Quebec	537	(5.5)	547	(4.8)	535	(5.1)	513	(4.2)	-10.4	(2.0)
Ontario	542	(4.9)	547	(5.8)	551	(5.3)	524	(6.1)	-6.1	(1.9)
Manitoba	532	(5.2)	537	(5.3)	536	(5.6)	498	(6.9)	-12.9	(2.7)
Saskatchewan	521	(4.9)	525	(5.3)	527	(5.8)	496	(8.5)	-8.8	(3.3)
Alberta	551	(4.9)	555	(5.5)	557	(4.7)	540	(6.2)	-6.1	(2.5)
British Columbia	553	(6.5)	545	(6.0)	538	(5.3)	521	(6.9)	-13.6	(2.8)
Canada	540	(2.5)	545	(2.6)	542	(2.2)	520	(2.8)	-8.6	(1.0)
OECD average	517	(0.7)	515	(0.6)	503	(0.7)	472	(0.8)	-17.8	(0.3)

Note: Results based on students' self-reports.

Table B.4.15

Index of responsibility for sustainable development, by national and provincial quarters of the index

	Index of responsibility for sustainable development									
	All students		Bottom quarter		Second quarter		Third quarter		Top quarter	
	mean index	standard error	mean index	standard error	mean index	standard error	mean index	standard error	mean index	standard error
Newfoundland and Labrador	-0.22	(0.03)	-1.18	(0.02)	-0.54	(0.01)	-0.10	(0.01)	0.95	(0.04)
Prince Edward Island	-0.20	(0.02)	-1.30	(0.02)	-0.55	(0.01)	-0.07	(0.01)	1.12	(0.04)
Nova Scotia	-0.30	(0.03)	-1.38	(0.03)	-0.63	(0.01)	-0.18	(0.01)	0.98	(0.04)
New Brunswick	-0.13	(0.02)	-1.24	(0.03)	-0.50	(0.00)	0.02	(0.01)	1.19	(0.03)
Quebec	0.45	(0.03)	-0.84	(0.02)	0.01	(0.01)	0.73	(0.01)	1.90	(0.02)
Ontario	-0.05	(0.03)	-1.14	(0.02)	-0.48	(0.01)	0.09	(0.01)	1.32	(0.03)
Manitoba	-0.20	(0.02)	-1.22	(0.03)	-0.51	(0.01)	-0.08	(0.01)	1.02	(0.03)
Saskatchewan	-0.32	(0.03)	-1.30	(0.02)	-0.61	(0.01)	-0.21	(0.01)	0.83	(0.04)
Alberta	-0.16	(0.02)	-1.20	(0.02)	-0.51	(0.00)	-0.03	(0.01)	1.11	(0.03)
British Columbia	-0.14	(0.03)	-1.21	(0.03)	-0.53	(0.01)	0.01	(0.01)	1.18	(0.03)
Canada	0.02	(0.02)	-1.13	(0.01)	-0.42	(0.00)	0.20	(0.01)	1.42	(0.02)
OECD average	0.00	(0.00)	-1.10	(0.00)	-0.36	(0.00)	0.20	(0.00)	1.25	(0.00)

	Performance on the science scale, by national and provincial quarters of this index								Change in the science score per unit of this index	
	Bottom quarter		Second quarter		Third quarter		Top quarter			
	mean score	standard error	mean score	standard error	mean score	standard error	mean score	standard error	effect	standard error
Newfoundland and Labrador	489	(4.9)	510	(5.6)	536	(5.2)	571	(4.9)	34.9	(3.0)
Prince Edward Island	473	(4.8)	486	(4.8)	528	(5.8)	553	(5.4)	29.5	(3.1)
Nova Scotia	490	(5.0)	508	(5.6)	524	(5.1)	562	(4.3)	27.9	(2.6)
New Brunswick	474	(4.4)	490	(3.9)	520	(4.3)	544	(5.2)	27.0	(2.5)
Quebec	490	(4.9)	524	(4.9)	550	(4.8)	566	(4.9)	27.0	(2.0)
Ontario	514	(5.7)	528	(5.4)	549	(5.9)	572	(5.1)	21.6	(2.2)
Manitoba	501	(5.3)	506	(5.6)	537	(5.1)	561	(5.0)	24.9	(2.3)
Saskatchewan	489	(6.2)	503	(5.1)	527	(5.1)	551	(5.7)	28.9	(2.8)
Alberta	525	(6.0)	525	(4.3)	563	(5.6)	590	(4.9)	27.7	(2.2)
British Columbia	504	(6.3)	521	(5.9)	551	(5.2)	581	(4.7)	30.7	(2.7)
Canada	508	(2.2)	519	(2.3)	549	(2.9)	570	(2.6)	23.8	(1.1)
OECD average	466	(0.7)	493	(0.7)	514	(0.7)	534	(0.7)	26.5	(0.3)

Note: Results based on students' self-reports.

Table B.4.16

Percentage of students taking various science courses

	All students							
	General science course				Biology course			
	Compulsory		Optional		Compulsory		Optional	
	percentage	standard error	percentage	standard error	percentage	standard error	percentage	standard error
Newfoundland and Labrador	83.7	(1.0)	33.3	(1.2)	24.1	(1.3)	23.6	(1.2)
Prince Edward Island	67.9	(1.1)	18.3	(1.0)	24.4	(1.1)	12.8	(0.7)
Nova Scotia	82.1	(1.3)	34.6	(1.3)	26.6	(1.4)	25.0	(1.0)
New Brunswick	81.4	(0.8)	19.6	(1.0)	27.7	(0.9)	16.3	(0.9)
Quebec	68.8	(1.0)	12.8	(0.8)	32.8	(1.1)	10.4	(1.0)
Ontario	82.6	(1.4)	15.0	(1.0)	23.1	(1.3)	9.2	(0.6)
Manitoba	85.1	(0.9)	16.1	(1.0)	25.0	(0.9)	10.0	(0.8)
Saskatchewan	79.7	(1.1)	24.1	(1.1)	17.6	(1.3)	12.7	(1.1)
Alberta	84.3	(1.2)	19.7	(0.9)	40.9	(2.0)	13.9	(0.9)
British Columbia	80.1	(1.2)	17.6	(1.0)	34.7	(1.8)	10.0	(0.8)
Canada	79.1	(0.6)	16.6	(0.5)	28.8	(0.6)	11.0	(0.4)
OECD average	62.0	(0.2)	20.9	(0.2)	54.9	(0.3)	14.8	(0.2)

	All students							
	Physics course				Chemistry course			
	Compulsory		Optional		Compulsory		Optional	
	percentage	standard error	percentage	standard error	percentage	standard error	percentage	standard error
Newfoundland and Labrador	22.7	(1.3)	11.0	(1.1)	24.2	(1.4)	14.6	(1.1)
Prince Edward Island	26.5	(1.0)	11.5	(0.7)	30.8	(1.1)	14.2	(0.8)
Nova Scotia	18.6	(1.5)	7.6	(0.7)	21.4	(1.5)	10.6	(1.0)
New Brunswick	27.2	(1.0)	8.1	(0.7)	31.2	(0.9)	14.3	(0.8)
Quebec	40.7	(1.2)	7.1	(0.5)	10.6	(0.8)	3.1	(0.3)
Ontario	24.2	(1.2)	6.5	(0.5)	25.4	(1.3)	7.8	(0.8)
Manitoba	27.8	(1.1)	7.7	(0.7)	31.5	(1.2)	9.8	(0.7)
Saskatchewan	14.8	(1.3)	8.4	(0.7)	19.1	(1.7)	9.2	(0.8)
Alberta	38.6	(1.7)	10.2	(0.7)	41.2	(1.6)	11.9	(0.8)
British Columbia	34.6	(1.8)	8.8	(0.6)	36.4	(1.7)	9.1	(0.8)
Canada	30.6	(0.6)	7.6	(0.3)	25.0	(0.6)	7.8	(0.4)
OECD average	59.9	(0.2)	14.9	(0.1)	58.1	(0.2)	14.7	(0.1)

Note: Results based on students' self-reports.

Table B.4.17

Percentage of students and performance on the science scale, by time spent on learning

| | Science | | | | | | | | | |
| | Less than 2 hours a week | | | | Four hours a week or more | | | | Performance difference | |
	percentage of students	standard error	mean score	standard error	percentage of students	standard error	mean score	standard error	difference (4 hours- 2 hours)	standard error
Regular lessons at school										
Newfoundland and Labrador	14.6	(0.8)	470.0	(5.3)	63.2	(1.1)	550.0	(3.4)	79.5	(6.1)
Prince Edward Island	26.3	(1.1)	475.0	(4.5)	60.6	(1.4)	537.0	(3.3)	62.3	(5.3)
Nova Scotia	19.1	(0.9)	484.0	(5.6)	65.8	(1.6)	539.0	(2.8)	55.3	(6.4)
New Brunswick	29.9	(1.0)	480.0	(3.8)	60.4	(1.0)	528.0	(2.9)	48.2	(4.4)
Quebec	28.4	(1.1)	481.0	(4.5)	38.6	(1.4)	571.0	(4.3)	89.6	(5.2)
Ontario	23.7	(1.4)	503.0	(5.7)	63.0	(2.0)	556.0	(4.0)	52.8	(6.1)
Manitoba	26.2	(1.4)	485.0	(5.6)	58.0	(1.8)	548.0	(3.8)	63.1	(7.0)
Saskatchewan	28.2	(1.4)	479.0	(5.9)	54.1	(1.8)	542.0	(4.3)	62.7	(7.4)
Alberta	19.2	(1.1)	507.0	(7.4)	69.1	(1.3)	567.0	(3.6)	60	(6.8)
British Columbia	17.3	(1.2)	487.0	(7.7)	58.5	(2.2)	554.0	(4.6)	66.8	(6.3)
Canada	23.6	(0.7)	492.0	(2.5)	56.8	(1.0)	557.0	(1.8)	64.9	(2.6)
OECD average	32.7	(0.2)	460.4	(0.8)	28.8	(0.2)	540.1	(0.7)	79.7	(1.0)
Out-of-school-time lessons										
Newfoundland and Labrador	88.0	(0.8)	530.0	(3.2)	3.0	(0.5)	523.0	(14.7)	-7.0	(15.4)
Prince Edward Island	90.0	(0.8)	516.0	(2.9)	2.0	(0.4)	459.0	(17.6)	-57.0	(18.1)
Nova Scotia	91.0	(0.9)	524.0	(2.4)	1.0	(0.3)	482.0	(22.0)	-43.0	(22.4)
New Brunswick	89.0	(0.7)	510.0	(2.3)	2.0	(0.3)	477.0	(14.5)	-33.0	(14.2)
Quebec	94.0	(0.5)	535.0	(3.8)	1.0	(0.2)	507.0	(24.2)	-29.0	(24.0)
Ontario	90.0	(0.8)	543.0	(3.8)	2.0	(0.4)	513.0	(16.4)	-30.0	(15.3)
Manitoba	93.0	(0.7)	529.0	(3.2)	2.0	(0.3)	483.0	(22.9)	-45.0	(23.5)
Saskatchewan	94.0	(0.6)	520.0	(3.3)	1.0	(0.2)	472.0	(26.5)	-48.0	(26.3)
Alberta	90.0	(0.9)	556.0	(3.9)	2.0	(0.4)	514.0	(14.9)	-41.0	(14.6)
British Columbia	90.0	(1.0)	542.0	(4.7)	2.0	(0.4)	520.0	(17.5)	-22.0	(16.4)
Canada	91.0	(0.3)	539.0	(1.8)	2.0	(0.2)	511.0	(9.0)	-29.0	(8.7)
OECD average	89.1	(0.1)	503.5	(0.5)	2.6	(0.1)	469.8	(2.6)	33.7	(2.5)
Study or homework										
Newfoundland and Labrador	64.5	(1.3)	519.5	(3.5)	8.3	(0.7)	552.9	(7.9)	33.4	(8.5)
Prince Edward Island	71.6	(1.3)	508.7	(3.0)	6.6	(0.6)	511.6	(12.0)	2.9	(12.2)
Nova Scotia	71.6	(1.2)	516.0	(3.0)	7.2	(0.6)	532.9	(11.0)	16.9	(11.9)
New Brunswick	74.5	(0.8)	504.4	(2.3)	5.1	(0.5)	522.0	(9.0)	17.6	(8.7)
Quebec	86.0	(0.7)	532.1	(3.9)	2.6	(0.3)	529.4	(15.1)	-2.7	(14.6)
Ontario	64.7	(1.5)	533.1	(4.7)	9.5	(0.8)	558.4	(9.8)	25.3	(9.9)
Manitoba	78.3	(1.1)	524.3	(3.7)	5.3	(0.6)	519.6	(11.7)	-4.8	(12.4)
Saskatchewan	78.6	(1.2)	515.5	(3.7)	4.1	(0.6)	523.6	(13.3)	8.0	(13.1)
Alberta	63.7	(1.7)	545.9	(4.1)	11.3	(0.9)	561.3	(7.9)	15.5	(8.2)
British Columbia	61.3	(1.6)	530.6	(4.9)	10.4	(0.9)	547.4	(8.4)	16.7	(7.7)
Canada	70.6	(0.7)	531.2	(2.0)	7.6	(0.4)	551.4	(5.5)	20.2	(5.4)
OECD average	75.1	(0.1)	497.8	(0.5)	6.4	(0.1)	511.8	(1.7)	-14.1	(1.6)

Note: Results based on students' self-reports.

Table B.4.18

Index of science teaching: Interaction, by national and provincial quarters of the index

	Index of science teaching: Interaction									
	All students		Bottom quarter		Second quarter		Third quarter		Top quarter	
	mean index	standard error	mean index	standard error	mean index	standard error	mean index	standard error	mean index	standard error
Newfoundland and Labrador	0.37	(0.03)	-0.82	(0.03)	0.10	(0.01)	0.61	(0.01)	1.58	(0.03)
Prince Edward Island	0.29	(0.03)	-0.92	(0.03)	0.05	(0.01)	0.55	(0.01)	1.50	(0.03)
Nova Scotia	0.20	(0.03)	-1.04	(0.03)	-0.04	(0.01)	0.51	(0.01)	1.39	(0.02)
New Brunswick	0.23	(0.03)	-0.96	(0.04)	0.01	(0.01)	0.50	(0.01)	1.38	(0.03)
Quebec	-0.07	(0.03)	-1.36	(0.03)	-0.31	(0.01)	0.27	(0.01)	1.13	(0.03)
Ontario	0.26	(0.04)	-0.92	(0.05)	0.02	(0.01)	0.52	(0.01)	1.40	(0.03)
Manitoba	0.22	(0.03)	-1.09	(0.04)	-0.03	(0.01)	0.53	(0.01)	1.47	(0.03)
Saskatchewan	0.24	(0.04)	-0.98	(0.03)	-0.01	(0.01)	0.50	(0.01)	1.44	(0.03)
Alberta	0.35	(0.03)	-0.85	(0.03)	0.10	(0.01)	0.63	(0.01)	1.53	(0.04)
British Columbia	0.17	(0.04)	-1.07	(0.04)	-0.07	(0.01)	0.45	(0.01)	1.36	(0.03)
Canada	0.17	(0.02)	-1.07	(0.02)	-0.07	(0.00)	0.47	(0.00)	1.36	(0.01)
OECD average	0.00	(0.00)	-1.16	(0.00)	-0.24	(0.00)	0.29	(0.00)	1.13	(0.00)

	Performance on the science scale, by national and provincial quarters of this index								Change in the science score per unit of this index	
	Bottom quarter		Second quarter		Third quarter		Top quarter			
	mean score	standard error	mean score	standard error	mean score	standard error	mean score	standard error	effect	standard error
Newfoundland and Labrador	523	(5.4)	525	(5.6)	527	(6.4)	536	(4.8)	4.7	(2.6)
Prince Edward Island	518	(6.7)	508	(5.2)	494	(6.5)	514	(6.0)	-3.1	(3.4)
Nova Scotia	524	(5.5)	527	(6.0)	511	(5.7)	526	(6.3)	0.3	(3.5)
New Brunswick	509	(5.0)	504	(4.8)	505	(4.5)	503	(4.7)	-2.0	(2.9)
Quebec	547	(5.1)	542	(5.6)	538	(5.8)	530	(6.8)	-5.3	(2.6)
Ontario	545	(6.2)	537	(6.5)	545	(5.9)	543	(5.5)	-2.2	(2.7)
Manitoba	540	(6.7)	524	(6.9)	524	(5.4)	516	(5.9)	-7.9	(3.2)
Saskatchewan	524	(5.7)	514	(6.4)	515	(6.1)	517	(7.6)	-2.1	(3.7)
Alberta	553	(5.3)	552	(6.1)	547	(6.9)	562	(6.0)	4.3	(2.6)
British Columbia	552	(7.0)	540	(6.2)	534	(6.9)	539	(6.3)	-7.0	(2.5)
Canada	545	(3.0)	536	(2.7)	537	(2.9)	539	(2.9)	-2.7	(1.3)
OECD average	513	(0.7)	507	(0.7)	501	(0.7)	492	(0.8)	-8.5	(0.4)

Note: Results based on students' self-reports.

Table B.4.19

Index of science teaching: Hands-on activities, by national and provincial quarters of the index

| | Index of science teaching: Hands-on activities | | | | | | | | | |
| | All students | | Bottom quarter | | Second quarter | | Third quarter | | Top quarter | |
	mean index	standard error	mean index	standard error	mean index	standard error	mean index	standard error	mean index	standard error
Newfoundland and Labrador	0.14	(0.03)	-0.91	(0.03)	-0.07	(0.01)	0.36	(0.01)	1.17	(0.03)
Prince Edward Island	0.26	(0.03)	-0.89	(0.03)	0.02	(0.01)	0.52	(0.01)	1.41	(0.04)
Nova Scotia	0.29	(0.03)	-0.81	(0.04)	0.05	(0.01)	0.57	(0.01)	1.37	(0.03)
New Brunswick	0.29	(0.02)	-0.76	(0.03)	0.04	(0.01)	0.54	(0.01)	1.34	(0.03)
Quebec	0.46	(0.02)	-0.52	(0.03)	0.23	(0.01)	0.70	(0.01)	1.43	(0.03)
Ontario	0.53	(0.03)	-0.40	(0.03)	0.30	(0.01)	0.73	(0.01)	1.49	(0.03)
Manitoba	0.36	(0.04)	-0.76	(0.05)	0.12	(0.01)	0.61	(0.01)	1.45	(0.04)
Saskatchewan	0.45	(0.03)	-0.55	(0.03)	0.18	(0.01)	0.69	(0.01)	1.47	(0.03)
Alberta	0.47	(0.03)	-0.60	(0.03)	0.26	(0.01)	0.73	(0.01)	1.46	(0.03)
British Columbia	0.44	(0.03)	-0.54	(0.03)	0.23	(0.01)	0.66	(0.01)	1.42	(0.04)
Canada	0.46	(0.01)	-0.53	(0.01)	0.24	(0.00)	0.69	(0.00)	1.45	(0.02)
OECD average	0.01	(0.00)	-1.16	(0.00)	-0.23	(0.00)	0.31	(0.00)	1.11	(0.00)

| | Performance on the science scale, by national and provincial quarters of this index | | | | | | | | Change in the science score per unit of this index | |
| | Bottom quarter | | Second quarter | | Third quarter | | Top quarter | | | |
	mean score	standard error	mean score	standard error	mean score	standard error	mean score	standard error	effect	standard error
Newfoundland and Labrador	524	(5.8)	529	(5.4)	546	(4.8)	513	(5.0)	-4.7	(2.9)
Prince Edward Island	521	(6.4)	525	(5.7)	502	(5.8)	486	(6.0)	-13.8	(3.5)
Nova Scotia	515	(5.3)	531	(4.3)	529	(5.7)	513	(6.4)	-1.2	(3.7)
New Brunswick	503	(5.6)	514	(4.8)	507	(4.3)	498	(5.1)	-5.4	(3.0)
Quebec	532	(5.8)	541	(5.0)	548	(6.2)	537	(7.2)	6.5	(4.1)
Ontario	536	(7.0)	552	(6.5)	550	(5.7)	532	(6.5)	-4.3	(3.8)
Manitoba	544	(8.3)	532	(5.7)	526	(5.8)	503	(6.6)	-15.0	(3.9)
Saskatchewan	501	(7.7)	525	(6.1)	535	(5.0)	508	(9.1)	4.0	(5.2)
Alberta	548	(5.0)	559	(6.2)	559	(5.5)	547	(6.5)	-0.4	(2.6)
British Columbia	554	(7.9)	538	(6.0)	541	(6.0)	531	(7.5)	-9.3	(4.3)
Canada	537	(3.1)	541	(3.3)	548	(3.1)	532	(3.3)	-1.3	(1.9)
OECD average	499	(0.8)	510	(0.7)	510	(0.7)	495	(0.8)	-1.1	(0.4)

Note: Results based on students' self-reports.

Table B.4.20

Index of science teaching: Student investigations, by national and provincial quarters of the index

	Index of science teaching: Student investigations									
	All students		Bottom quarter		Second quarter		Third quarter		Top quarter	
	mean index	standard error	mean index	standard error	mean index	standard error	mean index	standard error	mean index	standard error
Newfoundland and Labrador	0.11	(0.03)	-1.18	(0.01)	-0.17	(0.01)	0.47	(0.01)	1.31	(0.03)
Prince Edward Island	0.25	(0.03)	-1.11	(0.02)	-0.08	(0.02)	0.63	(0.01)	1.58	(0.04)
Nova Scotia	0.19	(0.04)	-1.11	(0.02)	-0.13	(0.01)	0.59	(0.01)	1.43	(0.03)
New Brunswick	0.24	(0.02)	-0.99	(0.02)	-0.08	(0.01)	0.58	(0.01)	1.43	(0.03)
Quebec	-0.02	(0.03)	-1.26	(0.00)	-0.44	(0.02)	0.32	(0.01)	1.30	(0.02)
Ontario	0.21	(0.04)	-1.04	(0.02)	-0.09	(0.02)	0.56	(0.01)	1.43	(0.03)
Manitoba	0.17	(0.03)	-1.21	(0.01)	-0.17	(0.02)	0.58	(0.01)	1.48	(0.03)
Saskatchewan	0.21	(0.04)	-1.07	(0.02)	-0.10	(0.02)	0.57	(0.01)	1.46	(0.03)
Alberta	0.16	(0.04)	-1.15	(0.02)	-0.14	(0.01)	0.52	(0.01)	1.43	(0.03)
British Columbia	0.06	(0.03)	-1.26	(0.00)	-0.26	(0.01)	0.41	(0.01)	1.36	(0.03)
Canada	0.13	(0.02)	-1.18	(0.01)	-0.18	(0.01)	0.48	(0.01)	1.39	(0.01)
OECD average	0.00	(0.00)	-1.15	(0.00)	-0.40	(0.00)	0.32	(0.00)	1.23	(0.00)

	Performance on the science scale, by national and provincial quarters of this index								Change in the science score per unit of this index	
	Bottom quarter		Second quarter		Third quarter		Top quarter			
	mean score	standard error	mean score	standard error	mean score	standard error	mean score	standard error	effect	standard error
Newfoundland and Labrador	552	(5.0)	544	(6.1)	520	(4.9)	496	(5.5)	-23.1	(2.6)
Prince Edward Island	549	(5.2)	526	(5.8)	497	(5.7)	464	(5.2)	-31.0	(2.5)
Nova Scotia	549	(4.6)	536	(4.6)	518	(6.1)	487	(6.3)	-23.6	(2.9)
New Brunswick	531	(5.8)	517	(4.8)	506	(4.4)	467	(4.7)	-26.2	(2.8)
Quebec	567	(4.4)	554	(5.1)	534	(5.1)	504	(7.2)	-24.0	(2.7)
Ontario	570	(4.7)	559	(4.6)	534	(6.3)	507	(5.6)	-26.7	(2.6)
Manitoba	562	(6.5)	541	(5.5)	526	(5.7)	476	(6.1)	-31.6	(2.6)
Saskatchewan	535	(5.6)	526	(6.8)	528	(5.3)	482	(6.4)	-19.6	(2.8)
Alberta	577	(5.2)	560	(5.8)	553	(5.5)	524	(6.0)	-18.8	(2.4)
British Columbia	580	(5.9)	553	(5.4)	532	(6.3)	501	(7.8)	-28.8	(2.4)
Canada	568	(2.3)	552	(2.6)	536	(3.0)	503	(3.2)	-25.1	(1.2)
OECD average	526	(0.7)	517	(0.7)	502	(0.7)	469	(0.9)	-23.9	(0.4)

Note: Results based on students' self-reports.

Table B.4.21

Index of science teaching: Focus on models or application, by national and provincial quarters of the index

	Index of science teaching: Focus on models or application									
	All students		Bottom quarter		Second quarter		Third quarter		Top quarter	
	mean index	standard error	mean index	standard error	mean index	standard error	mean index	standard error	mean index	standard error
Newfoundland and Labrador	0.35	(0.04)	-0.86	(0.03)	0.06	(0.01)	0.63	(0.01)	1.57	(0.03)
Prince Edward Island	0.32	(0.03)	-0.91	(0.04)	0.01	(0.01)	0.59	(0.01)	1.58	(0.04)
Nova Scotia	0.31	(0.03)	-0.92	(0.03)	0.01	(0.01)	0.60	(0.01)	1.56	(0.03)
New Brunswick	0.37	(0.03)	-0.86	(0.04)	0.09	(0.01)	0.65	(0.01)	1.62	(0.03)
Quebec	0.37	(0.03)	-0.92	(0.03)	0.09	(0.01)	0.67	(0.01)	1.65	(0.02)
Ontario	0.40	(0.04)	-0.85	(0.04)	0.14	(0.01)	0.69	(0.01)	1.63	(0.04)
Manitoba	0.40	(0.03)	-0.88	(0.03)	0.11	(0.01)	0.66	(0.01)	1.70	(0.04)
Saskatchewan	0.31	(0.04)	-0.91	(0.03)	0.01	(0.01)	0.60	(0.01)	1.56	(0.03)
Alberta	0.45	(0.03)	-0.84	(0.03)	0.18	(0.01)	0.75	(0.01)	1.72	(0.04)
British Columbia	0.39	(0.03)	-0.75	(0.03)	0.06	(0.01)	0.64	(0.01)	1.62	(0.03)
Canada	0.39	(0.02)	-0.86	(0.02)	0.11	(0.00)	0.67	(0.00)	1.64	(0.02)
OECD average	0.01	(0.00)	-1.20	(0.00)	-0.27	(0.00)	0.30	(0.00)	1.19	(0.00)

	Performance on the science scale, by national and provincial quarters of this index								Change in the science score per unit of this index	
	Bottom quarter		Second quarter		Third quarter		Top quarter			
	mean score	standard error	mean score	standard error	mean score	standard error	mean score	standard error	effect	standard error
Newfoundland and Labrador	508	(4.8)	529	(5.5)	534	(5.6)	540	(4.9)	12.0	(2.5)
Prince Edward Island	502	(6.1)	510	(5.9)	511	(5.8)	512	(6.5)	5.5	(3.3)
Nova Scotia	519	(5.8)	516	(5.4)	527	(5.7)	527	(6.5)	4.3	(3.3)
New Brunswick	494	(5.3)	505	(4.8)	510	(4.1)	512	(4.8)	7.3	(2.7)
Quebec	519	(5.2)	542	(5.5)	543	(6.2)	555	(6.3)	13.5	(2.5)
Ontario	534	(6.9)	541	(5.3)	543	(5.9)	552	(6.1)	3.7	(2.7)
Manitoba	521	(5.7)	529	(7.8)	522	(5.9)	534	(5.9)	4.3	(2.9)
Saskatchewan	507	(6.1)	514	(8.0)	529	(5.4)	521	(8.1)	6.4	(3.5)
Alberta	542	(5.1)	548	(6.9)	553	(5.8)	571	(6.2)	11.6	(2.5)
British Columbia	536	(7.5)	544	(6.3)	543	(6.1)	544	(6.6)	1.6	(2.9)
Canada	527	(3.0)	539	(2.9)	543	(2.9)	549	(3.2)	7.5	(1.3)
OECD average	494	(0.7)	507	(0.7)	508	(0.7)	505	(0.8)	5.1	(0.3)

Note: Results based on students' self-reports.

Table B.4.22

Percentage of students participating in school activities to promote the learning of science

| | Percentage of students whose principals report the following school activities to promote the learning of science | | | | | | | | | |
| | Science clubs | | Science fairs | | Science competitions | | Extracurricular science projects | | Excursions and field trips | |
	percentage	standard error	percentage	standard error	percentage	standard error	percentage	standard error	percentage	standard error
Newfoundland and Labrador	31.2	(3.00)	76.1	(1.60)	76.5	(2.90)	73.6	(2.40)	97.6	(1.40)
Prince Edward Island	27.6	(0.40)	95.7	(0.20)	70.7	(0.40)	64.9	(0.40)	94.3	(0.20)
Nova Scotia	42.3	(1.90)	68.1	(1.60)	60.4	(2.70)	59.8	(2.80)	97.9	(0.20)
New Brunswick	32.8	(1.10)	74.5	(0.90)	63.1	(1.20)	69.6	(1.60)	88.0	(0.40)
Quebec	45.4	(4.60)	68.5	(4.10)	58.2	(4.60)	65.2	(4.00)	84.8	(3.30)
Ontario	59.0	(5.30)	46.2	(5.30)	70.9	(4.90)	65.7	(4.80)	99.6	(0.00)
Manitoba	42.7	(2.90)	39.6	(2.70)	49.7	(2.90)	66.3	(2.80)	94.3	(0.40)
Saskatchewan	24.2	(2.50)	57.8	(4.40)	43.4	(3.80)	43.7	(4.50)	84.1	(2.90)
Alberta	42.5	(4.80)	49.3	(5.70)	55.6	(4.80)	65.4	(4.80)	93.6	(2.70)
British Columbia	36.5	(6.00)	59.6	(6.50)	70.6	(5.90)	60.0	(5.50)	98.5	(1.60)
Canada	47.9	(2.40)	55.3	(2.50)	64.5	(2.20)	64.1	(2.30)	94.6	(0.80)
OECD average	38.4	(0.51)	39.2	(0.59)	54.1	(0.54)	45.1	(0.61)	89.3	(0.38)

Note: Results based on reports from school principals and reported proportionate to the number of 15-year-olds enrolled in the school.

Table B.4.23

Index of school preparation for science-related careers, by national and provincial quarters of the index

	Index of school preparation for science-related careers									
	All students		Bottom quarter		Second quarter		Third quarter		Top quarter	
	mean index	standard error	mean index	standard error	mean index	standard error	mean index	standard error	mean index	standard error
Newfoundland and Labrador	0.40	(0.03)	-0.67	(0.03)	0.05	(0.00)	0.52	(0.02)	1.70	(0.02)
Prince Edward Island	0.30	(0.02)	-0.81	(0.03)	0.05	(0.00)	0.34	(0.02)	1.61	(0.02)
Nova Scotia	0.29	(0.03)	-0.89	(0.02)	0.03	(0.01)	0.43	(0.02)	1.61	(0.02)
New Brunswick	0.34	(0.02)	-0.82	(0.03)	0.05	(0.00)	0.49	(0.01)	1.65	(0.02)
Quebec	0.24	(0.03)	-1.02	(0.03)	-0.05	(0.01)	0.48	(0.01)	1.58	(0.02)
Ontario	0.35	(0.03)	-0.80	(0.02)	0.05	(0.00)	0.48	(0.02)	1.67	(0.02)
Manitoba	0.39	(0.02)	-0.73	(0.03)	0.05	(0.00)	0.53	(0.02)	1.71	(0.02)
Saskatchewan	0.31	(0.03)	-0.79	(0.03)	0.05	(0.00)	0.42	(0.02)	1.58	(0.02)
Alberta	0.42	(0.03)	-0.71	(0.03)	0.05	(0.00)	0.60	(0.02)	1.76	(0.01)
British Columbia	0.31	(0.03)	-0.79	(0.03)	0.05	(0.00)	0.43	(0.02)	1.54	(0.02)
Canada	0.33	(0.01)	-0.86	(0.01)	0.04	(0.00)	0.48	(0.01)	1.64	(0.01)
OECD average	0.00	(0.00)	-1.19	(0.00)	-0.30	(0.00)	0.21	(0.00)	1.28	(0.00)

	Performance on the science scale, by national and provincial quarters of this index								Change in the science score per unit of this index	
	Bottom quarter		Second quarter		Third quarter		Top quarter			
	mean score	standard error	mean score	standard error	mean score	standard error	mean score	standard error	effect	standard error
Newfoundland and Labrador	495	(5.7)	513	(4.8)	534	(5.6)	563	(4.6)	29.5	(2.8)
Prince Edward Island	480	(4.8)	507	(5.8)	514	(5.4)	538	(4.8)	24.1	(2.5)
Nova Scotia	494	(4.7)	510	(4.1)	528	(4.8)	553	(5.6)	24.5	(3.0)
New Brunswick	474	(4.3)	502	(4.2)	513	(3.7)	537	(3.8)	24.5	(2.0)
Quebec	505	(4.4)	527	(5.6)	538	(5.1)	563	(5.3)	23.4	(2.0)
Ontario	513	(5.4)	537	(4.9)	544	(6.0)	569	(5.6)	21.8	(2.6)
Manitoba	498	(6.3)	522	(5.5)	531	(5.3)	553	(4.5)	24.2	(2.9)
Saskatchewan	490	(5.0)	520	(5.0)	515	(5.6)	544	(7.3)	23.0	(3.3)
Alberta	520	(5.3)	540	(4.3)	558	(6.5)	585	(5.4)	26.7	(2.4)
British Columbia	512	(7.4)	531	(5.6)	550	(4.6)	564	(5.8)	23.1	(2.5)
Canada	508	(2.6)	530	(2.3)	543	(2.7)	566	(2.8)	23.5	(1.3)
OECD average	487	(0.7)	499	(0.7)	505	(0.7)	518	(0.8)	13.2	(0.3)

Note: Results based on students' self-reports.

Table B.4.24

Index of student information on science-related careers, by national and provincial quarters of the index

	Index of student information on science-related careers									
	All students		Bottom quarter		Second quarter		Third quarter		Top quarter	
	mean index	standard error	mean index	standard error	mean index	standard error	mean index	standard error	mean index	standard error
Newfoundland and Labrador	0.34	(0.03)	-0.88	(0.04)	0.07	(0.01)	0.67	(0.01)	1.52	(0.03)
Prince Edward Island	0.42	(0.02)	-0.84	(0.03)	0.14	(0.01)	0.76	(0.01)	1.61	(0.02)
Nova Scotia	0.35	(0.03)	-0.94	(0.03)	0.07	(0.01)	0.73	(0.01)	1.56	(0.02)
New Brunswick	0.32	(0.02)	-1.00	(0.03)	0.05	(0.01)	0.68	(0.01)	1.56	(0.02)
Quebec	0.07	(0.02)	-1.20	(0.03)	-0.23	(0.01)	0.44	(0.01)	1.30	(0.02)
Ontario	0.39	(0.03)	-0.90	(0.03)	0.09	(0.01)	0.71	(0.01)	1.66	(0.02)
Manitoba	0.22	(0.03)	-1.11	(0.03)	-0.10	(0.01)	0.62	(0.01)	1.46	(0.03)
Saskatchewan	0.14	(0.03)	-1.08	(0.03)	-0.16	(0.01)	0.49	(0.01)	1.30	(0.02)
Alberta	0.36	(0.03)	-0.92	(0.02)	0.04	(0.01)	0.70	(0.01)	1.60	(0.03)
British Columbia	0.28	(0.03)	-1.06	(0.03)	-0.02	(0.01)	0.67	(0.01)	1.55	(0.02)
Canada	0.28	(0.01)	-1.03	(0.01)	-0.03	(0.00)	0.65	(0.00)	1.53	(0.01)
OECD average	0.00	(0.00)	-1.22	(0.00)	-0.28	(0.00)	0.31	(0.00)	1.18	(0.00)

	Performance on the science scale, by national and provincial quarters of this index								Change in the science score per unit of this index	
	Bottom quarter		Second quarter		Third quarter		Top quarter			
	mean score	standard error	mean score	standard error	mean score	standard error	mean score	standard error	effect	standard error
Newfoundland and Labrador	521	(5.1)	529	(4.6)	524	(5.3)	532	(5.7)	3.8	(3.2)
Prince Edward Island	503	(5.3)	516	(5.8)	499	(4.9)	523	(5.6)	4.0	(2.8)
Nova Scotia	516	(4.2)	527	(5.0)	515	(5.4)	528	(4.9)	2.7	(2.1)
New Brunswick	495	(3.8)	510	(4.4)	504	(4.1)	517	(4.3)	7.5	(1.8)
Quebec	514	(4.7)	531	(4.2)	542	(4.7)	544	(5.8)	11.9	(2.2)
Ontario	536	(6.1)	542	(5.3)	536	(5.7)	549	(5.3)	4.7	(2.3)
Manitoba	515	(5.9)	539	(6.0)	532	(4.8)	519	(4.7)	3.5	(2.6)
Saskatchewan	510	(4.6)	522	(4.4)	516	(5.2)	520	(7.9)	3.8	(3.4)
Alberta	544	(5.3)	555	(4.4)	547	(4.6)	558	(7.4)	5.6	(2.4)
British Columbia	524	(6.5)	546	(5.4)	542	(6.1)	544	(6.2)	6.5	(2.1)
Canada	524	(2.7)	542	(2.0)	537	(2.7)	544	(2.8)	7.1	(1.0)
OECD average	493	(0.7)	505	(0.7)	506	(0.7)	505	(0.8)	5.6	(0.3)

Note: Results based on students' self-reports.